"This book pulled me straight into the world of fantasy . . . and I've never looked back. Having never read a fantasy novel before, I was surprised at how quickly it hooked me. The writing was vivid and colorful, clearly coming from an artist's heart with all the imagery it paints. The story itself was deeply satisfying and kept me on the edge of my seat. And those cliffhangers at the end of each chapter? Infuriatingly brilliant! I stayed up way too late because I just couldn't stop turning the pages."

—Faith Reynolds

"*Silver Steps* focuses on what makes fantasy so much fun with whimsical magic that captures the 'awe' that I love so much with deep characters who explore all its facets, for both good and evil. I would recommend this book to anyone who shares a love for magic, mystery, and a satisfying ending where it all comes together."

—Paul Ray

"*Silver Steps* is an engrossing read with rich characters and a fun new world to explore. Interesting and entertaining from beginning to end!"

—Ely Reynolds

Silver Steps

The Heretics Cycle: Book 1

Stephen Ray

LUCIDBOOKS

Silver Steps

The Heretics Cycle: Book 1

Written and Illustrated by Stephen Ray

Published by Lucid Books in Houston, TX
www.LucidBooks.com

ISBN: 978-1-63296-939-2
eISBN: 978-1-63296-940-8

Special Sales: Most Lucid Books titles are available in special quantity discounts. Custom imprinting or excerpting can also be done to fit special needs. Contact Lucid Books at Info@LucidBooks.com

To my wife, Krysten, who makes me hope, and to my daughters, Brooklyn and Belle, who make me smile.

Table of Contents

CHAPTER 1

"When I searched for a blessing, there was none to be found.
So, I feasted on curses where plenty abound."
—The Book of Heretics

"DEATH TO THE WITCH." The black letters covered my cottage door for all the villagers to see. I gritted my teeth and scrubbed the charcoal message with my palm, ignoring the splinters from the rough wood.

Tightening my grip on the sack of coppers, I turned, but the streets remained empty. No sign of Father. I scrubbed harder, but the words remained fixed as if they were seared into the wood. This couldn't be happening! On the best of days, Father hated the messages, and if he was drunk…I couldn't imagine.

Other phrases covered the doorposts. "LEAVE THE VILLAGE." "DROWN YOURSELF." "LIKE MOTHER, LIKE DAUGHTER."

I struck the last message with my fist. "She wasn't a witch!"

Sucking blood from my knuckles, I sighed. My palms, normally a light olive tone, turned as black as the letters that I rubbed, but the words remained. I still didn't see any sign of Father, but I couldn't spare another moment. Suthian, the smaller of the two moons, climbed over the hills, showing it was already passed noon.

From the side of the cottage, I retrieved a wooden sign I made months earlier which read, "Dried fruit for sale." It never attracted customers, but it would help me now. Dusting off the dirt and leaves, I nailed it on the door. I nodded in satisfaction as only a few smudges showed at the corners. There was nothing to cover the doorposts, but the sign would do until I could properly clean it.

When I entered the cottage, a single shiver ran through me. Home was always cold, even when I dried fruit in the oven. It wasn't refreshing like a cool breeze on a summer's day but rather a stagnant chill that burrowed deep inside where not even the angriest flames could reach.

I pulled back a patched gray curtain from the kitchen window to illuminate the portrait of my mother. I ran my fingers across the stitches of the canvas where I had mended it after Father threw it in a drunken rage. Much like mine, a braid of raven black hair hung to one side of her amber face. When black streaks smeared her necklace, I realized my hand was still covered in charcoal.

"She was not a witch," I repeated. "And neither am I."

The memory of her death itched in my head, but it was always out of reach. I remembered hearing the screams as she gave birth to my sister. The door to the Healing House opened, and then… blackness. It was only three years ago; I was twelve. There was no reason why I should forget such an event.

A faint voice whispered in my mind. "*She was a good mother, and she died giving birth.*" The words rang again and again, but I didn't know why, nor did I remember her body burning on the funeral pyre.

CHAPTER 1

Pulling out the sack of coins, I knelt beneath the painting. Fifteen coppers rested inside, nearly a record for a day of selling dried fruit, and for just a moment, I considered taking tomorrow off. When I removed the loose floorboards, I picked up a wooden box with a sheet of parchment on top.

Unfolding the paper, I stared at the sketch of a cottage I had seen in Lanvire. It was small with only two windows, but it was quiet and safe, perfect for two girls starting a new life. I planned to weave blankets, sew clothing, and sell preserved fruit to provide for us. No longer would I have to walk on eggshells around Father.

When I opened the hidden box, my stomach dropped. I thought he wouldn't find it this time, but of course he had. Four hundred and twelve coppers had been in there, leaving 1,588 needed to buy the cottage. Six months of saving, gone! I let myself hope again, and hope was for the fool.

My father walked in, several bottles of mead in his bear-like arms. Gray dust coated his ebony face from his mason work, and he stood a hair short of hitting the doorframe. Locking eyes with me, he froze. A flicker of guilt crossed his eyes, but it slipped away, replaced by irritation. He looked from the empty box to me but said nothing.

A familiar feeling washed over me—numbness. It would come suddenly and leach away all emotion, leaving me a hollowed husk. The parchment fell from my limp fingers. "Is any left?"

He slammed the first bottle on the wobbly table. "I had debts."

Debts with the tavern, no doubt. I knew I should be angry, or sad, or… something. But I had been wrung dry for too long.

Father squeezed the remaining bottles, and his breathing grew heavy. The sign was all too familiar: he ached to drink more. He was desperate, like a starving dog near a slab of meat, and I was standing between them.

No. He wasn't like a starving dog; he was like a swarm of bees. Dogs were predictable, but you could never tell with bees. People say they only sting when provoked, but that was nonsense. I never provoked them, just like I never provoked Father. He would sting without warning. Without realizing it, my meandering mind slipped into how bees made honey, and honey made mead, and Father drank mead, and—

"Sashel, did you hear a word I said?" His sharp tone shook me from my thoughts.

"Uh—I—"

"The forest!" he yelled. "Were you in the Scarlet Forest today?"

"No!" He hated the place, and every day he would ask the same thing.

Sweat beaded on his brow, and his eyes drifted towards the bottles. "Keeping your attention is like holding water in a basket. How can you be so dense?"

He doesn't mean it. He'll apologize in the morning.

Placing the rest of the bottles on the table, he said, "I'm guessing you forgot the potatoes I asked for."

I winced. "Yes." For the thousandth time, I cursed my wandering mind.

His face hardened. "Useless! Your mother couldn't even leave me with a son. Just a simpleton and one miserable mutt who isn't even mine. Why do I bother with you two?"

Pain pricked at me, and I tried to hold onto the numbness. I wasn't a simpleton. My focus was shattered, and my memory abysmal, but I wasn't a simpleton. *He's just drunk, and he'll apologize in the morning.*

"Did you really think you could buy that cottage?" he asked.

My eyes blurred as I stared at the sketch on the floor. "I had to try."

"Did you?" He struck the table hard enough for me to feel it across the room.

One of the bottles toppled to the floor and shattered. Amber liquid pooled around the table, filling the air with a sweet, earthy aroma. As he stared in disbelief, terror gripped me. He saw every drop as precious as jewels.

Placing a cautious hand on the other bottles, he spoke as though restraining a beast. "Get out."

Those two words ripped away the numbness. I backstepped and scrambled for the door, slamming it shut behind me. Father shouted a string of profanities and hurled the broken bottle through the window.

I leaned against the outside of the door and whispered a prayer to Suthian. "Let him stay inside. Please let him stay inside." Silence reigned followed by a slight pop of another bottle opening. A deep ache formed in the pit of my stomach, one that wriggled its way up my throat and made my lips quiver. I had to be strong.

As I strolled down the street and away from the cottage, the tension in my chest eased, which bothered me. *I should feel safe when I come home, not when I leave it. Maybe I should just live in the Scarlet Forest. Father would never look there for me.* Realization struck. The Scarlet Forest! He was terrified of it and forbade me from entering. It would be perfect for hiding my earnings. That was it. I would save up again, and he wouldn't be able to steal from me. But this would be the third time starting over. Could I do it?

Without realizing it, I found myself walking towards Elder Grinda's cottage, the honorary matron of the village. Her house rivaled the size of the mayor's, and she adored the children of Ashwood, allowing them to play inside with her countless trinkets. She even welcomed my little sister, despite the two of us being pariahs. I was forced to leave her with Grinda more often as I strove to save money while Father squandered his own.

Something bumped my leg, and two bright blue eyes stared up at me. "Sorry, Sash," Minessa said. "I get Papa's hat. I'm a backsmith today."

I let out a faint laugh. My sister, the "mutt" as Father called her, was so innocent. Instead of saying, "I'm three," her childish speech would make it sound like "I'm free." If only we were free.

With her cinnamon brown complexion and button nose, Elder Grinda said she looked like me when I was younger. The main difference was Minessa's blue eyes which Father hated, and I loved. No one else in the village, not even fair-skinned Grinda, had eyes like hers. This was why Father didn't believe she was his daughter as his eyes were nearly black like Mother's had been.

She stuck out her lower lip in a pout. "I need a hat."

I knelt and brushed red leaves from her hair. "I know, but Papa is...sad right now. Why don't you see if Grinda has one you can wear?"

"She only have a cook hat."

What did a blacksmith's hat even look like? I'd seen the men work a few times but couldn't recall what they wore. I cinched Minessa's belt, ensuring each of the three knots around her waist was evenly distributed. "A three-knotted chord is the safest ward." I didn't know if the saying was true, but we needed all the luck we could get.

Minessa tugged at my tattered, azure dress, and I winced at how distracted I'd gotten. I grabbed my sister's hands, running my thumb over the two nubs where her index and middle finger had been. "I'm sorry, but you can't go home right now," I pleaded. "I can make you a hat later."

I hated sewing, but I would do it if it kept her away from Father today. What was I going to use to make her a hat? I think Father had an old shirt he didn't use. Maybe I could use the material to—

"Sashel? Sashel?" Minessa asked.

I gritted my teeth as my mind once again ran off without me. "Please stay at Grinda's house until I get back. Promise me, and I'll make you your very own hat."

"Alright, but I want a backsmith hat."

"Say 'black.'" I drew out the 'l' sound to enunciate.

"Black," she said slowly.

"Now say, 'blacksmith.'"

"Backsmith."

I sighed. Mother would have been so much better at this. After I led her back to Grinda down the street, I grabbed an empty basket and headed for the Scarlet Forest. Dread filled me at the thought of saving up for a third time, but I would do it for Minessa.

When I entered the forest, I was underwhelmed. The most dangerous creature was a fox which scampered away. The place seemed like any other, save for the deep red leaves and black bark. Although the forest was over a mile from Ashwood, its crimson leaves would make their journey all the way and cover the village's streets like rivers of blood.

I twirled my copper bracelet in thought, then something pushed against my mind like a strong wind. *It's not safe here. Run! Run away!* I was used to my wondering thoughts, but this was different. It was strange because the voice had no origin. A sense of dread pressed down on me as I gazed deeper into the forest. It whispered to me. The words were nearly tangible, prodding me like an angry lady with a cane. They warned me I would receive scars that went far deeper than flesh.

The numbness tried to cover my mind like a thick blanket, protecting me as it had so often. But a spark of defiance pushed it back. I was tired of watching my life unravel like a tale thrice told. Much of my life I couldn't change, but that didn't mean I had to obey this strange voice. I would not be pushed any further.

I faced the direction where the warning was loudest and ran straight for it. Each step was strengthened by the next. My pace quickened as I ran downhill, through thickets and over streams. I ran faster and faster on bare feet, passing tree after tree at a blurring speed. Creatures had no time to flinch before I shot past them. While dread pushed against me, the forest itself wanted me to move, branches bending out of the way and the wind blowing me forward.

Something flickered in front of me, and I slowed. My eyes watered from the wind, and I stopped to rub them. When I refocused, I froze, the empty basket falling at my feet.

A silver staircase meandered upwards in a contorted pattern, fading like mist into the highest branches. The steps were the strangest part. They were alive, growing and shrinking like the flickering flames from a funeral pyre. The first word I thought of was "beautiful," but that wasn't quite right. There was beauty, but it was wrong, like a wedding dress torn apart, then sewn together at odd angles, creating a grotesque elegance.

What was a staircase doing in the middle of a forest? Perhaps a house once stood here and then decayed, leaving only stone steps behind. But that wouldn't account for the steps waxing and waning, and there was no sign of a house ever existing here.

I circled the anomaly, looking for any clues as to who or what made it. There were neither columns nor banisters, yet it stood tall and firm. Soft earth surrounded it, not a single leaf within a few paces. Neither lizard nor beetle dared touch its surface, and not a strand of a spider's web rested on its steps.

Grabbing a handful of velvety leaves, I tossed them, but they blew to either side, leaving the steps untouched. I threw a stone, and… nothing. It was right where I retrieved it as if I never threw it.

Despite myself, I leaned forward to climb it but stopped. What was I doing? I was like a child wanting to touch fire, unaware of the consequences. But there was something about these stairs. Then it occurred to me. It was change. The anomaly didn't conform to the rules of nature. I knew as much as I knew my own name that if I climbed the stairs, my life would forever change.

Contrasting desires swirled within me. I wanted change, but I was also terrified of it. Deep down I knew that things would always be the same. I saved up money already knowing Father would somehow find it. Like a wheel caught in a rut, I needed something to get me out. But using the staircase seemed excessive, like hurling a mountain. The wheel would undoubtedly be free, but at what price? Still, it promised change.

I reached the edge and placed my bare foot on the first step. I half expected it to sink through like it was a mirage, but it held, and the earth around me rippled in white light. The first step froze while the rest moved like waves. My chest burned and my head spun, causing me to flail my arms for balance. *I should run! This wasn't natural. It wasn't right. I should—*

As always, my thoughts shifted. *Minessa wanted a hat. What color did she want again? What design should I do? What material should I use?*

My mind snapped back to the present, and the oppressive fear faded like a distant dream. Before I could take another step, an angelic voice sang out, searing its words into my mind.

"All that was lost, the new and the old,
Will be given in full when the story is told."

The air rippled before me, and visions flooded my senses. A loving father free of drinking, a thriving business selling preserved fruit, Minessa safe from harm, and… was that Mother? A woman stood tall and regal, much like in the painting. And she smiled, her raven hair whipping in the wind. She hugged my father and sister, and the three were at peace.

I stretched my hand out, but it passed through the images like a shadow. Every fiber of me yearned to hug my mother, to speak with her just one more time. If I continued climbing, the staircase promised all this and more. Everything I had lost would be given in full.

"No!"

For the barest moment, I dared to think she could return, and I quenched the thought as soon as it came. *If I don't hope, I can't be hurt.*

The vision vanished, and I leaped off the step, landing awkwardly on my ankle. It throbbed, and putting even the slightest weight on it was unbearable. As the pain intensified, something inside me reached out for help.

The air in front of me warped and then tore in half. Reality itself ripped like old parchment, and beyond the rift was another world. Through the portal, a powerful waterfall roared with an emerald rainbow arching over it. Unlike the vision of my family, this was real. The waterfall thundered in my ears, and the cool vapor dampened my face.

A translucent thread shot out from my hand and tugged at something beyond the rift. Like a fish on a line, something resisted, but I instinctively yanked. A flash of silver shot through the opening and over my head, colliding into a pile of leaves behind the stairs. Whatever it was moved in the foliage and grunted. A creature from the other world had escaped into my own.

Before I could get closer, a second rift appeared, this one singed black with smoke wisping at the edges. While the first realm was beautiful, the only word to describe the second was rotten. Until today, I would have sworn only my world existed. Now I was seeing multiple, both glorious and corrupt.

Through the second portal, a pale creature as tall as a tree turned to look at me with bulbous yellow eyes. Its right arm was human-like with black talons while its left arm resembled a scorpion's stinger. The creature smiled, revealing hundreds of black teeth. Most of its body wouldn't fit, but its one taloned arm reaching through the rift was longer than my whole body. Letting out a shriek like a hawk, it lunged at me.

I lurched toward the staircase for cover, pain shooting up my left leg. The air sparked and crackled as the creature's hand drew near the steps. It snarled as it raked at the invisible barrier protecting the stairs, but it found no opening.

The wind howled and stirred, but I felt nothing. Only then did I realize the wind was coming from the other side of the rift, pulling the monster back into it with the force of a cyclone. The creature clawed for a purchase, snapping trees and digging deep trenches in the earth, but the force never wavered and pulled it back. After long, agonizing moments, both portals closed, and all fell still.

Nalorath
Suthian Ocean
Gran Schorol
Gran Mala
Ithri
Char Kaltha Dominion
Vorc Sea
Tash Sea
Malvic Gulf
East Tantha
West Tantha
Threscia
Kingdom of Telavast
Torinth Sea (Merchants' Passage)
Bevric Gulf
Gavnian Ocean
Cralfira
Talva Sea
This region is detailed in a separate chart
Serulian Sea
Sennavian Empire
Robius Ocean
N
W
E
S

The Great Spires
Scarlet Forest
West Vallik Lake
Ashwood Village
Tannekin Village
Thornvale Village
Lanvire
Morggis River
Sennevar
N
W
E
S

CHAPTER 2

"All those who climb the stairs shall be corrupted or cleansed. Choose wisely."
—*The Book of Heretics*

I lay on the earth, motionless save for my quick breathing. *I imagined it. That must be it. But then why do I still see the staircase above me?*

I tried walking, but the slightest weight on my foot sent a wave of agony. Hopping several paces, I retrieved a thick branch for a crutch. I broke the twigs off, grabbed my basket, and headed for home. *How long would it take to get back like this? Minessa may have to spend the night at Grinda's house.*

A voice spoke behind me. "Human, where am I?"

I screamed and spun to look. The motion made me lean on my left ankle, and another jolt of pain shot up my leg, causing me to scream again.

"You're a… loud one, aren't you?" the voice asked.

It sounded young, male, and commanding with a regal tone. I looked all around, but there were only piles of soft, red leaves.

CHAPTER 2

"What is this place? How did I get here?" The questions cracked like a whip, firm and demanding an answer.

Before me stood a white weasel with large, furry bat wings and a long tail tipped with a sharp spike. The creature sniffed my bare feet, then scowled up at me. "You summoned me, didn't you?" His tone was more accusing than questioning.

"Summoned you? I never—" Wait. When the portal opened, a strand connected me to something from the other world. When it resisted, I pulled harder, and something flew into my world. I didn't realize it, but I must have pulled him through. The creature that landed in the leaves must have been him.

He bared his sharp teeth and growled. "Do you have any idea what you've done? Do you know what I was in the middle of when you stole me away?"

I knelt, wincing at my sprained ankle. "You're talking."

He gave me a condescending stare, something I never expected to see on a weasel's face. "Of course."

"Great judgment! You're talking. You're a weasel, and you're—"

"Sprackin."

"What?"

He flapped his white wings. "I'm a noble sprackin, not a common weasel. Now send me back to my realm at once!"

His realm. My mind still reeled at the fact that there were other worlds. "I didn't summon you," I said. "And—and animals can't talk."

"So, you're a liar *and* a simpleton. An unfortunate combination."

His words dripped with sarcasm and smugness in equal measure. I hated the word "simpleton." Many would whisper the word behind my back. I wasn't simple! I tried to slap him, but the sprackin dodged with a blurring speed.

"How dare you!" His eyes flickered from silver to purple, then back to silver. A second passed, then another. The creature cocked his head before trying again. His eyes turned blue this time then back to silver. If he expected more to happen, then he was disappointed. Stiffening his muscles, he grunted in concentration.

"Are you… pooping?" I asked.

He gave me a disgusted look. "No. I would never."

"You never poop?" Only afterward did I realize what he meant, but it was too late.

He growled as he paced around before his eyes widened in realization. "You've melded with me!"

"And what does that mean?"

He remained silent for over a minute, pain and defeat evident on his face. When he finally spoke, it was as though he had given me some devastating news or confessed a dark secret. "It means I can only access my blessings through you."

"Your blessings?"

He slumped, speaking in a more defeated tone. "Search your soul. You'll find a fire burning within. If you transfer some to me, I can demonstrate."

Search my soul? It sounded like something Cleric Shoff would say in his sermons. When I shut my eyes, I saw it. A tall candle stood in my mind with a silver flame burning atop. I felt the same thread I had earlier connecting my candle to the sprackin. I sensed his mind, his frustration, and even his fear. Like an old patch ripped from one garment and hastily sewn onto another, this creature had been taken from his world and forced into my very soul. He felt powerless, completely reliant on me for abilities that rightfully belonged to him.

I imagined a bit of the fire transferring to the creature, and silver flames danced across the invisible thread, igniting his soul.

The sprackin perked up. "I see you found it."

I nodded, dumbstruck by what I'd experienced.

He lifted his long snout. "I suppose I acted unbecoming for one in my station. You seem ignorant of all this; so, I doubt you purposely melded with me." Straightening, he said, "My name is Nittles, and I believe we can come to an arrangement. You provide me with your fire, and I'll use my blessings to aid you until I return to Tal Miral."

"Again, what are these blessings?" I felt more ignorant by the second, asking things that seemed rudimentary to him.

"I'm proficient in two of the three noble gems as well as a master in Agrariance, a skill you would probably call magic. Simply provide me with fruit, and I'll do the rest."

"Fruit?"

"Yes, little tasty things that grow on plants."

His condescension returned, and it rankled me. I considered trying to slap him again, but I took a calming breath. "Please explain how this works."

He rolled his eyes. "When we find some fruit, I'll show you."

After a few minutes of him flying low and me hobbling on my stick, we found a blackberry bush. I held a handful of berries out to him and poured more of my silver fire into the sprackin, causing the candle in my soul to shrink ever so slightly. He flapped his wings and sparks shot out. Silver flames licked at the berries, but there was neither heat nor smoke. Instead of charring, they turned egg-shaped and glowed a golden brown.

"These are called 'lifespur,'" Nittles said. "And one should be plenty to heal your injury. You can become ill if you eat too many."

I hesitated. Could I trust this creature? If I didn't try, it would take forever for me to get back, and Minessa needed me. I took a bite, and a mixture of sweet and tart blended in my mouth followed by a sensation of pins and needles washing over my ankle. The swelling retreated, and the pain vanished. Gingerly stepping on it, I braced for the agony, but none came. I moved it around, then jumped without the slightest twinge of pain. I clutched the remaining fruit and jumped as high as I could. "This is incredible!"

Nittles folded his wings and spoke in a dry tone. "Yes. I suppose jumping can be incredible if one is dull enough."

I ignored his barb as we walked toward Ashwood Village, me skipping and him flying. Four precious fruits remained in my hand. Lifespur. The ability to heal wounds in an instant. The clerics could use magic, but this was different. Their rune-covered staves could do all sorts of things like read minds or grow plants, but I'd never heard of anyone healing wounds.

There was a soft crackling like dry wood in a fire. I spun around, but everything seemed normal. A moment later, the crackling stopped, and I returned my gaze to the fruit in my hand. "We have to make more of these," I said. "We could make a fortune!"

All levity vanished from Nittles' face. Even his mocking sarcasm was gone. Slowly turning to me, he said, "No."

I stopped, then jogged to catch up. "What do you mean 'no'? You just made some."

"That was to heal you, not to sell them."

My anger simmered as he spoke. This was the one chance I had at taking my sister away from Father. "I sell fruit all the time. What's the problem?"

"Lifespur is sacred."

The word took me by surprise. Sacred. It made me think of items in the temple like Neerion's staff. The cleric had pointed it at me and called me broken, saying I had evil spirits. After trying to perform an exorcism on my fractured mind with his staff, my father called the man every vulgar thing he could think of and all but threw him out of our cottage. Although Father wasn't as tender as he once was, he was still protective. Something bothered me. Did my mental ailment start before or after Mother died?

"…going back fifty generations."

I snapped out of my reverie as Nittles finished whatever he was saying. "Uh—What did you say?"

The sprackin gave me an incredulous look. "Are you mocking me?"

"No. I just have a hard time focusing. What do you mean the fruit is sacred? You let *me* use it, but you won't let others?"

"For one, we're melded; so, I didn't give you the fruit. We made them together. For another, selling the healing fruit is akin to being a harlot."

"Excuse me?"

He descended and walked beside me. "Think of it this way. If you're anything like humans in my world, you see intimacy as sacred, correct? It's special. It's more than just a physical process like breeding cattle."

"Well, some would argue it's just physical." I didn't believe this, but I needed the fruit.

"Some can argue about anything. Your point is moot."

Nittles spoke like a judge dismissing an argument. Was he a judge back in his world? A prince perhaps? I reluctantly nodded. I hadn't slept with anyone, but I knew it was special. Still, there had to be a way to convince him.

"But why is lifespur sacred?" I asked.

"Healing touches the very soul of a person as does intimacy. To sell either of them like common merchandise is sacrilege to my kind."

I racked my mind for a rebuttal. "I've seen harlots in other cities. They seem happy, and some of them just need the money."

"They undoubtedly have pleasure, but there is a deeper joy that slowly fades without a deep connection. And as for those who need the coin, well, the most horrid things imaginable are done in the pursuit of gold."

Was I really being lectured by a flying weasel? What would he know about life in my world?

"But—"

"That being said," he interrupted. "I can help you create other kinds of fruit. They won't be as valuable, but they will still sell."

I bit back a reply. How much would someone pay to have their injuries healed instantly? I could sell them to kings and lords for a ridiculous amount. My sister and I could live in luxury far away from Father. Still, I would follow Nittles and see what else he could make.

When we arrived at the edge of the forest, Nittles flew to a blueberry bush. Silver sparks shot out from his wings and morphed several berries into a single, tear-shaped fruit with a purple hue. As I ate them, time slowed around me, and my body felt limber and energetic. I leaped in the air and instinctively performed a perfect backflip.

I threw two stones high in the air. Throwing two more, I giggled as they collided with the first two. In a blink, I snatched another pair and tossed, hearing a satisfying clack as they struck the second pair before colliding with the first pair. It was effortless precision.

"This!" I exclaimed. "This, we can use."

Nittles nodded. "In Tal Miral, it's common to sell glaidens. They have many uses as you can see, but they don't last long."

I nodded as the supernatural feeling was already fading. I rubbed the amethyst fruit with my thumb as ideas blossomed in my head. Hunters would pay heaps to have this uncanny precision with a bow and arrow. I could make quite a few silvers selling glaidens, but lifespur was worth its weight in gold. It rankled me that we couldn't sell the latter.

The same crackling sounded around me, but when I turned, there was no sign of anything following us.

"So," Nittles said. "I expect compensation if we sell the glaidens."

"Of course. Fifty percent."

"No. I wish to return to my realm."

"I don't know how." I threw up my hands. "I don't even know how I melded with you in the first place."

"It doesn't matter." He stared at the bright blue sky as if just seeing it for the first time, then turned back to me. "Since you climbed the stairs, the goddess will send you trials. If you pass them, you'll be able to travel to Tal Miral. Promise to take me with you if you pass, and I'll help you make as much fruit as I can."

I headed toward Ashwood but stopped. "Trials?"

"Of course. Don't tell me you climbed the stairs without knowing what it all entailed."

"Uh..."

He closed his eyes and sighed. "The trials are unique to the one who climbs, so I don't know exactly what you'll go through. But I know they'll test you in every way. They may come tomorrow or a month from now. Again, it's different for each person. Just promise me that if you pass, you'll bring me back to my world."

This was a lot to take in. I had to pass trials? And if I passed, I'd be able to travel to a different world? I remembered how beautiful it looked when I saw it in the emerald portal, but I shuddered when I thought of the dark one. Then I thought of the deal. Nittles wasn't asking for much, just to take him with me if I passed. And for Minessa, I would do much more than that. "I promise."

"Excellent," Nittles said. "Now who will you sell the glaidens to? Traveling acrobats would pay well for their abilities."

An idea struck me. "Soldiers."

"Interesting choice. I'm fine with that, but when all is said and done, you must bring me back to my world."

As we neared the village, it occurred to me that Nittles would draw attention even if he didn't talk. The villagers already viewed me as the witch's daughter, and bringing back a magical creature would only confirm their suspicions.

When I said as much to him, he considered this, then pressed his furry wings across his back. It would look odd under scrutiny, but he would pass as a weasel instead of a sprackin. Even a normal weasel as a pet was strange but not supernatural.

When we entered Ashwood, Jocksin sat near the cobbler's house, one of his mangled legs protruding from under his tattered blanket. He gave a wide grin, showing a scattering of teeth nearly as black as his weathered skin. Holding out a hand, he asked, "Copper for the cripple?"

"Sorry," I said, "I don't have any on me." This was true since I had buried the coins near the staircase before leaving.

Pressing his fingers to his chin, he stopped himself, but I caught the sign. He still saw me as the daughter of a witch and was attempting to ward off evil. He scratched his chin in a weak attempt to cover the gesture. "Come now," he said. "You mustn't forget the cleric's reading. 'Give to the lowest and receive from the highest.'"

I considered. Jocksin had been crippled for decades, trapped in this town with no hope of change, and I could relate. When I gave Nittles a questioning look, he nodded. He would be fine with me giving a lifespur as long as I didn't sell it. Again, the thought of not selling them bothered me, but I ignored it the best I could.

When I handed him one, he eyed it warily. "Ain't seen nothing like it before."

"Trust me. It's delicious"

I hesitated to tell him what it would do. Jocksin was a devout man to the temple, and if I told him the fruit would heal him, he might refuse for fear of witchcraft. At the thought, part of me regretted giving him the lifespur. Cleric Neerion would have me arrested and possibly hanged given the chance. *I should have thought this through. I could have slipped it into his food to avoid suspicion. I always act before thinking!*

Jocksin gave it a quick sniff before popping it in his mouth. "Say, it's not bad."

I gave him a wave and left, regret filling me with each step. If he healed, I could say I found it in the woods. They may not believe it, but they wouldn't have enough evidence to execute me, I hoped.

The same crackling sounded beneath my feet, and finally, I saw the source. The crimson leaves around me turned charred black. As I knelt, more leaves darkened. With a nagging suspicion, I waved a handful of glaidens over another pile of leaves, and they turned as black as obsidian.

"Strange," Nittles said. "No fruit does this in Tal Miral. How many steps did you climb on the staircase? Tell me it was more than one."

My stomach felt like I swallowed a sack of stones. It was evident I should have climbed more, but I couldn't. The stairs seemed to promise to bring back everything I had lost. I didn't know if that meant my mother, but I couldn't risk it. I tried everything to bring her back. I chanted prayers every night and even tried reading tomes about necromancy in the temple, but the clerics forbade me. Every time I failed, the pain grew worse. I wouldn't dare hope again; it would be too painful when I inevitably failed.

"Sashel, how many steps did you take?" he repeated. He seemed worried like the leaves were an omen of something worse. If I admitted I didn't go past the first step, he may refuse to make more glaidens. I had to make this work. Minessa needed me.

"Four," I lied.

Nittles sighed in relief. "Good. The staircase appears in many realms, but few can see it, and even fewer can make it past the first step. Most cannot resist the hypnotic pull on their minds. I may have misjudged you."

"What happens if they don't make it past the first step?"

He sniffed a black leaf. "Best not to think about it. You've climbed four. The first step ignites your heartfire, and the rest will allow you to summon special items from Tal Miral during your trials."

Leaning closer, I asked, "But what happens if they only climb one?"

"Any number of things, the worst being the Rending, where reality fractures and monstrous creatures from other worlds break free." He eyed me for a long moment before saying, "But of course, you climbed more than one step, right?"

I stared at the pile of black leaves. I thought of my father and what the mead did to him. I could almost smell the foul drink. Then I thought of Minessa, and my will became solid. If we ever wanted to be free, I needed this to work.

"Yes," I said slowly. "I climbed four."

CHAPTER 3

"The fallen fruit shall rot."
—The Book of Clergy

I raked the leaves with my hands as fast as I could, shoving them in an old potato sack. Father would be back soon, and the ground was covered in those wretched black leaves.

At the time, I thought making glaidens close to home was a good idea. The plan was to pick plums from our tree, change them to glaidens, then take them right inside to dry them. Styrcle wood burned in the oven at a lower heat for much longer, making it perfect for drying fruit. But I hadn't considered that the leaves would darken where we worked. I was an idiot.

"You're an idiot!" Nittles said as he flapped his wings, blowing piles of foliage away from the cottage.

"Well, you didn't object to my idea," I shot back.

"That was before you told me what your father would do."

The fear of his wrath made me work faster. Father hated witchcraft and hated the Scarlet Forest even more. I didn't want to imagine how he would react if he discovered our cottage was the only one surrounded by dark leaves while everywhere else had red. I might as well make a sign saying, "Dark arts performing here."

"What would your father do if he discovers I'm a sprackin?"

I cinched the sack shut and opened a fourth one. "Nothing good. My best guess is he'd kill you out of fear. Then again, he might try to sell you to buy mead. He's sold almost everything else."

Minessa held up three leaves in her tiny hand. "Here you go."

"Thanks," I said, shoving them in the sack. "Why don't you go to the front and tell me if you see Papa coming."

"I did that twice." She held up her pinky and ring finger as the other two were missing.

"Look again."

Now that the major piles had been dealt with, I picked up individual leaves.

"He's coming!" Minessa clapped excitedly as though this were a game of hide and seek.

I snatched up one last handful and cinched the sack shut. As I surveyed the area, only a few scattered leaves remained, but it shouldn't be noticeable. Nittles folded his wings and pressed them to his back just as Father opened the back door.

"What are you doing?" he asked.

Since my hands were covered in dirt, I used the hem of my dress to wipe sweat from my forehead. "Just tidying up."

He looked around and nodded.

"I got one." Minessa held out a fist then slowly opened it.

I winced. All that work, and she just walked right up and showed him. What would he do? My heart raced as her hand opened wider. Before I could distract him, Father bent down and plucked the leaf from her hand. Between his thick, dark fingers was a single crimson leaf.

A grin stretched across his face, then his eyes widened in exaggerated shock. "Wow! That's the prettiest leaf I've ever seen."

Minessa puffed up her chest. "Yes."

He examined the leaf more intently then looked around and asked, "Did you clean up all by yourself?"

Minessa laughed. "No. Sashel helped."

My eyes stung, and I wiped them quickly. I'd grown used to seeing Father drunk. He was either drunk, recovering from being drunk, or itching to get drunk. But today, we were safe. Today, this was sober Father. My heart ached as I remembered how he always used to be this way. But the mead would return. It always returned.

* * *

Once more I raised my hand and tried opening a portal to Tal Miral. Nittles described his land as a field of golden lilies beneath a green sky. Instead, the same patch of deep red trees stood before me. No portal opened, and no green light appeared.

"You failed," Nittles said.

"I know."

"Try again."

"I have."

"Again."

Even though I hadn't climbed past the first step, I thought I might be able to open a portal. After all, I did it once when I summoned Nittles. I tore my gaze away from the staircase just a few paces away. No. I wouldn't dare climb them. It would only bring hope which always led to misery.

As I shut my eyes in concentration, I felt something in front of me. In my mind's eye, an opening appeared like an endless chasm staring back at me. It was as dark and hungry as a rabid dog, whispering in a language without words. It wanted to be free, to be loosed from its cage, and I was the only key.

"Sashel, stop!"

As I opened my eyes, a dark tear in the air yawned open. Countless shadows stirred inside, anticipating their release. Reflexively, I waved my hands like swatting a hornet, but they passed right through it.

"Pour your fire into it and force it shut," Nittles shouted. "Bend it to your will!"

Trying to ignore the writhing figures in the darkness, I imagined a thread connecting the silver candle in my soul to the dark rift. The flames leaped across the invisible string and ignited the opening.

The shadows pressed against the entrance, but I gripped it tight with my will. *What was happening? How was I doing this? Were there more rifts? What kind of creatures were moving inside?*

It widened, and I forced myself to concentrate. Never had my wondering mind been such a detriment as it was right now. As I refocused, the dark portal shrank. I was doing it! What would it be like once it completely shut? How would I know when to stop? Maybe I needed to put more fire into it.

"Sashel!"

The rift widened to an arm's span. I cursed and poured more fire into it. After what seemed like an eternity, the portal winked shut.

My shoulders slumped in relief. "What was that?"

"The Sprawn Lands. It's a corrupt part of Tal Miral that has been cut off from society like a rotten branch. Never open it again!"

For the last two days, the sprackin had reminded me endlessly of my failure to open a portal, emphasizing it was my fault we had melded. If I couldn't do it in the next few weeks, I'd have to tell him I hadn't made it past the first step on the staircase.

The small sack of glaidens shined purple in my hands. We made five more today before my silver magic he called "heartfire" dimmed. I still had some left and Nittles told me the fire would replenish when I slept, but saving a bit seemed prudent in case another rift opened.

I stared at the dark line in the air, whisps of smoke still seeping through. A woman appeared, clothed in a gray dress down to her feet. She was transparent, like foggy glass, with silver hair flowing past her waist, and I squinted at the light shining from her jewelry. Before she could speak, the woman vanished.

"Eyes above! It was Kareli!" Nittles darted to the grass and sniffed where the apparition had stood.

"Who's Kareli?" I asked.

"The Silver One! The Great Goddess. She's the creator of Tal Miral."

A goddess? I had seen a goddess! My whole life I had gone to Congretory with my family, lighting lamps and hearing messages from the clerics. I considered myself a faithful worshipper of Suthian, but I had never seen visions of him.

"Sashel!" Nittles glared up at me, irritated as he had apparently been speaking.

"Sorry."

"I asked what Kareli said to you."

"Nothing. She gestured a bit, but she was silent. Do you think she was the one who spoke to me when I climbed the stairs?" I repeated the words verbatim as the memory was clear as day. "All that was lost, the new and the old, will be given in full when the story is told."

"Well, of course, Kareli said it, but she hasn't physically appeared to anyone in centuries, only spoken through the stairs or in dreams." The sprackin paced by my feet, muttering aloud. "The story must be referring to your trials. But why haven't they started yet? She rarely waits more than a few days before beginning."

My stomach knotted as the answer became apparent. I hadn't climbed further up the staircase. I shrugged. "What can you tell me about her?"

"Kareli is the Maker, the Sacred One. Goddess of knowledge and wisdom. If you use enough heartfire, she'll appear in your dreams to refill it, but she never appears in the waking world."

"Maybe I saw her because of the staircase?"

He shook his head. "Several have climbed them in my realm, one I know personally, but no one has seen a vision, only dreamed of her. You are not the first who was brave enough—" He eyed me. "—or foolish enough to climb the steps."

"I'd like to see *you* climb them."

"No!" His sardonic tone was gone. "I'd rather have my wings clipped and thrown off a cliff. Also, I can't see the steps. As I said, very few can, and even fewer can overcome the crippling fear they bring. It is unnatural, and those who climb are cursed or driven mad."

"So, you've told me, but I don't feel cursed."

"And you don't seem to be suffering from madness either."

I hesitated. It was the closest thing to a compliment he'd given me.

He smirked. "Your mind can't be broken if you've never had one to begin with."

Before I could retort another dark rift appeared, this one near a blueberry bush at the edge of the forest. Several blueberries morphed together like before, but instead of the purple, tear-shaped glaidens I'd come to expect, they turned inky black. Three large fruits hung from the branch like slimy deer hearts dipped in tar.

Nittles hissed. "Don't touch them!"

His words echoed distantly. The black fruit called to me. *I need them. They're mine!* My hand reached out of its own volition, and I let it. *I deserve it after all.*

A furry wing smacked me across the face. "I said don't touch them!"

I blinked and looked away.

"Those are drethals," he said. "They'll turn you into a Kral, the pale creature you saw near the staircase."

My eyes drifted toward the fruit, but I shook myself. They were so hypnotic. "The Kral. The giant monster with the stinger for an arm?" I asked.

"Yes. But you'll be dead long before you transform. The Kral will make sure of it. It's quite territorial."

"Then why did you make them?"

He huffed. "I didn't. The dark rift *you* opened corrupted the bush. Are you sure you climbed past the first step? This might be a sign of the Rending."

I hated lying to him, but I wouldn't climb the stairs. "I'm sure. Now, what exactly are drethals?"

"They're a corruption of mandrils, a bright blue fruit that brings fertility and strength. But when they rot, they bring nothing but pain and destruction."

I focused on the small rift and imagined it closing. As before, it was difficult with my slippery mind, but eventually, the silver candlestick in my soul shrank as the opening in the air faded away.

A squirrel darted to the bush and snatched a dark fruit. Black, pulpy juice ran from its mouth as it ate with a savage hunger. Its bushy tail morphed into a scorpion's stinger and its fur fell from its pale skin. Black teeth elongated in its mouth as it shrieked in pain.

I screamed and stumbled back as the animal grew to waist height. What was happening? Nittles whipped his spiked tail forward, impaling its neck. The squirrel snarled and writhed, then fell limp as blood pulsed from its open wound.

"That would have become an inkthid," Nittles said. "They're nasty little things. Only humans can become a Kral."

I stared at the grotesque creature as it morphed back. Soon, it was an ordinary squirrel, an ordinary dead squirrel with its throat wide open.

CHAPTER 4

"The fruit calls to me, like a worm on a hook or bait in a snare.
I know its end is death, but when I look upon it,
I find I do not care."
—The Book of Heretics

As the great city of Sennevar drew near, Nittles attacked me with questions as he pretended he was the constable I was selling to. "Do glaidens have seeds? Can they be grown?"

"No. They're made, not grown."

"Why do you want to sell to soldiers?"

He had asked me this several times, but I knew he wanted my answers to be crisp and concise. "To reduce crime in the city."

He scurried up my dress and onto my shoulder. "I'll give you four coppers per fruit. Take it or leave it."

I halted. "Um…Will you do ten?"

"No!" Nittles hopped off and glided beside me. "You emphasize the worth of them before you make a counteroffer. We've been over this. And ten is the minimum we should take. At least offer fifteen or twenty. Set the price high to leave yourself room to haggle."

My heart sped up as I could now make out the details on the city walls. On each side of the city gate, a giant red and yellow banner displaying a tree shaped like a hand reaching up toward a crescent moon waved. This was happening too fast. Yesterday, I could haggle much better with Nittles, but today my mind was a jumble. Was I really going to sell the fruit to the city guard? We had made fruit for nearly a week and traveled six hours, but now all I wanted to do was turn around and head home.

"Are you sure you're up for this?" Nittles asked.

I fastened the cobalt fabric around my nose and mouth as I walked. "Yes. Sennevar is far enough that no one will recognize me."

"But what of your veil? Will it not seem odd?"

I shrugged. "A few women have passed through Ashwood wearing them. It's some kind of religious thing."

"A ceremonial garb?"

"Uh, sure." I had to try hard not to let Nittles' vocabulary intimidate me.

Nittles crawled onto my shoulder and inspected the veil. "Hmm. Well, it's an improvement to your face; so that's something."

"You're a great encouragement, aren't you?"

"I should say so. May I suggest covering up the upper half of your face as well?"

I shifted the bulky sack to my other shoulder. "You could at least carry some of the fruit. I have plenty of empty sacks to put them in. Even carrying a fraction of them would help."

"I keep telling you, dear one. The sacks are for your face, not the fruit."

"I have half a mind to shove *you* into one of the sacks."

"But then you'd have to carry me as well."

"Oh, I wouldn't carry the sack," I grunted "I would throw it in the river."

Nittles barked a laugh. “Well done! Your words were quick and morbid. If you hadn’t ripped me from my world and forced me to meld with you, I’d start to like you.”

His words cut deep, and I didn’t know whether to take them as a compliment or an insult. By the look on his face, he was amused at my confusion.

“I didn’t—”

“Yes, yes, I know,” he interjected. “You’ve apologized. Nevertheless, the deed is done.”

I couldn’t help but think of my father. I thought something similar when he took my money. He’d apologized, but I didn’t care since it wouldn’t bring back all the coppers he’d stolen. Was what I did to Nittles any different from what Father did to me? Yes. Father knew what he was doing, and I did not.

I took a deep breath as the city drew closer. We’d made as many glaidens as we could, and I couldn’t go back empty-handed. I had to make this work.

“Honestly, Sashel, why the ridiculous veil?”

“Now and then, people here pass through Ashwood, and I don’t want the slightest chance of anyone recognizing me. The last thing I want is for my townsfolk to see me as a witch.”

“It seems the word ‘witch’ means something different in your world. In Tal Miral, a witch is any woman who can perform magic, whether it be for good or evil. What you think of as a witch is what I would call a sorceress, one who worships the Corrupt One and makes dark sacrifices for power.”

I placed the sack down to catch my breath. “The clerics have power. I’ve seen their staves turn rotten meat fresh and make old wood as strong as the day it was chopped. But I was taught theirs is the only good kind of magic.”

He rolled his eyes. "And if the clerics say a sword is only good if they wield it, would you believe them? Magic is neutral. It is the motive behind the magic that matters. There is nothing wrong with being a witch."

I remembered all the horrible messages written on my cottage door. "I'm not a witch, and I never want you calling me that."

He descended and pressed his wings to his back. "There's a lot of emotion behind the word. I sense it's not just because of what the clerics say."

My steps slowed as I met his gaze. "About four years ago, strange things happened to Ashwood. Phantoms and monsters appeared. Even the plants started attacking us. During that time, my mother died giving birth to Minessa. Around the same time, the attacks stopped. Ever since then, the villagers have believed she was a witch."

His white, furry face softened. "I see."

"No, you don't. We've been shunned. Not a day goes by that I don't see someone bring their fingers to their forehead to ward off evil when they see me."

"I'm sorry. I didn't—"

"Do you know what the townsfolk do on my sister's birthday?"

He shrugged. "They celebrate?"

I laughed, but there was no mirth in it. "Yes, they celebrate. Not for my sister's birth, but because it's the anniversary of my mother's death!"

The sprackin stared at me, and I realized I'd been shouting. Why was I taking out my anger on him? He had helped me more than anyone else had.

"Sashel," he said softly. "I had no idea that happened, and you have my condolences. I will never call you a witch."

I nodded, and we continued our pace. Trying to lighten the mood, I said, "Besides, I'm far too beautiful to be a witch."

He scrutinized me and the blue veil I wore. "Hmm… are you sure you won't reconsider covering up the rest of your face? You might have better luck making the sale."

As we arrived at the city gates, I was flabbergasted by the immensity of the place. The outer walls stood five stories high with an iron gate at the entry, making the small wooden gate in Ashwood flimsy by comparison.

Inside, an endless marketplace overwhelmed me with a cacophony of noises. Venders proclaimed their goods, circus performers juggled and danced, and women wore dresses that would be scandalous back in my village.

More than once a passerby jostled me, but I clung to the coppers in my pocket the whole time. Several men eyed me, and I had the distinct impression they would jump me given the chance. I stuck to the main roads in clear view of the public until I arrived at the constable's office. After an hour of waiting in line, a short, thin man holding a quill and parchment greeted me.

"Name?"

"Tenari," I answered, picking the name of the only woman I remembered who wore a veil.

"Tenari." He scribbled the name. "Daughter of?"

"Tamble." I winced as I realized I had said my father's real name. Idiot! I just blurted it out, not even thinking. I hadn't expected they would even ask.

The man wrote the name on the paper. "And are you a citizen here?"

This time I thought before speaking. I didn't want to tell them I was from Ashwood. Sennevar wasn't at war with my village, but neither were they friendly. There was talk of Sennevar wanting to expand its territory, but I didn't know how true the rumors were. If I said I was a citizen, they may ask where I lived and possibly have some complicated tax I had to pay.

"I'm from Lanvire." I hoped picking a nearby territory that Sennevar controlled would be good enough. The cottage I intended to purchase was there.

The man eyed my blue veil as well as Nittles by my feet. He wrote something else down, then said, "The constable will see you now."

When I entered the office, we made brief introductions, then I placed a single slice of dried fruit on the table, all my hopes resting on such a small thing. "This is a glaiden, and it gives supernatural speed and agility to whoever eats it."

The constable raised it to eye level and sniffed. "The color is certainly different, but I'm afraid the story is the same."

"What do you mean?" I asked.

The man placed it back on the table and swirled his finger around it. The red freckles and orange hair on his fingers were captivating. I'd seen a few people pass through Ashwood with freckles, but this man seemed to have been bathed in them, nearly making him look solid red instead of fair-skinned like most others in Sennevar. And why did he have orange eyebrows but a white beard? That wasn't natural, was it?

"...at least once a month," he said.

No. I told myself I'd pay attention. It was crucial I didn't lose focus!

"I'm sorry. The journey here was more taxing than I realized. Can you repeat what you said?"

I rubbed my eyes, feigning fatigue. It wasn't difficult. At my feet, Nittles let out a frustrated sigh.

The constable gave me a patronizing look I was all too familiar with. "I said I see your kind all the time," he repeated with growing irritation. "They come with charms or potions that will supposedly bring my soldiers luck. When it doesn't work, they say I just need to give it more time. Some even say I have to *believe* before it can work." He bent his meaty finger back and flicked the glaiden across the room, thudding off the stone wall. "I'll spare you the trouble and refuse now."

A soft crackling sounded in the office. Although the constable barely noticed, my eyes darted around in panic. Behind him in the far corner, ivy grew through the window. The leaves turned black with whisps of smoke rising above them. No! Not here. Not now!

"I traveled many miles on foot!" I yelled, trying to keep their attention away from the corner. "I waited over an hour just to meet with you, and you won't even try it?"

"You were fortunate to see me at all today, and doubly fortunate I don't string you up for being a charlatan."

Near the ivy, the air cracked like glass, dark, hairline fractures stretching an arm's span. It was like strands of black thread hovering a few feet in the air with something beyond the cracks, something alive.

I focused on the constable. "I'm not a charlatan."

"It's one thing to swindle young men into buying a love potion. But draining the magistrate's coffers with…purple fruit?" His laugh turned into a cough before he continued. "Now, away with you."

My mind spun. What was beyond the cracks? What would happen if he saw them? He was going to throw me out. I had to make the sale, but I couldn't let him look in the corner. Minessa needed me. What she really needed was a mother. Mother would be much better at this. But instead, my sister had me, me, and this bag of dried fruit.

I grabbed a slice and shoved it in my mouth, chewing only a few times before swallowing hard. "Then you'll have to throw me out!"

The constable raised his bushy eyebrows, and then his face firmed. "If that's how you want it."

He reached his massive hands to grab me, but the fruit had already taken effect. His body slowed, like he was moving through water, and I leaned backward till my head nearly touched my ankles.

Cocking his head, he lunged, but I leaned to the side, only to see two guards closing in, swords drawn. I swatted the flat of the blade from the first guard only to realize hitting metal still hurt regardless of my dexterity and speed.

I kicked the hand of the second guard at just the right angle. I somehow knew what would happen. Sure enough, the man dropped his weapon, but before it touched the ground, I kicked the hilt. After three full rotations, I caught it.

I realized I was now holding a sword and pointing it straight at the constable of the city. As the other guard lurched toward me, I threw the sword. The handle struck just below his sternum, making him grunt as the air rushed from his lungs. He keeled over, and slammed against the corner of the room, directly towards the black ivy.

With my heightened perception and time slowed, I focused on the dark rift. The glaidens worked against me as it seemed to take an eternity for it to close, but at least no drethals appeared.

The other guard picked up the sword, but the constable raised a hand. He surveyed my small frame several times before his eyes landed on the sack of fruit at my feet.

"I think I'll have a second look at that fruit of yours."

The two of us sat down as if I hadn't just assaulted his guards. Every few seconds, my eyes darted to the corner, but the rift stayed closed.

The man twirled his beard before asking, "How long will the fruit last?"

"About five minutes, maybe more depending on how much you eat."

"And how much can someone eat?"

I paused. I itched to tell him what he wanted to hear, that there were no side effects. But he would find out eventually, and he would be livid if I wasn't upfront with him. I learned years ago not to focus on making a quick sale but to work on creating a continual customer. As much as I ached to withhold the information, I told him.

"You can become ill if you eat more than a few at once."

"Is it lethal?" he asked.

"No, but I wouldn't recommend it."

He furrowed his brow. "I can't have my men keeling over while fighting. That would be just as lethal to them."

"They can eat one or two, every few hours, but no more."

He laced his fingers in front of him. "Then eat another."

"But—"

"Eat another or there's no deal."

I let out a breath. My mother would be strong, and so would I. Reaching into the sack, I ate a second one. Time slowed further, and I could sense even the slightest movement around me.

"Another," he said.

"I can't."

"Now."

Nittles bumped my leg, urging me not to, but I ignored him. I imagined Minessa and me in the small cottage in Lanvire, safe and far away from Father. I ate another glaiden.

He raised a finger. "One more."

Nittles let out a savage growl, but I placed a calming hand on him. My fingers shook as I pulled out a fourth and ate. My heart felt like it would burst out of my chest. I could sense the very blood flowing through me, the slight breeze in the air, the breathing of the guards.

Letting out a slow breath, I stood firm. "They'll only last for a few minutes, but in that time, the city guards will be unstoppable."

He nodded as if it made perfect sense. Of course. He was a realistic man. Everything had pros and cons.

"A few minutes isn't enough to win a battle," he said.

The comment seemed half-hearted as his eyes never left the sack of fruit. I recognized the look. He had already decided to buy the glaidens; he just wanted to haggle. Since Nittles and I had gone over countless objections, I was ready for this.

My stomach churned, and bile rose up my throat, but I held it in. "It's perfect for law enforcement in the city. If a purse snatcher is on the run or a prisoner escapes, five minutes for your men would be invaluable."

"Invaluable" was the word Nittles suggested. He said by using it, the implication would be the fruit is priceless, and I'd be hard-pressed to part with it for any amount.

Clenching a fist to steady myself, I offered the constable to eat one at no cost, something most charlatans would never do. After accepting, he laughed uproariously as he juggled four knives, two cups, and a wet stone with ease. He sat down and dabbed his brow, turning even more red than his freckles.

"How much for the lot?"

As the room spun, I said another line from Nittles. "How much is it worth to have the best soldiers in the country?"

* * *

Ever so slowly, I left the constable's office, each step intensifying my nausea. I shut my eyes and focused on the sacks of coins in my hands. I made twenty-one silvers and eight coppers, a half silver per fruit depending on the weight. Since one silver was worth twenty coppers, I made 408 coppers in one day. That was almost what I saved over several months before. The best part wasn't the coin but the promise to buy all I had when I next visited. A few more trips like this and Minessa and I could move out. I couldn't believe it!

I would have giggled like my sister, but once I left the city gates, I could hold back the vomit no longer. I had just enough time to rip off my veil before giving up everything I'd eaten that day, then dry-heaved for several minutes. My entire body convulsed with each retch, and my limbs shook like reeds in the wind. I lay on my back just off the main road as passersby gave me a wide berth.

"You shouldn't have eaten so much," Nittles whispered.

"I had to prove they worked." I panted the words, then spat another mouthful of bile. Clutching the bags of coins, I relaxed. My plan had worked! It had actually worked!

"I did it!" I exclaimed.

"Yes, you did." Nittles turned toward the pile of vomit. "You did it there, and over there, and on the city wall too. You did it quite spectacularly."

The mention of it sent a twinge of nausea through me once more. "You can stop, now."

His eyes widened. "And the way it came out your nose was incredible! Masterfully done."

I retched again then glared at the sprackin. He only grinned as though it was exactly what he wanted. Was he doing this because I took him from his world, or was he always a pain in the neck? I suspected it was the latter.

My damp dress clung to my body, and the stench of vomit burned my nostrils. My hands still trembled, and my legs felt as weak as a blade of grass. I planned to head straight back, but in my state, I'd never make it. I would have to spend the night in the city.

Minessa was staying at Elder Grinda's house; so, she'd be fine, but I was hoping I could make it back by nightfall. Squeezing the sacks tighter, my worries eased, and I entered the gates once more. Despite all that happened, I succeeded, and hope was beginning to bloom.

CHAPTER 5

"Beware of luxury, lest it strangle you in your sleep."
—The Book of Clergy

The goddess stood before me, her face shining so bright I couldn't make out any details. The light wasn't blinding like the sun but soothing like moonlight.

A stone chamber surrounded us with ornate tapestries of green and silver. In the center stood the silver candle that had mostly burned up. The goddess placed a hand on the candle and said, "Remember."

The candle grew and radiated power. Nittles had said this might happen as she visited him in his dreams to refill his heartfire, but seeing it was something else entirely.

Before I could speak, silver light flashed, and I awoke. The bed in the inn was softer than anything I had slept in, and the room was warm as soft sunlight. As the smell of savory meat wafted through the air, I threw on the dress I'd washed and hung to dry the night before. It was still damp, but I didn't care. The smell of breakfast pulled me downstairs.

Whatever they sprinkled on the eggs made me devour them in seconds, and the juicy sausage was better than anything I could make. The fried potatoes burned my tongue, but a tiny bit of lifespur fixed that. Everything was incredible!

On the same street as the inn, I entered the marketplace. I bought a forest green dress with white sleeves which tugged at my waist and shoulders. It was beautiful, and strangest of all it was new! I also bought a yellow knitted hat that would fit Minessa. I even bought a pair of shoes, which the cobbler said matched the belt on my dress. I didn't know what the belt had to do with anything, but it sounded fancy.

I packed my old blue dress neatly in my sack. After all was said and done, I'd only spent two silvers, and it was well worth it.

As we left the city gates, Nittles turned to me. "I don't want to sound childish for saying this, but I don't want to leave this place."

Part of me wanted to shoot back a retort like usual, but he seemed sincere for once. The truth was I agreed. Despite the rough start and my brief illness the day before, this had been one of the best times I had since Mother died.

I looked back at Sennevar and the thought struck me. "We can move here."

"I wasn't expecting you to agree."

"I hadn't realized how nice parts of the city were, and I definitely wasn't expecting the constable to be so enthusiastic about the fruit."

"Well of course he wanted more. Glaidens are one of the most powerful fruits."

"What about the blue fruit you mentioned? The one that gives strength?"

"Mandrils. They provide fertility as well, but I can't make those, nor do I wish to. They rot far too quickly and turn to drethals. The last thing we want is an army of Krals."

The thought made my hair stand on end, and I moved on. "We can move here within a month. I can't believe it."

"What were you expecting? Selling the glaidens was a sure thing. The only question was how much we would make."

"I guess I was so used to things not turning out well that I didn't dare imagine moving. The constable may even help us find a place to stay. He'd be delighted to know I want to live here and continually sell to him."

"And what of me?" he asked. "Living in Sennevar is better than that cold shack of yours, but I wish to return to my world."

"I know, but you said we're connected, right?"

"Melded," he corrected. "Yes, I have no flame without you, which was all your doing, I might add."

"I'll find a way to get us both through. We can travel back and forth together. We'll find a way to get your fire back."

Nittles flew on my shoulder and locked eyes with me. "Do you swear you will do this? Do you swear on your fire you'll do everything you can to make this happen?"

I had never seen him so intense. Even when he insulted me, there was always a hint of playfulness. Now, his icy stare warned me not to make light of this.

I slowly nodded. "I swear."

* * *

As we approached the staircase in the Scarlet Forest, two black rifts smoldered nearby. Luckily, they weren't near any fruit trees; so, no drethals appeared. It cost me a good amount of silver fire from my soul to close them, but it needed to be done. I saw what the dark fruits did to the squirrel, and I couldn't imagine what would happen if a wolf or a bear ate them.

I buried the five sacks of silver coins at the base of the staircase. The city's crest was engraved on each of the silver coins, a tree shaped like a hand reaching up to a crescent moon. The sacks also bore the same image along with a receipt from the constable. Since Ashwood wasn't on good terms with Sennevar, I wouldn't risk anyone seeing them. The coppers, however, had the more common engraving of a stag, a sign of the old empire before it fell. These would be fine to use.

No other creature would come near the stairs, not even Nittles. Other people must have passed by this before, meaning they either couldn't see it or had the same compulsion to leave. Either way, it seemed like the best place to hide the coins.

As we made our way into Ashwood, Jocksin sat by the road, hands cupped in front of him as always.

"Copper for the cripple?"

I tossed him a copper coin and waited till we were out of earshot before turning to Nittles. "You and I saw him eat the lifespur, didn't we?"

"Indeed," he said. "It should have healed him. You said his legs were crushed as a child, correct?"

"Yes. They're mangled."

The sprackin nodded. "Lifespur is powerful, but it has its limits. For instance, it can't cure diseases or bring someone back from death. But mending bones and muscles is no problem. Are you sure his back wasn't injured? There are complicated nerves that lifespur can't cure."

"Healer Fendin told me they were broken, but I don't know the details. You're saying they can't heal all wounds?"

"Everything has limits."

That was a thought. I just assumed the fruit could heal anything. Although I felt bad for Jocksin, part of me was relieved he hadn't healed. It would cause quite a stir, and I would be at the center of it.

The rattling wheels of a cart and the braying of a donkey pulled me out of my thoughts. The fresh smell of river fish wafted towards me as two men leading the cart argued.

"The folks won't pay, no matter what you tell them!" a plump man said.

The gangly one leading the donkey tipped his straw hat and spat. "We're always finding new breeds in the Morggis. Won't be no different from the others."

"No different?" the shorter one asked. "Anyone with half an eye can tell these ones be cursed!"

"Half an eye? What in the five gods does half an eye do?"

"Well…it's like me gran's eye. She only had one, and it didn't work too well."

"Fish guts! I know your gran well, and she has a good pair of eyes." The gangly man elbowed the other in the ribs. "Too bad you don't got a good pair to match. Eh?"

"I'll have you know I have the sharpest eyes in Ashwood."

"'Twasn't the pair I was referring to."

Upon seeing me, the tall man removed his hat. "Beg your pardon. Those weren't the proper words for a lady."

I eyed the crate on the cart. "What did you mean the fish are cursed?"

The taller man elbowed the other again. "There. See what you did. Spreading rumors and the like." He turned to me and smiled. "Good lady, I am Bordig, and this is Grad, and these magnificent creatures aren't cursed. They're a rare breed never before seen."

The portly one lifted the lid and waved me over. Each fish had two emerald horns jutting from its head with five sharp dorsal fins across its back. Instead of tail fins, the fish's body tapered off in a point like a snake.

I stepped back. "What are they?"

The shorter man gave them another look. "They're called… demon fish."

For the third time, Bordig elbowed him. "No one will buy them if we call them that."

"How about the Finnigan fish?" Grad asked. "You know… since they got lots of fins. So, it's fin again fish. Get it?"

Bordig gave the shorter man a blank look. "I worry about you, Grad." He handed me a copper. "If anyone asks, they're called 'horn fish,' and they be a delicacy in Torinth."

"Hey! Stop that!"

I turned as Grad pulled a fish from Nittles' mouth. The sprackin growled, causing the man to stumble back. Seizing the opportunity, Nittles bit into another fish and hopped onto my shoulder.

Bordig held him back and laughed. "Let him have it. At least we know someone will like them." As the cart pulled away, he yelled back, "Remember, they're horn fish, and they're a delicacy."

I waved and then turned to Nittles who licked his paws. "Do you know what they are?"

Blood dripped from his mouth as he said, "They're grakes. I take it you don't have them in your world."

I shook my head, and he hopped off my shoulder. "Your world is being influenced by mine. More rifts must be opening."

"Is there any way to close them all at once?"

"Only through dark arts can it be done, and I will have no part in that. They involve human sacrifices, mutilating family members, and worse things that are too deplorable to speak of. You will not ask of this again."

As we neared the village, my stomach dropped as all of Ashwood began to change. In sporadic places the air rippled like a heat haze, but there was no fire. Vegetables in the market held strange patterns on their skin, and vines covering cottages were tinged a deep blue.

Most shocking of all were the leaves. The soft, red leaves covering every street had turned inky black.

"Sashel, look!" Nittles cried.

Hovering a few feet above the smithy was another smokey, black rift. A large, yellow eye peered through the small opening. The Kral!

I held out my hand and willed it to shut, pouring silver fire into it. The flames weren't visible, but I felt the candle in my soul shrink. A snarl came from the other side, but it faded as the portal shut.

Only two people had seen me raise my hand. The mother and her child stared at me and then at where my hand had been pointing. Before they could say anything, I sped up and rounded a corner.

"Did they see the portal?" I asked Nittles.

"I don't know. I suppose I was a bit distracted with a Kral staring at us like we were its next meal!"

"I know."

"No, you don't know!" He grunted in frustration. "If I had all my abilities back, I might stand a chance against some of the smaller creatures, but not a cursed Kral!"

"Keep it down!"

"You didn't make it past the first step on the stairs. Did you?"

"I—yes I did."

"Liar! That's why the rifts are opening. Do you realize what you've done?"

"It'll be fine."

"You don't know that. You've weakened me by melding with you, and now you've started the Rending. Creatures from the Sprawn Lands are escaping!"

I pinched the bridge of my nose and sighed. "I'm sorry I lied to you." When he continued glaring at me, I went on. "I promise I'll close every rift that opens, even if it takes every bit of heartfire I have, even if it takes all day and all night. I swear."

He considered. "Very well. But I won't make a single glaiden with a dark portal nearby. Closing them takes priority. Agreed?"

"Agreed."

He folded his wings to his back just as a family walked by. I waved weakly, and when they passed, a wall of tension formed between Nittles and me, arresting my words before they could escape.

Despite the tension, something he said forced me to ask, "What did you mean you've been weakened since we're melded? How strong were you before?"

He faced forward as we neared the cottage. "It doesn't matter. I am not that sprackin anymore."

When I opened the cottage door, I was greeted by my sister's wails. She covered her left eye, curled up in the corner. I had to pry her hand back before I could see. All around was swollen, and the white of her eye was red from burst blood vessels.

"Who did this?" I asked, already knowing the answer.

"Papa," she said through sobs. "He was mean again."

Across the room, the portrait of Mother lay on the floor. The frame was cracked in one corner where it had collided with the wall. Drunken Father had returned.

Minessa's crying didn't stop until I pulled out the soft, yellow hat I bought in Sennevar. She cradled it like a doll, and I pressed her head to my chest. Rocking her gently, I rubbed the nubs on her left hand where her severed fingers had been.

After giving her a lifespur, her eye healed but the nubs on her hand remained the same. Not for the first time I wondered if Father had sliced her fingers as well, but I couldn't remember. How many more injuries could she take? In less than a month, we would move out, and that day couldn't come soon enough.

CHAPTER 6

"What separates the clerical powers from witchcraft? Both may grow crops and bring protection. Look not at the product but at the cost. One requires strength of mind; the other, human flesh."
—The Book of Clergy

The next few weeks passed relatively the same. Tension remained between my father and me, and I kept Minessa at a safe distance from him. His outbursts grew worse, and later he'd apologize, but the cycle continued.

Nittles helped me make glaidens under the agreement that I continue trying to open a portal to his world. Each day I failed to open one, he'd scowl at me and urge me to try harder. Occasionally, I'd catch him playing with my sister, but he'd immediately stop when he saw me looking. Whether he simply enjoyed children or was upset that she was being beaten by Father, he seemed to have a soft spot for her.

Once, I made jam from the fruits, only after realizing it was a bad idea. It was difficult to get enough honey to make them, and it would be cumbersome for the soldiers to carry jars of jam everywhere they went. Sacks of dried fruit were more portable, plus I found I didn't like working with honey as it reminded me of Father's mead.

Once a week, we'd travel to Sennevar, always burying the silver near the staircase afterward. A villager taking one glimpse of the Sennevar crest on the coins could ruin everything. The last time I buried them, I could swear I heard someone following us, but it was just my paranoia. Deep down I knew all of this was too good to be true. Surely someone would steal them, and I didn't dare to hope. Hope was for the fool.

Finally, the day came, and even Nittles looked excited. Father was at work with the masons, and Minessa played in the back. There was so much I wanted to bring, little mementos, my sister's toys, and mother's portrait, but I needed to pack light. Whatever we couldn't carry on our backs had to be left behind as I still had to retrieve the buried silver. Minessa's sack was neatly packed, but I still struggled with mine.

"You're stalling," Nittles said. "Having second thoughts about leaving?"

"No. Today just snuck up on me."

The sprackin gave me a sideways look. "Did you not know we were leaving today?"

"I did. I just…thought I'd have more time."

Father had a locked box under his bed with mother's most precious belongings, but I didn't bother with it. I ached to know if mother's necklace was inside, but leaving soon took priority.

"She was a good mother, and she died giving birth," the voice in my head whispered.

Why did the voice keep saying that? I shut my eyes, but I couldn't remember just as I couldn't remember the day she died.

I folded my old blue dress and placed it in the sack. I would wear my new dress as we left, and I didn't care if the villagers noticed.

Next came a small knife, scissors, and a brush. What else did I need? I could buy everything else in Sennevar, but I felt like I was missing something.

The front door creaked open, and my father stepped in. Upon seeing me, he froze.

"You're home," I said numbly.

His eyes moved from the sacks to me then around the room to stare at the opened drawers and items strewn across the floor. "We ran out of building lime, so I left early."

I wanted to sink under the floorboards and crawl away. I felt like I was a child again, caught doing something wrong, but this wasn't wrong. He was in the wrong, and I was doing what was needed.

"I'm leaving with Minessa."

His face went from puzzlement to shock and then firmed to anger. "I see."

My stomach dropped as his right hand clenched and unclenched as though grasping for something, a tell-tale sign I was all too familiar with. He wanted a drink, which meant he was unstable.

As cautious as a rabbit near a sleeping lion, I placed the sack on the kitchen table. "It's better for all of us if we leave."

My father gave me a cold stare. Dust coated his grey, frizzy hair, and his brown eyes seemed black in the dim light. "Where'd you get the dress?"

The dress! I'd forgotten about it. I had kept it hidden from him to avoid questions. "Sennevar," I said.

"Must have cost a good silver."

As he stepped towards me, I clutched my dress and said, "I needed a new one."

His eyes grew hungry, and his thoughts were plain as day. Sell the dress to buy mead. "Where'd you get the coin?" he asked with a dry voice.

"I sold fruit."

"No way you made that much from selling jars to old widows. How much do you have left?"

"None."

"Then we'll sell the dress. You'll ruin it within a week anyway. And leave the weasel behind."

"Why do you want my weasel?"

"Never mind that." His hand clenched faster and beads of sweat formed on his face.

"You want to sell him like you sold everything else."

"Just go change."

"No."

He pointed a thick finger at my room. "Go change now." Each word was clipped with frustration.

I grabbed a pan and pointed it at him. "No!" It wasn't about the dress. It wasn't even about Nittles. I hated how he wanted to bleed me dry before I left. He didn't even try to convince me to stay. I thought I didn't care about my father, but the swirl of emotions inside me said otherwise. I told him I was leaving, and all he cared about was his next drink. He didn't see my dress; he saw money for mead. He didn't see his daughters; he saw mouths to feed which would cost money that could have been spent on drinks.

I stepped in front of the sprackin, and my father lunged. I swung but only grazed his shoulder, which did nothing to his burly frame. I raised the pan again, but he grabbed my wrist. His massive hand swallowed my entire forearm. I was an idiot for not keeping a few glaidens on me! I jerked and pulled, but he didn't so much as budge.

He ripped the pan out of my hand, sending a lance of pain up my wrist. "In this house, you do what I say, or—"

He cried out as Nittles bit deep into his calf. Father kicked and swung his leg, but the sprackin held tight. Father released my arm and then gripped me with his left to have a better position to strike him, but he froze.

He stared, not at Nittles or me, but at something behind me. I didn't have to look to know it was the painting of Mother. His watery eyes looked from me to the painting and his lip quivered.

I tried to hate my father, but at that moment, I couldn't. His face seemed to say, "What have I become?" I missed who he used to be when Mother was alive.

There was a strange moaning, but it didn't come from Father. It came from behind the cottage. He must have heard too as his grip loosened. I yanked my hand free and darted to the back door, swinging it open.

A smoking rift hovered above the plum tree, corrupting several branches, but no fruit remained. At the base of the tree sat my sister wearing her yellow hat. Dark sludge covered her dress as she bit into the last of the drethals with her monstrous, black teeth.

CHAPTER 7

"The rifts are too many. They surround me by day and whisper by night. What power or might shall seal them tight?"
—The Book of Heretics

Little Minessa still wore her yellow hat I bought her as black, pulpy juice covered her white apron. She bit hard into the last fruit, not caring she bit several fingers as she ate. Blood dribbled down her hands and wrists, mixing with the black sludge coating her small body. She moaned in savage delight, licking her fingers and even the nubs on her left hand, smearing the juices across her pudgy face.

"Minessa!"

I ran, but something pulled my dress back. Nittles held tight with his mouth and flapped his wings hard. I batted him aside and reached my sister, but her blue eyes had already morphed into bile yellow.

"No, no, no!" I yelled.

She let out a blood-curdling scream as the nails on her right hand lengthened into black talons. Gritting her teeth in anguish, she clutched my arm and gave me a desperate look. She was helpless, confused, and wanted her big sister. I wanted to hold her, to hug her, to tell her everything would be fine.

"Sashel, we need to go!" Nittles cried.

"There has to be a cure."

"There isn't!"

"What's going on?" Father asked.

His mouth fell open at the sight of Minessa. After another spasm, she raked her claws down my arm. I only had time to scream before she slashed my leg. She grew to my height and raised her left arm which had morphed into a scorpion stinger. Nittles lunged at her face, obscuring her vision. Her swing went wide, and I scrambled back.

"Sashel!" Father pointed at Minessa. "Look out!"

I dropped to my knees as the air whooshed over my head. Minessa's stinger lengthened, and she shrieked like a hawk. She swiped at Nittles, but he dodged.

Father grabbed me under my arms and swung me away from her. I focused on the silver candle in my soul and poured heartfire into the sprackin. He dove at her face and struck her with more force than his small body should allow.

The smoking portal near the tree stretched and ripped, revealing the Kral on the other side. I focused on the opening and willed it to close, but the creature resisted, pulling it wider with its taloned hand and thick stinger.

"One shall stand," the creature growled.

Minessa glared up and responded, "All others fall!"

The creature could only fit its one human-like arm through, yet the appendage stretched longer than my sister's entire body. Catching the stinger, the Kral snapped it like a twig. In a single motion, it rotated the stinger then thrust it through my sister's chest, nailing her to the tree. The Kral roared in victory, then pulled its arm back and let the portal shut.

My sister's pale skin darkened once more, and her yellow eyes turned their natural blue. Her elongated arm shrank, and the stinger holding her to the tree vanished. She was back to normal, save for the gaping wound in her chest.

My father let me go, and I darted towards her. I pressed my hands to her wound, but the blood seeped through my fingers and continued to pour.

Tears welled in my sister's eyes. "I'm so cold."

I pushed harder with my slick fingers. "You're gonna be fine."

"It hurts, Sash. It hurts!"

"Lifespur!" I told Nittles. "She needs lifespur!"

He shook his head. "They only turn human just before death."

There was fruit drying in the oven. That's what I was forgetting earlier. I couldn't wait for them to cool. How would I get her to eat them? Maybe I could summon something through the portal that could help.

Her small hands clutched my arms. "I'm scared."

Her breathing slowed, and her head slumped into my chest. I lifted her face and shook her, but her body was limp and lifeless.

"Minessa?" a quivering voice asked. My father grabbed her body from me, cradling her in his massive arms. He rocked her back and forth as his tears pattered on her head. "My little girl, please, please, no!"

I'd seen my father weep many times, but never with such absolute hopelessness. His face wrinkled and contorted as he squeezed her tighter. Brushing her hair, Father sobbed as he sang a lullaby. I hadn't heard him sing in years, and the sound of it hollowed me out as the reality sank ever deeper. Minessa was dead.

"Father, I—"

"You did this." The words were barely a whisper, yet it shook me.

"No."

"The dress. Your trips to Sennevar. You're somehow responsible, aren't you?"

"I—I didn't mean to—"

"Go!"

I ran. With a torn, bloody dress, I ran. My vision blurred and my lungs burned, but I couldn't stop. I couldn't look back. I had to get to the staircase. For once in my life, I was focused, focused on the Scarlet Forest ahead.

CHAPTER 8

"The clergy claims the staircase was created through devilry, meant to cause mayhem and destruction. I denounce this. Look not at the weapons it brings but how the wielder is tempered. Look not at the charms they summon but at the trials that purify."

—The Book of Heretics

I gazed at the silver steps, my heart racing as I prepared to climb. This could make things worse; I knew. But there was a chance, a sliver of hope, that things would be fixed. Hope. I dreaded the word. Hope was empty promises. Hope made people desperate. But I *was* desperate, and I needed my sister back.

Then I remembered my mother and hesitated. I had tried everything to bring her back, and every time I failed, the pain grew worse. That's why I couldn't climb the stairs. I feared one more failure would push me over the edge. But now I was ready to leap. I missed my mother, but I couldn't live without Minessa. It was my fault she died.

The thick branches around me blocked out much of the sunlight, leaving only the dim silver glow of the stairs. The goddess was nowhere in sight, but the celestial song still echoed in my mind. How many steps would I have to climb? Nittles told me everyone was different, but I had to keep climbing until the song began.

As I raised my foot, Nittles spoke behind me. "What are you doing?"

"I'm climbing the stairs."

"You told me you stopped at the first one."

I turned to face him as he flapped in the air. "I did, but I could have gone further."

The sprackin gave me an incredulous look. "Then why didn't you?"

"It—" I swallowed, trying to hold myself together. "It sounded like I could get my mother back if I kept climbing."

"I fail to see the problem. You told me you loved your mother."

"I do. That's why I couldn't go further."

Nittles huffed. "You're not making any sense."

"I know." I faced the stairs and took a deep breath.

"Beware!" he said. "If you try climbing again and don't go high enough, the Rending will escalate. The consequences would be disastrous!"

"Then help me."

"I can't. I don't even see the stairs; even if I did, I would be stopped instantly. You must climb them alone. Are you sure you can do this?"

My heart thundered in my chest. Was I sure? I remembered stepping off willingly last time, but was that the stairs' subtle influence? No. I stepped off because I didn't want to hope. "I'm sure."

He nodded. "Then listen closely. You'll hear a section of the song with each step you take, clues for the trials to come. Continue climbing until you hear one additional line after the trials conclude. You'll know it when you hear it."

"Alright." I let out a slow breath and took my first step. The celestial voice, the goddess's voice, sang out as it had a month ago when I first climbed.

"All that was lost, the new and the old,
Will be given in full when the story is told.

The same panic I had last time struck me. *I have to get off. This is wrong. It's unnatural. I have to –*

The thought occurred to me. Why was Father so sad about Minessa dying? He hated her. He never saw her as his daughter. Yet he looked so empty upon seeing her. His sobbing lullaby still echoed in my ears.

My mind focused, and I was back on the stairs. The urge to leave faded like before; however, this time I took a second step.

"First will come visions that cut to the bone.
The greatest of lies you find on your own."

The goddess appeared, gesturing wildly. Although her mouth moved, no words came out. The light from her necklace and bracelets was blinding, and her face was so transparent I couldn't read her lips. What was she trying to say?

"Keep going!" Nittles cried. "Don't stop!"

I took a third step.

"Next is the serpent that swimmeth below.
The depths are its friend but also its foe."

Dark rifts opened around me, and a bear-like rock monster peeked through and spewed fire. The heat was intense, like opening an oven. I ducked, but the flames moved to either side of me. A force stronger than the beast protected the stairs.

Nittles flew a safe distance from the flames but continued watching. The pale Kral drew near another rift and clawed at me like before but to no avail.

At the fourth step, my stomach grew queasy like when I ate too many glaidens. Each word from the goddess's song was seared into my mind.

"Sand in the glass will fall from on high.
Live in the past if your wish is to die."

Swallowing hard, I stepped again.

"The spirits within come out to play.
Burn their name or drink them away."

I groaned as the nausea intensified. How many trials were there? With trembling legs, I climbed higher.

Secrets are heavy and shouldn't be borne.
Speak them aloud or flesh will be torn.

Still no sign of the trials ending. My heart pounded, and I struggled to breathe, but I rose to the seventh step.

"Travel the forest that sees you as prey.
The scepter of runes will make them obey."

My legs gave out, and I fell to my knees. Everything around me spun faster and faster, and I clung to the steps. I had to keep going. For Minessa, I had to keep going! Raising a hand, I crawled to the eighth step, begging the gods for mercy.

After the trials, the beast will arise.
The head of an eagle will bring its demise."

Finally, it was done. It wasn't just the words, but the tune and the way it faded out, I knew it was over. Colored spots littered my vision, and I tumbled backward. Pain shot from my side, then my knee. The last thing I felt was the soft, cool earth beneath me.

* * *

"I warned you,"

I tried to open my eyes but couldn't muster the strength.

"I warned you," the voice repeated. "I told you the Rending would come if you didn't climb the stairs. Now your world is tearing apart."

As I raised my hand, my arm throbbed. Was that from my father hurting me? No, this was from falling down the steps. Rubbing my eyes with my other hand proved far better, and the first thing I saw was Nittles' white furry face glowering at me. I winced as I sat up. It felt like a dagger was embedded in my side, probably a cracked rib.

His face softened as he said, "I'm…sorry about your sister. She meant a lot to you."

"Yes." I cleared my throat as it was dry and ragged. "You were right. I shouldn't have lied to you, and I should have climbed the stairs the first time."

He looked surprised at my admission. "Well, yes."

Silence rested over us, not out of tension like before but from exhaustion and defeat. The sprackin was the one to break the silence by making a lifespur for me, and my pain eased.

Instead of broken bones and deep cuts, they became light bruises and faint scars. Although I wanted to eat another and completely heal, I wouldn't risk getting sick. As I washed the blood and grime off in a nearby stream, I recited the song I heard from the stairs.

"Anything else?" he asked.

"That was it."

Nittles lapped at the cool water. "If you pass the trials, you will get your sister back. Kareli is powerful and keeps her word. And I must confess, I'm impressed with you climbing so many stairs. Very few have done so."

With my bare hands I dug up the silver coins by the stairs. Deep down I knew I was just distracting myself by doing this. Maybe if I knew the coins were safe, I could hold onto the fading fantasy that my sister would come back, and we could have a life away from Father. Upon seeing the coins, I again felt like someone was watching me, but I ignored it. As I told Nittles about the goddess, I mentioned how she seemed mute.

He nodded. "I saw her. She seemed worried about something. I still don't know why she is appearing in the real world when she's only appeared in dreams until now."

After burying the sacks, I brushed off my tattered dress. "We should be going."

He perked up. "You know where the first trial will be?"

"No. I'm going back to Ashwood…for my sister's funeral." The words felt wrong as though "sister" and "funeral" didn't belong in the same sentence. Still, I went on. "If someone dies in the morning, they will be burned in the evening. I missed my mother's funeral. I won't miss Minessa's."

CHAPTER 9

"When we are deceived, we hate ourselves more than our deceiver; for we have proven ourselves the fool."
—Words of Shoffilem

The sun bled red on the horizon by the time we reached Ashwood. I had no idea what Father told the villagers, but I needed to honor my sister's death.

At the front of the temple stood hundreds of people around the stone slab. Cleric Shoff stood before them reciting a passage from the Meritori in his soft voice that nevertheless carried across the crowd. "We are planted and sown, purged and grown, and in the end cometh the reaping."

As I crept closer, I gasped. There was not just one body on the slab but four, all clothed in white burial shrouds. Two adults lay side by side. The third was a woman whose womb was swollen from pregnancy. By far the youngest was little Minessa who hadn't reached her fourth year. Her body didn't belong there. Mine did.

I closed every rift I could find, but how many others were there? The Kral must have killed them. Then again, maybe other creatures had gotten loose. This was all my fault! Nittles was right. I didn't know what I was doing.

From the back of the crowd, Grinda turned to see me. "Great judgment!" she exclaimed. "Sashel!"

Several others turned, muttering to each other as they saw me. The old woman hugged me and then examined my torn and bloody clothes. "Oh, my dear! What did that monster do to you? You must've been so scared. And poor Minessa. I'm so sorry."

I was relieved she didn't suspect me, but I preferred not to have this much attention. Soon half the crowd was facing me and peppering me with questions. "How did this happen? Did you see the creatures? Was this witchcraft? Did you do this?"

Cleric Shoff looked up from his notes. "What is this? What's going on?"

The villagers led me to the front until I stood before the stone slab. Wood and straw laid beneath the bodies, making the funeral pyre ready for burning.

The cleric bent his lanky frame and placed a bony hand on my shoulder, eyeing my tattered clothes. "I've seen gutted fish in better shape than you. We'll get you cleaned up after this. The families have already said their peace, but if you wish to say something before we light the pyre, you may."

"Has Father spoken yet?"

Shoff's white-whiskered face wrinkled in concern. "He didn't come."

I should have guessed he wouldn't come. He was probably home drinking.

The cleric must have seen my anger because he added, "We all grieve in our own way. Don't be hasty to pass judgment. But since no relative of Minessa has spoken, I encourage you to if you can."

The crowd silenced as all eyes fell on me. As I turned to her body, my heart dropped. A flood of tears begged to escape, but I held them at bay. I had to be strong. Mother would be strong. I had to believe I could bring my sister back. Gently clutching her small foot, I was reminded again of how young she was.

Letting out a shuddering breath, I faced the crowd, but before I could speak, the earth beneath my feet turned hard as stone. I looked down, but there was only soft soil and leaves. Moving my foot around, it all felt like…the stone steps from the staircase. A flash of silver lit the sky, but instead of gasps or exclamations, there was only dead silence. The crowd stood still as statues.

At first, I thought they were too stunned to speak, but the torch near the pyre removed all doubt. The flames were motionless as a painting. The same sonorous voice I heard near the stairs spoke again. "The Trial of Visions hath begun."

The trial! Not now. I wasn't ready. My mind raced to the song, and I whispered the first two lines. "First will come visions that cut to the bone. The greatest of lies you find on your own."

"Indeed."

I spun as a man five paces away gave a resounding clap. Everything about him seemed off. His beard wasn't blonde but glittering gold, matching his eyes. His violet shirt seemed too bright for the dark evening light, and the rapier at his side didn't just glint; it glowed. He seemed too perfect, with no blemishes or wrinkles on his face or clothes even when he moved.

The man waved a hand, and the crowd vanished along with the funeral pyre. Instead of the village, a grand arena surrounded me with blue marble pillars supporting several stories of cheering fans. At least, it looked like they cheered. The arena was deathly silent, yet the people waved banners and opened their mouths as if roaring applause, yet there was no sound.

"You may call me Vision Master, and you are in my domain," the man said. "The cowardly goddess has stopped time until we conclude our bout. Once one of us concedes, the trial will end and time will resume. Any questions?"

My mind raced, but nothing else was said of the trial.

"How does this work?" I asked. "Do we…fight?"

Vision Master chuckled. "A fight would imply there's a minuscule chance of you succeeding. No, this is merely sport."

I shoved the purple fruit in my mouth and chewed quickly.

The man's golden eyes glowed brighter. "Ah, glaidens. Summoning a sprackin was clever. The few who make it past the first step of the stairs usually summon charms or amulets before I slay them."

With a snap of his fingers, five spiders as tall as a man appeared. Their size wasn't the only thing that made me jump back. They were made entirely of blades.

He sauntered forward. "You see, pain is a fascinating concept. We all have vices to numb ourselves from reality. For some it's women. For others, it's sweets, the bottle, or even sleep. For me, my vice is pain itself. When I inflict it on others, my own seems to alleviate."

The spiders were just visions. The song said so. But it also said they could cut to the bone. Was that a metaphor? The first spider swung its metallic leg, scoring a deep gash in my thigh. A scream leaped from my throat as I clutched the wound. This was real!

He let out a giggle that lasted far too long before chanting in a sing-song tone.

"Clickety-clack
The spiders lack
Their webs needed to spin.
They slit and slash.
They bite and gnash
And make their homes with your skin."

A flash of light blinded me as another spider punctured my calf. When my sight returned, Vision Master scratched his cheek and looked around as though nothing had happened.

"I like it here." A section of the arena dissipated, revealing the temple of Ashwood. "So many colors. In Tal Miral, there's only a green hue in the sky. My visions work even better here. Maybe I can escape from Kareli once and for all. She only lets me out for trials, you see, but they're so few and far between."

Another spider struck, but I dodged, the glaiden doing its job. I threw a rock with perfect precision, but the man moved unnaturally quickly and continued speaking.

"The last few I fought became my prisoners. Would you like that? I'll allow you to see your loved ones, but you'll be unable to interact with them. They will see you as a wraith, a haunting spirit. Truly wonderful. Wouldn't you say?"

In unison, the five spiders charged. I dodged the first then flipped over the second, but the third slashed my back.

"I've been watching you," he continued. "Every rift you've inadvertently opened I see through. And I've seen much. Vision Master sees all!"

I swung a fist, but he vanished, and my arm was slit from wrist to elbow.

"Clickety-clack. Clickety-clack."

I dropped to my knees as searing pain radiated from my hip to the base of my neck. I was no match for him. This was insane. Every second that passed, I was being sliced to ribbons. I turned and ran. Between the marble columns and under the archways I sprinted, a crazed cackling resounding behind me.

Beyond the arena was the mundane village of Ashwood. I bolted through the streets at a breakneck speed, my lungs burning in my chest. What was I going to do? A weapon. I needed a weapon!

The butcher shop was locked as was the smithy. I looked back several times, but Vision Master didn't pursue. Was he toying with me? Maybe he simply waited for me to return. The streets were eerily empty, everyone having gone to the funeral, everyone but Father. Father…that was it! My father may be a drunk, he may be broken, but he was built like a wild bull with a temper to match. If Vision Master came near him, he would regret it.

I ran home and swung open the door to his room, but no one was there. Was he at the tavern? No, every shop would be closed for the funeral. Even if I found him, would he be frozen like the rest of the villagers?

Rushing to the kitchen, I opened the drawers, but they were all empty. Not a single knife remained. My arm throbbed from the deep cut, but I couldn't think about it now. My eyes darted around the room, searching for anything that could be used to fight. I paused at the portrait of Mother. What would she do in my situation? She would be strong. She would be cunning. She would—

My mother blinked. Her portrait turned to face me, and she gave a wide grin. "Clickety-clack. Clickety-clack." She lunged from the painting and grabbed my throat with both hands. Her umber skin darkened until she was pitch black, a shadow made solid.

The shadow's grip was strong, but I grabbed one of its fingers and bent it back with everything I had until something snapped. Its grip loosened as it cried out, and I ran. The streets twisted and turned in ways they never had in reality, but this wasn't reality. It was Vision Master's realm.

I collapsed; every bit of strength leached from me. Blinding light blurred my vision, and when my eyes adjusted, I was back in the arena. The crowd roared its silent cheer, and Vision Master gave a broad smile. "Well, well, the fighter has returned. Out for a stroll, were you?"

I lay panting on the ground as the crazed man spoke. "I used to wallow in misery, but then realization struck. If the goddess didn't prevent my pain, she wouldn't prevent me from harming others either. Her carelessness works in my favor." He knelt and caressed my face. "You're a pretty thing, aren't you? My son would be about your age. After I climbed the stairs, I obtained the power to find the bandits who killed him. I made them swallow their own swords." He let out a cackle that went on for far too long. "You could say it was their last meal."

I shakily took the healing fruit from my pocket, but he flicked it from my fingers and tsked. "None of that, now. Remember my vice. I need to see your anguish."

I closed my eyes and concentrated on the thread that connected me to Nittles. A silver chord ran fifty paces out from me. I couldn't see him, but I knew he was there and in the same frozen state as the rest of the village. I gave it a mental pull and…nothing.

"Ready to concede?" he asked.

Focusing on my soul, I paused. I'd grown used to seeing a single candle fueling my magic, but now something more stood before me. The tall silver candle stood to my right, but on my left was an ornate candelabra. A thick emerald candle stood in the center with three branches stretching from either side, making seven in all.

Climbing the stairs must have created them. When I took the first step, I was given heartfire from the silver candle. The second time I climbed, I took seven more steps, creating the candelabra. Eight steps, eight candles. I ignored the green ones for the moment and poured the silver flames through the strand, feeling the sprackin quiver.

"I take it you're the stubborn type." Vision Master smiled and scratched his beard "Perfect. Most aren't gracious enough to let me really enjoy myself. I cut out a man's tongue so he couldn't concede, but the goddess knew his thoughts and ended his trial. Such a shame."

He dug his heel in my foot and my toes fractured. It was too much. The pain was too much! My stomach churned and I vomited.

"Clickety-clack. Your bones will crack."

As he spoke, I stared at his silver sword at his side. Something gnawed at my mind, but I couldn't think. My toes, my back, my legs!

"Get off me, you little rat!"

What was happening? It was the man's voice, but his mouth wasn't moving. He and the spiders stood motionless like sculptures. Scuffling and scratching came nearby, then something thumped near my feet.

"Sashel, eat the fruit!"

It was Nittles' voice. He'd come! I grabbed the fruit with numb fingers and ate. Sweet relief flooded my body as my cuts closed and my bones mended.

Climbing to my feet, I looked all around. Vision Master and the metallic spiders stood still, yet the sound of fighting continued. All of this must have been an illusion while the real fighting continued beyond my perception.

"I will rip those wings off your back and shove them down your throat!" There was a whoosh through the air as Vision Master continued. "You were a legend when we first met." Another whoosh sounded like metal swinging. "Now look at you, melded to a pathetic girl. Oh, how the mighty have fallen!"

Nittles spoke through ragged breathing. "Better to fall with virtue than stand in corruption."

"Spare me your piousness. The goddess abandoned us both. Don't you see? She wants us to suffer, to beg, to grovel for scraps."

"I do not claim to understand the ways of Kareli, but I know my own," Nittles said. "Even if she were the devil you claim she is, what of you? You claim you wish to be free of her, yet you lean on her to justify your sadistic pleasures."

"I lean on her for nothing!"

"Every atrocity you do, you claim it is because Kareli made you this way. You need her."

"No!"

Metal sliced through the air as Nittles' wings beat rapidly. I squinted, but the motionless image of the spiders and Vision Master still stood before me. All I could do was pour more heartfire into Nittles and hope it helped.

The sprackin spoke louder. "If the goddess freed you today, you would have no excuses, no veneer to hide behind. You deceive yourself more than any illusion could."

"I am never deceived!" the man yelled. "Vision Master sees all!"

I needed to see what was happening, but how? Something deep inside me shifted. When I looked in my mind, the first emerald candle burned brightly. A rift opened, emanating green light, and a dagger sheathed in gold hovered before me.

As I grabbed it, it felt warm and glowed softly. Unsheathing the blade, I found one side was glittering gold while the other was solid black. At the slightest movement of the dagger, the air rippled. I slashed at the closest spider, and the creature burst into gold dust.

"Nittles, where are you?" I asked.

"Follow the strand!"

I did so and found a blur several paces behind me. Another spider struck, but one swipe of my blade dissipated it.

Nittles spoke again, but his words were directed at Vision Master. "You look through windows but never a mirror. You are broken, and Kareli seeks to heal you."

"Kareli was the one who broke me!" Another swoosh of a blade sounded.

"Others cannot break us," Nittles said. "We choose to be broken."

"Then choose this!" There was a sickening slice followed by a yelp of pain. Nittles fell at my feet, bloody gashes stretching across his limp body.

Nothing made sense. Why were the illusions harming us? His sword! The spiders weren't cutting me. Vision Master was casting an illusion of himself while striking from behind with his rapier.

I swung the dagger wildly around me, and the remaining spiders vanished. The vision of the man faded as well, revealing the real one a few paces away panting with a blood-stained sword in hand.

"Your sprackin has proven quite the pest." He raised his hand, and a silver eagle flew at my face. I swung the dagger, but the bird continued its barrage of attacks.

"Merely swinging the blade won't stop my stronger visions," he said. "I layer them, you see? You need a bit more heft to cut through them." His eyebrows raised and he dismissed the eagle. "I see you've healed. Perfect. More pain for me to give."

His golden eyes held a crazed look, the same look my father had right before drinking. His excitement was palpable as he itched to torture me.

"Why are you doing this?" I asked.

He stepped forward. "Do you blame a starving man for eating? I need this."

He needed this. I hated that phrase. Countless times my father would say it as he drank himself into a stupor. I needed a father. Minessa needed a father, but he needed his mead.

"You don't need it! You *want* it. You have a choice. Everyone has a choice!"

He cracked a smile. "This isn't about me. Is it?"

I backed up and swiped the dagger around, ensuring he wasn't casting another vision.

"You think I didn't notice your reaction earlier?" he asked. "When I spoke of vices, you grew angry. When I mentioned the bottle, I could tell I was spot on. Vision Master sees all."

"Shut up!"

"Yes." His smile widened. "It's not *your* vice but someone close to you, I think. A friend?" He cocked his head. "No. Your face says I missed by a league. Mother? Again, no. Father? Ah, yes. Now I see."

I swung the dagger faster and looked all around me.

"Your face betrays so much. Don't be dismayed. My abilities give me unparalleled sight and understanding. The twitch of the brow, the flare of the nostrils, rapid blinking. Your thoughts might as well be painted on your face." He swung his blade as though it were a walking cane. "And I can't blame your poor father for drinking. Who wouldn't be disappointed with a daughter like you?"

"I said 'Shut up!'"

With the dagger blocking his visions, I might have the upper hand. I still had the glaidens giving me speed. But what did he mean about the dagger needing more heft? Was there a way I could cut through stronger visions?

I lunged, my body reacting on its own. He thrust his rapier, but I parried. He swung twice more but I batted them harder and harder. He stepped backward to regain his stance but slipped, falling hard on his back.

"I concede. You win." He raised his hands in mock surrender and chuckled. "And by the rules I've laid forth, you must cease."

He conceded, but he didn't mean it, did he? He said the goddess could read thoughts. I'd never done this before, but every fiber of my being wanted to kill him. He was a monster.

"Was that your sister I saw earlier?" He shook his head. "Her body had all the signs of someone who ate drethals, and we all know what happens after that."

I clutched the dagger and looked around warily.

"She probably ate them on purpose," he said. "I think she'd rather die by the Kral than live with a pathetic sister like you."

The dam holding back my anger burst, and I leaped beside him, plunging the dagger deep into his chest.

He shook his head as not one drop of blood spilled from his wound. "I told you; your blade is weak."

Something was wrong. It was like a bad dream. I stabbed again and again as tears streamed down my cheeks, but he just laughed, making no effort to stop me. I felt a connection to the dagger just like I had with Nittles. Pouring silver fire into the weapon, I thrust it down once more.

This time, a burst of light rippled outward, and every illusion vanished. The goddess's voice rang out, *"The Trial of Visions hath ended."*

My heart leaped. I won! I—

Vision Master's voice whispered the same lines of the song. "First will come visions that cut to the bone. The greatest of lies you find on your own."

The villagers stared at me in utter horror. I sluggishly pulled out the dagger, not from Vision Master, but from the cold corpse of my sister.

CHAPTER 10

"When we only see our enemies as monsters,
we are destined to be the same."
—Words of Fremma

Once again, the goddess Kareli stood in my mind, her silver hair as radiant as ever. Her face, still too bright to make out her features, turned to the candelabra in the center of the chamber. Her fingers brushed the first candle stick that was now empty, leaving two emerald candles on the left and three on the right of the silver candle.

When I played the song through my head, I realized I could use one emerald candle per trial to summon a weapon, leaving the final candle to help battle the beast, whatever that was. It was daunting to know how difficult the first trial was and how many more I had left.

The goddess circled the candelabra before touching the silver candle in the center which had burned low.

"Remember," she whispered.

There was a flash of light, and the candle was tall and bright once more. When I blinked, I was back in bed, warm sunlight covering my face. I tried to rub my eyes, but my wrists were bound together. Moving my legs proved equally fruitless. I wasn't bound to the bed, but if I wanted to move, I'd have to hop around with my ankles together.

What happened last night? After realizing Vision Master tricked me into stabbing Minessa, everything grew hazy. Had I fainted? Maybe I passed out from exhaustion or even shock. I remember the villagers were shocked as well, and angry, especially angry. Cleric Shoff tried to placate them, but pandemonium ensued. Everything went dark soon after, but there was one thing I vividly remember hearing— "Kill the witch!"

Shaking off the memory, I looked around. My bed stood in the center of the room where sunlight reached through blue and yellow stain glass windows. That meant I was in the Healing House, but it didn't explain the white chord surrounding my bed tied in three even sections to ward off evil. "Kill the witch," the voices echoed in my mind.

"You're awake!" Triska looked up from her knitting, causing a jingle from the copper loops and clips throughout her hair. At sixteen, she was already a head taller than I and perpetually hunching as she hated her height.

"That is—of course you're awake," she stammered. "I just wasn't expecting you to wake up. I mean, I knew you'd wake up, just not so soon."

I didn't respond. How could I after what she did?

Triska squirmed in her chair. "It's… been a while since we really talked."

"Not since my mother died. Not since she was labeled a witch. Is that a coincidence?" The words spilled out of me, and I couldn't help it. I could take the shunning I received from most of the villagers, but not her, not Triska.

"No," she said. "I mean, it's not a coincidence, it's just..."

"It's just what?"

"It's—" She huffed then stood, her copper hair loops rattling as she did. "I'll go get my grandfather."

As the door shut behind her, the sheets rustled at my feet. "I've seen amputations that were more comfortable than that."

"Nittles?"

The sprackin reached out his paws and stretched like a cat.

"But you were bleeding," I said. "You were barely alive."

"A pleasant memory to be sure." Walking to a patch of sunlight warming the middle of the bed, he lay down. "Lifespur has saved my life many times over. I'm more interested in your little squabble you just had with the young lady."

I plopped back on my pillow. "She was my best friend."

"I assume the word 'was' would be the key word here."

"Yes!" I took a calming breath then spoke in a more measured tone. "How much do you remember of last night?"

He eyed me, clearly realizing I was changing the subject. "Through our connection, I could sense everything taking place, but I wasn't able to fight Caster until you poured heartfire into me."

"Caster?"

"I'm sure he called himself 'Vision Master.'" He rolled over and spoke quietly. "We served together in the royal court."

"Court? Wait, you worked with that madman?"

There was a long pause before he answered, "He wasn't always that way."

I thought back to what Vision Master told Nittles. "He said you were great. It was like you used to be better before we melded."

He stared at the window and sighed. "I was...powerful, very powerful."

"Why did melding change that?"

He scowled at me before he softened. "It significantly decreases what I can do." I opened my mouth to speak, but he beat me to it. "I know it wasn't your fault. In fact, I think Kareli orchestrated it for some reason. Regardless, I used to be much more than what you see now."

My heart sank at his words. It seemed I messed everything up just by existing. "I—I'm sorry."

The doorknob jiggled before Cleric Shoff hobbled inside. "That Triska is as tense as a snake charmer with a broken flute." His hand shook as he pulled up a stool and sat. "Sashel, good to see you're awake."

His wispy white hair grew long on the sides of his head, but the top was as bald as an egg. His weathered ebony skin spoke of years working in the fields before joining the clergy. Placing a hand on Nittles, he ruffled his head, not noticing the glare the sprackin gave him.

Shoff gave a loud sigh. "How are you feeling?"

"Better."

What did he think of me after last night? Did father know what I had done? Maybe he was still hungover and hadn't been told.

"And…you haven't heard a word I said, have you?" he asked.

"Oh, sorry." I rubbed my bleary eyes awkwardly with my bound wrists.

He pulled his hand away from Nittles and rested it on his well-worn staff. "The town's worried. Creatures appearing out of nowhere. Four dead. Some say Gronin didn't die by a beast yesterday, but that strange vines came to life and strangled him. Another swore he saw the earth itself rise like a wave and crush poor Mara. And then there was your… escapade last night. If things were any stranger, water would be dry, and Neerion would be pleasant."

My stomach clenched. The fruit. The more fruit I made, the more corrupt my world became. I had to find a way to close the rifts.

He opened a drawer and retrieved the golden dagger. "This was the weapon you used last night. We washed the blood off."

I winced as the memory struck me like an arrow.

The cleric cleared his throat. "I would write it off as merely an expensive heirloom, but these runes across the sheath and blade give me pause. They're similar to the ones on my staff. Where the hel—helper did you find it?"

I stifled a laugh at his slip up. Old Shoff had a rough life before he joined the clergy, and no amount of sermons would cleanse his mouth completely.

A lump formed in my throat as I considered his question. What could I say? I found it lying on the ground?

"No need to explain," he said. "You've been through enough."

I couldn't bear the tension. "Are you going to ask why I stabbed my sister?"

"No. I came to ensure you're in your right mind. Some folks say you were possessed. They tied you here after you collapsed and insisted you be examined by both clerics."

"And am I possessed?" Heat rose in my voice.

"I think you're hurt."

He unsheathed the blade and tapped it against his knee. He squinted as the air around him rippled. If he discovered its powers, he'd have no choice but to try me as a witch.

I blurted out the first thing I could think of. "Why does Suthian allow monsters to live?"

Shoff looked up. "When you say 'monsters,' do you mean the creature that attacked?"

"Yes."

He shrugged and absentmindedly rubbed the flat of the blade. "I can't say. I don't know if it was a bear or if the stories are true. As to why Suthian allows such beasts to harm us, I gave up on such silly questions long ago."

"It's not silly."

As he scratched the back of his neck with the hilt of the dagger, his head vanished, but he continued speaking.

"I'm too old to dance around the sleeping wolf. I say what I mean, and I say it's a silly question."

I stared at where his head should have been. "Uh—Why?"

"We naturally give anyone smarter than us a bit of faith."

"Why do they need face—uh, faith."

His head reappeared, but he seemed unaware. "How much do you know about blacksmithing?"

"N-not much."

"So, if a blacksmith did something with metal that you didn't understand, would you be surprised?"

"Probably not." It took all my willpower not to stare at the dagger. "I don't know much about blacksmithing."

Shoff nodded and sheathed the knife. "Then why are you surprised when Suthian does something you don't understand? Is he not wiser than a blacksmith? Why give one the benefit of the doubt but not the other?"

"Yes, but if the blacksmith covered his hammer in entrails, I'd still question him. The benefit of the doubt only goes so far."

He tossed the dagger on the bed and smiled. "Well, some blacksmiths use horse urine to quench their metal; so that's not farfetched."

Whether it was the words or the tone, something about his answer irritated me.

"So, you're saying anything a god does is just excused away because he's smarter than us? That could be your answer for everything. I could ask why the grass is green, and you could say 'We may never know Suthian's secrets.'"

He gave a loud cackle. "I knew a cleric who gave that very answer to every question, but he was lazy. I've seen puddles deeper than that man's mind. True scholars seek the best answers, not the easiest ones."

"Then why did you give me the same answer?"

"Because in this case it's the right one."

I tried to roll over, but the ropes made it difficult. Part of me wanted to study the dagger more closely, but I also wanted to prove Shoff wrong. I hated how dismissive he was being. I couldn't argue with him about gods, but perhaps I could about man.

"And what about people who are monsters?"

His smile faded. "I hesitate to call anyone a monster. There's an old saying in the clergy. 'The hurt will hurt.' Sometimes people who suffer will in turn cause suffering to others. Suthian forbid, but if my granddaughter was robbed on the road, she may grow bitter. She may get so angry she'll hate humanity altogether. Before long, she's robbing others, thinking she deserves whatever they have more than they do. In the end, she becomes the same as the one she hated. We often become the thing we hate."

"So, you're saying it's never their fault? Everyone is a victim and nobody takes the blame. I don't buy that."

He reached to pet Nittles, but the sprackin rolled off the bed. "Now I didn't say that. We're all responsible for our actions. I'm saying we shouldn't just write them off as evil. They were all sweet, innocent children at one time. No one comes bursting out of the womb carrying a knife ready to murder."

"But it doesn't give them the right to hurt others, no matter what they've gone through!"

His face softened. "No, it doesn't."

"So why doesn't Suthian stop them? He could judge them all!"

"And he will. The Moritori speaks endlessly about the day of judgement. What you're asking is why he doesn't stop them *now*. Right?"

"Yes."

"When you dry fruit, you understand it takes time. If someone wanted it now, you'd tell them to wait."

"It's not the same."

"Then here's something that *is* the same. Should Suthian have passed judgement on you last night after what you did? Half the town is terrified of you. They think you killed not only your sister but the others as well. They want judgment, and they want it now."

"That..."

What could I say? The mere mention of the staircase or magic would have me hung for witchcraft. The gold dagger had nearly given me away already.

"You wouldn't understand."

"You're right," he said. "I wouldn't understand because you're a person, and people are complex. They're not just one or the other, monsters or martyrs. They have nuance, your father included."

My father. That's who I'd been really thinking about, not the Kral and not even Vision Master. I didn't care how he used to be before mother died. All I knew was today he was a miserable old drunk.

Shoff tried to untie the ropes, but his feeble hands only jiggled the knots and chafed my hands. He unsheathed the knife and prepared to cut them but stopped and shook his head.

"I'd probably cut you as much as the bindings with these da— dangling hands. They're flopping around like a fish on a line. Triska, come in here!"

She burst in as though she had been listening the whole time. Her hair clinked as she spun her head. "Are you alright?"

"No. They tied these confounded knots too tight. I swear it was someone from the fishery. They love showing off their knot-tying skills."

Her eyes widened. "You're untying her?"

"Trying to is more like it. I think spitting on the ropes would be more helpful than what I'm doing. Be my favorite granddaughter and help me."

She deftly untied my wrists, never making eye contact. Once my ankles were freed, the cleric touched Triska's shoulder and said, "Tell everyone I deem Sashel as clean. She is not possessed and presents no danger to the public."

Her eyes darted from him to me. She opened her mouth, then closed it and nodded. Once she left, I stood from the bed and felt the soreness from the prior night. I never knew how exhausting a few minutes of fighting could be. It was only then I realized I wasn't wearing my dress but a burgundy robe. The bottom fell to my ankles and the sleeves were rolled up twice to fit.

Shoff nodded as I examined it. "Triska was kind enough to loan it to you. What you wore last night was little more than shredded ribbons. I've seen skinned dear more covered."

"Why did she do that?"

"She's a caring soul and knows you've been through a lot." He gave me a wink that seemed to say, "It's almost like she sees you as more than just a monster."

I tripped on the white chord surrounding the bed and caught myself on the stand.

"Sorry about that," he said. "I kept telling everyone you just needed rest, but they insisted on taking precautions. 'A thrice-tied chord makes the safest ward.' More superstition than scripture, but they wouldn't listen."

I nodded and rolled my sleeves up higher. "I understand. Thank Triska for the robe. I'll return it—"

The door opened again as Cleric Neerion stormed in. If his thick Gren Mallish accent didn't give him away as a foreigner, his olive skin and connected eyebrows surely would have. His braid of black hair whipped around like a serpent as he strode toward me.

"You are evil or possessed!"

"Come now," Shoff said. "We all grieve in different ways."

He stamped his ornate staff which was wrapped in white fabric. At the top rested a four-legged silver eagle which seemed to glare at me.

"This witch has disturbed the dead!"

While Neerion's staff was decorative and used to ward off evil, old Shoff leaned against his weathered one for balance. That is, until he poked the young cleric in the stomach.

Neerion bent over. "You struck me! Robius forbids this."

Shoff furrowed his brow. "Struck you? I did no such thing."

"You mock me."

"Never. Back when I plowed the fields, I'd have a stubborn mule that needed a good prod to get going. I didn't strike you; I merely prodded."

"You call me a mule then?"

Shoff scratched his bald head as though taking the question with absolute seriousness. "I suppose not. Your ears are far too short."

"You *do* mock me! You forget I represent Robius, god of judgement. You cannot hide behind Suthian's weakness forever."

"Compassion is not weakness. Judgement needs understanding, and understanding knows when to show mercy."

"Your use of words does not make you right. The temple needs a bringer of judgement, not a weaver of words."

Shoff nodded. "A weaver of words. I like that."

"Play games if you wish, but I have just as much right to examine her."

He pressed the silver eagle on his staff against my forehead, causing the runes that were not covered by fabric to glow.

"Why did you desecrate your sister's body?" he asked.

I stiffened as the power of his staff took effect, and words flowed from my mouth. "I was tricked."

A flash of Vision Master surfaced in my mind, and Neerion cocked his head. "Curious."

He probed deeper, and the image of metallic spiders appeared slashing at me.

"You've seen visions?" he asked.

"Yes." Again, I spoke against my will.

The light from his staff flickered then faded. Growling in frustration, Neerion shook it. "This thing has a mind of its own sometimes."

"You're too young to be using mental magic," Shoff said.

"Maybe for you who grew up in the back woods of nowhere, but I was raised in the temple. I know what I am doing."

Shoff shook his head. "You're not weak for admitting you haven't mastered the craft yet. You shouldn't be practicing on a girl who just lost her sister."

Neerion gritted his teeth and slammed the staff down, causing the runes to glow once more. "Was stabbing your sister's body part of a pagan ritual?"

"No," I answered.

Another flash of Vision Master appeared, and the cleric scowled. "What do you know of this man you saw?"

I wanted to curse at Neerion and shove that staff away from my face, but my mouth was already speaking against my will. "I had never seen him before yesterday. He tricked me into stabbing Minessa."

"That's enough," Shoff said. "You have your answer."

Neerion pulled his staff back, and I relaxed. My body was under my control again.

Neerion rubbed the base of his braid with his thumb and index finger in thought. "Her visions make no sense."

"None of this makes sense," Shoff said. "Beasts appearing, the leaves turning black, it's all concerning, but you can't prove she's responsible."

"But if she is, she must be dealt with swiftly. Some must die for the village to live."

Neerion turned to me. "I see you did not mean to stab the body. But you still might be a witch like..."

"Like my mother?" I stood. "She wasn't a witch! She was a good mother, and she died giving birth." The last statement came out unbidden.

"But she was a thief!"

"A thief?" I wanted to argue, but the word caught me off guard. I'd heard her referred to as a witch many times but never a thief.

"It is nothing," he said.

"No. What did you mean by that?"

"It is nothing!"

He slammed his staff down, and the runes flashed silver. His eyes widened, and he raised the staff, but it was too late. Against his will, his own memory poured into me.

* * *

My mother's fingers wrapped around the staff and lifted it from the floor. The gray strands in her hair seem to glow in the light of the shining runes.

"Thrella, what are you doing?" Neerion asked.

She pressed the staff against her chest. "I'm sorry, but I need it more than you do."

"I trusted you!"

She shook her head. "You shouldn't have."

As Neerion reached out his hand, the runes flashed, and his body locked up.

"As long as I hold it, the staff cannot be taken," she said.

He gritted his teeth. "That is a temple artifact. Only the clergy is worthy to wield it!"

She shook her head as her eyes watered. "I never should have climbed those cursed stairs."

CHAPTER 11

"There are many worlds and many realms, all connected by the great tree Eurethelim. The staircase is its root, and the runic staves are its branches."

—Words of Tarendi, Emerald Lordmage of Tal Miral

My mother climbed the stairs. The truth pressed down on me, and I couldn't make sense of it. Why did she take the staff? Why didn't she tell me? And why didn't Neerion report it to the clergy?

He seemed both embarrassed and outraged when he realized he'd shown me his memory. Healer Fendin entered and shooed the two clerics out, warning she'd sit on them if they didn't leave. With her portly frame and strength like an ox, it was a legitimate threat. She opened the windows, letting cool fresh air in the muggy Healing House, then she brewed a cup of herbal tea and placed it on the stand.

"You will drink it all, or I'll pour it in your ears and hope it goes down your throat."

"I don't think it works that way."

"I know it doesn't, but I'll do it all the same."

As I sipped the steaming tea, I tasted lemon, honey, and mint. I set the cup down and rubbed my wrists where the ropes had been. "Healer, did you know my mother well?"

"That I did." She placed a basket on the floor and folded white strips of cloth. "I helped deliver both you and Minessa, and I even helped relieve your mother's maladies."

"What maladies?"

She lowered the cloth. "Didn't you know? She had complications with you. Since then, she couldn't bring a child to term."

"She was barren?"

"Not quite. She could conceive just fine, but she kept miscarrying. Had five or six, I think. Poor soul."

"But she had Minessa."

Fendin looked down and pinched the bridge of her nose. "That she did."

"Could—could Neerion's staff have helped her?"

"Of course not. It does a good job of keeping away the rot from meat, but it doesn't heal people. If it could, my work would be far easier. All he really uses it for is interrogating people like you." She slammed the folded cloth on the table and grabbed another. "Miserable Gran Mallin! I know the perfect place he can shove that staff of his."

Then why did my mother steal the staff? This was the question I wanted to ask, but I didn't know how much Fendin knew. Instead, I asked, "If my mother couldn't bear children, how was Minessa born?"

She shut her eyes. "She stopped coming to me for herbs and the like. She had horrible morning sickness with you, but she seemed perfectly fine carrying Minessa. I remember how large her belly was and you by her side. You always wanted to feel the baby kick in the womb. And you were so excited to be a sister."

My eyes watered at her words. I tried remembering the day she gave birth, but like before, there was only blackness. Then it occurred to me. Fendin was there.

"Do you remember how she died?"

"She—She was a good mother, and she died giving birth."

There was that line again, but this time it came from Fendin.

"But *how* did she die?" I pressed. "Blood loss? Infection?"

"You were there." She grabbed another cloth and resumed her folding. "You saw what I saw."

"Then tell me."

She slammed the cloth down. "I don't know!"

"What do you mean?"

She softened. "I've—I've never told anyone this, but I can't remember that day. It's like a shroud covering everything. I can't recall a thing."

"What's the first thing you can remember?"

"Well, I remember preparing her for birth. I had extra linens, hot water, a sharp knife for the chord, herbs… and then nothing. After the blackness, I remember little Minessa crying in your arms with two of her fingers cut clean off. I must've done it while cutting the chord, but I've never made a mistake like that."

"And my mother?"

I didn't remember any of this, not even holding her.

Fendin shook her head. "I'm sorry. I don't remember."

* * *

I knelt beneath the waterfall and brushed my hair back. Fendin had the same memory loss. I kept going over it, but nothing made sense.

"I said to turn around."

"You're joking," Nittles said. "I'm a sprackin. I don't care about the decency of—"

"Just do it!"

He rolled his eyes and turned. "Humans!"

The waterfall was chilling but the pond I sat in was merely cool and the warm breeze felt amazing. The lichen-covered boulders and tall reeds gave me ample cover and the lily pads on the surface provided even more concealment as I bathed, not that anyone would want to bathe near the daughter of a witch.

Triska's robe lay on the shore and next to it sat my gray trousers and myrtle green tunic. This was supposed to be a quick rinse, but once I stepped in, I couldn't resist taking a swim. It had been ages.

As the sunlight pressed against my face, I felt the stress wash off as easily as the dried blood coating me. I remember swimming here when my mother was pregnant with Minessa. She was stern, never letting me near the deep end. I could still see her by the edge of the water. She had strange cravings with her pregnancy and poured a bright blue sauce on sliced bread. Father would jump in and splash her, claiming it was an accident. Then he'd do it again, claiming that too was an accident.

He was the fun one, a perfect counterbalance for her. I missed Father's smile. I missed his laugh, his jokes. What would it be like if all four of us were here today? I wracked my brain, but I still couldn't recall what happened the day she gave birth. Why couldn't I remember? Why couldn't Fendin remember?

"Nittles, is it possible for someone to forget an important event in their life, something that would normally be unforgettable?"

He cocked his head, still turned away from me. "If it happened long ago it's possible. Or if it was traumatic enough, your mind can block it out. Why do you ask?"

"I—I don't remember my mother dying."

"That is understandable. It's a rare occurrence but I can see it happening in your case."

"That's not the strange part." I wasn't sure how to explain it, but I had to try. "The healer can't remember it either."

Nittles turned around and stared at me. "What did you say?"

I sank farther under the water. "I said no looking!"

"Enough with that nonsense. Please explain what you know."

I sighed but didn't rise any higher. "It's like a dark veil covering that day. And both of us have the same words echoing in our heads. 'She was a good mother, and she died giving birth.' What do you make of it?"

"Fascinating."

"That's it? That's all you can say?"

He shrugged. "There are several possibilities. The best I can do is theorize about what is most likely."

"Which is?"

Nittles considered his words for a while before answering. "You told me creatures had been attacking the village around the time your mother died, correct?" I nodded, and he continued. "I also know Minessa was missing two of her fingers. My best guess is that a creature attacked your mother shortly after giving birth. Maybe it attacked Minessa, biting off her fingers, and then your mother intervened."

I turned his words over in my head. It fit. "But why wasn't her body publicly burned?"

"It seems like the village already suspected her of being a witch and wouldn't honor her death. On the other hand, her body may have been disfigured during the attack and they burned her body in private out of respect. Again, I'm only theorizing based on what little information I have."

"What about the blocked memory and the repeating words in my head?"

He ruffled his white furry wings. "I am no expert in the human psyche, but my best guess is both you and the healer were traumatized, and she whispered the words to you repeatedly for comfort. Again, this is not my field of expertise."

That reminded me. "And what is your expertise? You mentioned you were in the royal court back in your world. What did you do?"

He looked away. "I was many things."

"Like what?"

"An advisor for one, but I had many duties."

I never had to pry for details from the sprackin before. Now I felt like I was pulling teeth to get him to talk. "What other duties?"

He sighed. "You could say I was the king's sword, an enforcer if you will. I would use diplomacy whenever possible, but I had many methods to defend the kingdom. Van Kordin is light, and the king is might." He recited the last line like a mantra or a pledge.

I ran a hand through my wet hair. "And I took you from your position, didn't I?"

"Well, yes, but…there's something I haven't told you. I—"

Silver light flashed across the sky. The roar of the waterfall silenced as the goddess's voice echoed. "The Trial of Water hath begun." We both froze.

"Sashel," Nittles whispered. "What was the next line of Kareli's song?"

I thought for a minute. The song was still clear as day, but I had to skip the first two lines since they pertained to the first trial. "Next is the serpent that swimmeth below. The depths are its friend but also its foe."

"Get out! Get out now!"

I scrambled to rise and sprinted for the shore, not bothering with decency. My feet slipped on the slick stones, but I made it out. Yanking off the lily pads clinging to me, I put on my trousers and tunic. "Nittles, what is it?"

"The Canthi. It's a myth, which is why I didn't think of it before, but now…"

"What? What is it?"

The earth shook like thunder as the boulders around us stretched into steep cliffs. The waterfall roared as it grew from five feet to ten, then thirty then sixty, filling the air with thick white mist. The small pond rippled outward until it was a vast sea. I ate a glaiden and clutched a healing fruit in one hand with my dagger strapped to my side.

The sprackin flapped his wings. "There's no fighting it. We need to go!"

"No! Passing the trials is the only chance of saving my sister."

"It's suicide."

"I passed the last trial."

"Caster let you win, and you know it!"

Near the shore, the sea frothed and swirled in a cyclone. The waves rose high and crashed into me, consuming me in a single sweep.

My limbs locked up in shock as the water turned from warm pond water to a frigid sea, and I was completely submerged. I thrashed and kicked in the darkness. Finally, my head reached the surface, and I gasped for air.

"Sashel, grab my tail!"

Grasping the furry tail, my hand sliced on the sharp barb at the tip, but I hung on. I poured my silver fire into him, and Nittles sped for the shore.

A tall sharp rock sprouted from the depths, and we halted. No, it wasn't a rock but a horn. Two more joined the first as the head of the Canthi emerged. Its eyes, larger than my entire body, glared at me. A deep rumble sounded beneath it before bursts of misty air shot from its horns like a whale's spout, filling the air with the scent of dead fish.

Terror gripped me as I craned my neck up to take in the enormity of it. Its serpentine head rose higher and higher like a mighty tower.

When it opened its mouth, hundreds of teeth the size of spears retracted and extended independently of each other.

A low rumble burbled down its neck before another gout of air shot from openings on top of its horns, making them more like nostrils. Snapping its head back, the Canthi struck.

Even with the magical fruit granting me speed, the creature was fast, and I was in water. Just before impact, I pushed against its nose and flipped so I was on its head.

Nittles flapped beside me. “Are you insane?”

The Canthi shook its head, and I clung to the top of its horn. Too late I realized my stupidity as a burst of air shot me upward.

Hanging in midair, I could only watch as the creature swung its tail. The blow was like a battering ram, but with the glaiden in my system, I rolled with the impact and then struck the water in a perfect dive. The surface felt like solid rock, but I broke through. I swam as far as I could before coming up for air.

The water chilled me to the bone, and the wind felt even colder. As my shoulders shook and my teeth chattered, I was convinced I was going to die. The only question was whether I would drown, freeze to death, or be eaten.

Nittles swooped low and extended his tail. “Grab on.”

Careful to avoid the sharp barb at the end, I grabbed and poured more heartfire into him. The sprackin shot off like an arrow, and it was all I could do to hold on, my feet skipping across the icy depths.

As the Canthi pursued, I poured more and more fire. The serpent struck, and Nittles was forced to fly away from the shore. When my grip weakened, Nittles wrapped his tail around my wrists. The tail glowed a deep blue before hardening like stone. Instead of fur, it felt like sturdy chains coiling around my hands, linking us together.

We flew for what seemed like an eternity, dodging strike after strike with me flailing behind. Finally, we made it to the shallow end of the shore, and the Canthi stopped. We splashed in the knee-high water and walked the rest of the way with the chilling wind battering us from behind.

When we made it to shore, neither of us could speak. Nittles lay panting in the wet sand, his abilities spent, and I sat beside him. His tail softened, but it took over a minute to pry my hands off since the muscles were stiff and cold. As my breath turned visible, I shivered violently, not able to feel anything below my knees.

Thick grey clouds blanketed the sky, and the relentless wind sapped the life from me. A hundred paces away stood a small cave in the cliff walls. When I tried to stand, I fell flat on my face. Rubbing my feet was like touching a frozen corpse. I felt nothing. With few options, I pressed the sprackin to my chest and crawled on my knees. Sand and shells dug into my skin, but I pressed on.

The cave was smaller than I thought, the inside barely as wide as my bedroom and half as tall, but it blocked the wind. Teeth chattering and arms trembling, I held the sprackin out.

"N-N-Nittles, w-wake up."

He curled into a tight ball and shook.

"Nittles, you need to d-do something."

His eyes sluggishly opened and drifted around the cave. "The moss."

I looked around, but it was so dark, only the dim gray light from outside peering in. I reached out my shaky hand and felt around. At the other end, farthest from the entrance, I felt soft moss growing on the walls. I laid the sprackin next to it and poured my silver flames through our connection.

He grunted as he flapped his furry wings, but nothing happened. He flapped again, weaker than the first, then fell against the rocks.

"Nittles, y-you have to do this."

He gave a deep sigh but said nothing.

"I'm s-so sorry for getting you into this mess. I took you from your world, and now you're stuck with me. But the only way to get my s-sister back and bring you back to your world is to p-pass this trial."

My vision blurred and I swayed on my knees. All I wanted to do was lie in the soft sand and sleep. I didn't even feel cold anymore. My shivering eased, but I knew that was a bad sign.

"Nittles, we both need you to do this. You served in the royal court. You fought Vision Master. And—and you're the only friend I have. You can do this!"

His eyes opened a crack, and he raised his wings. Taking a deep breath, his face firmed and he brought his wings down. Bright sparks shot out in all directions, landing on the moss-covered rocks. The silver flames licked across the moss, then faded. Darkness filled the cave once more.

No. This couldn't be happening. It couldn't end like this. I needed to bring my sister back. I hadn't gone this far just to freeze to death.

The moss all around us glowed a bright copper and lit the walls with warm light. As the cave heated, my feet tingled as the feeling returned. The Canthi roared in the sea, but I had to rest before continuing the fight. How was I going to defeat it?

As Nittles feebly tried to roll toward the copper moss, I reached out and pushed him closer. My last memory was of Nittles purring softly before my eyelids finally shut.

CHAPTER 12

"Better to die with a friend than prosper alone."
—Words of Fremma

A thunderous roar shook me awake. Where was I? I sat up and looked around, the copper moss lighting the cave. I was still in the trial. The roar had to be the Canthi unless there were other creatures in the sea.

I stood stiffly as my whole body ached. My pants were torn, and my legs were covered with cuts and scrapes from crawling in the sand.

"If you think the Canthi was loud, you should hear your snoring." Nittles sat at the cave's entrance near a pile of red ivy.

"I don't snore," I said.

"Then what woke me up this morning? I think the Canthi started roaring because he heard your bestial snoring and took it as competition."

I rolled my eyes. "What are those plants you have?"

"These are frenlock vines. I transformed them this morning with what little plant life I could find. They're not as powerful as lifespur but give them a few hours and you'll be as good as new. Plus, you need sustenance, and they're quite filling."

I picked up a strand as long as my arm. The crimson vines were warm, and blue veins stretched across their sinuous leaves.

"Do they taste good?"

"They're quite filling."

The vine coiled around my forearm like a small snake, and I shook it free.

"That's just its reflex," he assured me. "It can't eat you."

"Thank you. Whenever my mother said the meal won't eat me, I knew it would be delicious."

"You can eat sand if you don't like it."

My stomach rumbled. I was so hungry I felt sick. The Canthi roared and a loud splash came from the sea.

Nittles cocked his head. "If your snoring wasn't enough, I think he's competing with your loud stomach as well. You're really challenging him today."

Ripping the frenlock off my arm, I took a bite. Warm juice filled my mouth that tasted eerily like blood, making me gag. I clenched my teeth and forced myself to swallow. The sprackin had done the best he could, and I needed food. True to his word, after only a few more bites, I was filled, and my energy returned.

Sitting outside the cave's entrance, I stared at the sea. Four crushed ships in different stages of decay rested on the shore about three hundred paces away. I hadn't noticed them last night because I was barely conscious. Large sections were missing from the vessels as if they had been bitten off. Although I knew little about shipbuilding, I knew none would sail again.

"How can I defeat the Canthi?" I asked. "It ripped those ships apart like they were slabs of meat."

"You can't defeat it." He peered at the wreckage. "The one on the far right bears a striking resemblance to the Luthman, one of the fastest ships in Royal Fleet. It went missing in the Toral Sea, never to be seen again. There are legends of other ships going missing in that area. I think they were all taken to this realm. There are magical storms that can transport things from one world to another."

"But how do I kill the Canthi?"

"Have you tried summoning?"

Summoning. Why hadn't I thought of it sooner? Remembering how I nearly drowned the previous night and then skipped all over the sea while tied to Nittles, I could understand why it didn't occur to me.

Focusing on the emerald candle in my soul, I ignited the wick. Or rather, I tried to. The green candle stood motionless as before with no fire illuminating it. I tried again, but no fire appeared and no portal opened.

"It's not working."

He dropped the red vines in his mouth and looked up. "What do you mean?"

"I mean my candle isn't lighting. I can't pull anything through."

"We need that portal opened. There's no other way of defeating it! Each scale is the size of a dinner plate."

"There has to be a way." I thought about the song from the staircase. "'Next is the serpent that swimmeth below. The depths are its friend but also its foe.' Does that mean anything to you?"

"It's nonsense."

"It must mean something."

"I'm sure it does," the sprackin said. "But it's too vague. It could all be metaphorical, symbolic, or a reference to some ancient story lost to time. That's the problem with the staircase. It surpasses time and space. It is the key to every world. The possibilities are endless."

Part of the Canthi's back surfaced before submerging again. I sighed. "The song explained the last trial and I know it can help with this one."

"Did the song actually help you last time?"

"Well, no, but I didn't have time to think."

"Think?" He gave me a flat look. "I'm surprised you know that word."

"You're not helping."

"Nothing is helping. If we don't pass these trials, I can't get home."

"I know! In case you've forgotten, I have a lot riding on this as well."

Nittles went quiet and stared at the sea beneath the gray sky. After a minute, he sighed and asked, "Did you mean what you said last night?"

It was my turn to go quiet. I didn't know if he would remember since he was so exhausted. "Uh...which part?"

"I already know I'm the best sprackin. I'm curious if you meant the part about being friends."

"I..." Why was this so hard? I said it last night, but now it was far more awkward. "I need to fight the Canthi. I don't know how much longer the trial will last."

"There's never been a record of time limits in the trials, but I agree. The sooner this ends, the better. But as I said, the Canthi can't be defeated, especially not by a single human and a sprackin."

"I have to try something."

"You'll die."

Reaching out with my mind, I sensed my dagger. A similar thread linked me to Nittles, and I found it quickly, resting at the bottom of the sea. When I poured a bit of silver fire through the connection, the dagger sprung from the depths and shot straight at me. *I did it! I…made a dagger fly directly at me.*

I dropped to the ground just as the blade collided with the back of the cave. Nittles gave me a look that spoke volumes, but I ignored it. Dusting myself off, I retrieved the dagger and examined it. Not so much as a nick on it.

"What good will that do?" he asked.

I examined the runes on the dark side of the blade. What had Shoff done to make it work? His head disappearing wasn't something I would easily forget. Hadn't he scratched himself with the hilt? I rubbed it against my arm, but nothing happened.

"Even if you made it fly at the Canthi, it can't penetrate its thick hide," he said. "Maybe you could blind one of its eyes before it eats you."

Half of the cross guard was gold while the other half was a strange black metal. When I rubbed the gold part back and forth against my arm, my skin shone bright gold.

Nittles' eyes bulged. "That's…different."

I flipped the handle around and rubbed the black half against my arm. After several back-and-forth movements, I vanished. When I looked down, I felt disoriented at not seeing my legs.

"Eyes above!" His head darted around. "Incredible!"

Holding the concealment grew harder by the second, like awkwardly carrying a heavy load. I let it fade and returned to normal.

"Yes," he said. "This will help, but…"

"It won't kill the Canthi," I finished. "There must be a way. What if we used rope from the ships and made a net?"

Nittles paused then burst into laughter. After a minute, he calmed down. He snorted, looked at me, then laughed again. "A net? You think simple rope can catch it? It's a monster of legend! It'll snap the ropes like a cobweb. It would—ropes!" His head snapped to the ships. "Ropes! That's it!"

"So…we can make a net?" I asked.

"Of course not. I stand by what I said, but we can use the ropes and lumber. Every ship in the fleet, including the Luthman, was required to carry tools of all sorts. With any luck, we'll have what we need."

My heart soared at his words. "Great! But, if we're not making a net, then what are we building?"

A wide grin stretched on Nittles' white furry face. "My dear, we are going to build a ballista."

* * *

I dug through the second ship, piling boards on the shore that weren't too rotted. Any tools went in a separate pile along with loose nails and rope. Nittles squealed in delight when he found a drill in the first ship as well as several hammers and a saw in the second.

I wiped the sweat from my face despite the cool day. "I still don't see how we can make a ballista. Isn't that a siege weapon, like a giant crossbow? I thought that took a lot of iron and special tools we don't have."

"Nonsense. They're mostly made of wood."

"What about the spring? I thought they used a giant metal spring to launch them."

A giddiness saturated the sprackin ever since the idea came to him, and he smiled again. "That's the beauty of it. Ballistae use twisted rope as torsion springs!"

The more he explained, the less I understood; so, I held up a hand and said, "Just tell me what to do."

As sprackins weren't designed for manual labor, the bulk of the work fell on me. He gave me the measurements, using the length of my hand for a standard length. The first step was cutting the boards into specific sizes using an old saw. Using two large stones as a makeshift sawhorse, I cut, asking Nittles what the other trials might entail.

He considered. "I can't give you details as the song is quite metaphorical, but there's a pattern. The first three usually try the will, body, and mind in that order."

I heaved and placed a thick board beside the others in the sand. "Well, this trial definitely symbolizes the body." I brushed my tender palms which had been rubbed raw from the rough wood. "The labor may kill me before the monster does."

"The more you work, the more you'll discover that strength isn't everything. Using the right angle and leverage, you can move things you never thought possible."

"Says the one who isn't lifting anything," I grumbled.

"Fine. Transfer some heartfire."

I did so, and his eyes glowed purple. He dove and struck the next board at just the right angle, flipping it onto the two large stones.

"Cheater!"

He chuckled. "There is no cheating when it comes to labor. If there's an easier way that accomplishes the same thing, I use it."

Sawing the next board, I asked, "What about the other trials?"

"The fourth is different. It tries the spirit. I doubt I'll be able to accompany you on that one."

"How does it try the spirit? And what's the difference between the mind, will, and spirit? They all sound the same to me."

"An excellent question." He gave me a surprised look. "The will is your resolve. The pain Caster inflicted on you in the first trial tested your endurance. The mind is more straightforward. It is your memories, personality, and reasoning. There are countless ways to test your mind."

"And the spirit?" I asked.

"Ah, yes. Think of the spirit like a great sea. It may be boisterous or placid as a lake. This trial will reveal what troubles you. For Caster, or Vision Master as he calls himself now, his revelation was bitterness."

I cast another board down and hefted another. "So, how do you defeat it? How do you win?"

"You must not only identify what troubles you but conquer it. Find a way to move past the pain, past the spirits that torment you. Caster failed this trial, and his bitterness ate him alive."

My stomach dropped. How was I supposed to pass? I didn't know what the spirit was I had to conquer. I knew I hurt deep down, but I couldn't put into words what was troubling me. All I knew was life stank, and I hated it.

When I sawed faster, Nittles took the cue to move on. "After the fourth, if anyone makes it that far up the steps, the trials become harder to predict. They usually rely on circumstances rather than introspection."

"So, the first four are inside my head and the rest are outside?"

He looked up in thought. "Crudely said…but close enough."

Sitting down, I ate another strand of frenlock vines. The pulsating plants were not only for food but also the only source of water.

"The pattern makes sense," I said through a mouthful. "But are there any specifics you can think of? Like what the sand or forest means?"

"The sand in the glass is a reference to the Great Hourglass. It's an intricate metaphor relating to our memories and how they affect us. It could mean just about anything; hence, I didn't comment on it. As far as the forest that sees you as prey, it could mean an actual forest or another metaphor."

I took another bite, trying not to choke on the lukewarm juices that tasted like blood. "Are there actual forests that are dangerous?"

"Practically all of them in my world are. Some even have a consciousness, but I repeat, we don't know for sure."

For the next two weeks, we worked. Nittles taught me how to tie intricate knots and how to weave rope that could function as a spring. We removed the helms, pulleys, and rope from every ship.

The sprackin even taught me some blacksmithing to make the large arrowhead for the missiles.

Every evening, I tried summoning an item from another world, but the emerald candle in my soul remained frustratingly still. I couldn't figure out why it wasn't working.

Finally, the day came. I ran a hand over the massive ballista, and Nittles gave me an approving smile.

"For building it with scraps from shipwrecks, it's quite impressive. It won't be as durable as one made in Tal Miral, but it should fire several shots with no difficulty."

I turned the helm on the right side of the ballista, and the rope cranked backward, snapping into place. I pulled a lever on the left, and the first of the twelve missiles slid into position. I took a deep breath and gazed at the Canthi swirling in the sea. We were ready.

CHAPTER 13

"Woe to them who see the black storm rage on the Toral Sea. It is where legends come to life and truth turns to fables."
—Captain Noravick of Tal Miral

We built the ballista close enough to the shore to shoot the monster but far enough that it wasn't in danger of being washed away. Nittles taught me to aim it, and we performed one practice shot. We couldn't waste any more of the massive arrows as they took too long to make, and the old wood wouldn't last too many more shots.

Next, I unwrapped the sack of coconuts Nittles had gathered. We split one the day before as neither of us could stomach much more of the frenlock vines. The rest we saved for this moment. The sprackin flapped his wings, and the coconuts morphed into a handful of glaidens and lifespur.

"I was expecting more."

Nittles shook his head. "Since coconuts are mostly hollow, they don't provide as much fruit as you'd think."

I placed the fruit in my pocket and held a single glaiden in my hand. The purple fruit didn't just speed up my perception; it made me understand direction, trajectory, and momentum on an unparalleled level.

"Better take two," he said. "I don't normally recommend it, but it will heighten your perception further, and the side effects should be bearable. But don't eat them till I bring the Canthi close to shore. Every shot counts."

I checked the candles in my soul, but the emerald candle still wouldn't ignite and no portal opened. The ballista would have to work. But what of the next trial? What if I couldn't summon anything else? My hands shook, and I took a calming breath.

"Peace," Nittles said. "I know this is important but try to focus on just two things: the ballista and the Canthi. Nothing else matters right now. With the glaidens, your aim will be nearly perfect. We will be victorious. You will be known as Canthi Slayer, death of mythical monsters!"

My voice quivered. "Alright."

"Courage before victory. Say it."

I cleared my throat. "Courage before victory."

"Shout it!"

"Courage before victory!"

"Excellent. Now, remember. Don't shoot until it draws near the shore."

Without another word, he took off. I poured half of my heartfire into him, and his speed increased. He flew low and struck the water again and again.

I rested my hands on the levers designed to aim the ballista. Silence reigned over the sea, and my heart sped up. I hated waiting. Weeks of work, countless hours of building this thing, and the creature wasn't even taking the bait. Why wasn't it—

The Canthi burst from the surface. It snapped at Nittles, but like before, the sprackin was quick. As he sped toward the shore, I ate two glaidens as instructed. As time slowed, I again was forced to wait. The glaidens let me understand how the beast was swimming and the patterns in its movement. Soon, I could predict where it would be a few seconds ahead.

I turned the helm on my right, adjusting the ballista's height a few degrees, then to the left one degree. The Canthi was a large target, but I wanted the first shot to be a killing blow. The moment it reached the shallow end, I fired.

A loud whoosh sounded as the bolt shot through the air. It missed. The Canthi halted and stared at the ballista. No, it stared at *me.*

Something stirred in my soul. The emerald candle flickered as if trying to ignite, but why now? For two weeks it hadn't changed no matter how hard I tried. At the roar of the beast, I made my decision. Summoning an item would take time, and like the dagger in the first trial, it would take trial and error to figure out how to use it. I didn't have that kind of time. Right now, I had a weapon aimed directly at the Canthi. I would try the ballista first.

I turned the other helm which pulled back the rope. After pulling the lever on my left, the second missile clicked into place. I assumed the first shot would be a miss, but it would give me understanding of how it worked. When I saw the bolt fly, I understood how the wind resistance affected it. The ballista was slightly off, but I compensated, by clicking it down a few degrees.

As the Canthi roared, I fired again. This time, it grazed the side of its neck. It thrashed in pain and lunged for Nittles. My third shot sank into the roof of its mouth and I couldn't stop the grin forming on my face. I was going to win.

I shot again, and the missile sank into the middle of its belly. I should aim for the eyes next. I understood exactly where the missiles would fly, and at this point, I could shoot each of its horns off if I chose. I imagined shooting a bolt into each of its three nostrils and chuckled. How many shots to the eyes would it take before it died?

"Sashel!" Nittles yelled.

I shook myself and realized my mind had drifted. No. Not now! Before I could adjust my aim, the Canthi dove beneath the surface. I looked all around, but there was no sign of it. Nittles flew closer to the shore, trying to get its attention.

Something felt off. The wind picked up and the water near the shore pulled back. The Canthi burst out, creating a massive wave headed straight for me. In the few seconds the monster was above water, I acted. Four degrees down, two to the right. I pulled the lever and fired.

Instead of a whoosh like with the other missiles, there was a deafening clack. The ballista had jammed. Several of the old ropes had snapped as well as one of the boards at the base. The force of firing the missiles must have been too much for it. With time slowed for me, I examined the ballista as the tidal wave approached. One of the main ropes at the top was snagged. If I could free it, there may still be a chance.

Grabbing the rope, I yanked, but it remained wedged in a notch in the wood. I tried a different angle. Nothing. I climbed on top and pulled. The rope snapped free and pain shot up my right leg. When I turned to where the arrow flew, there was only a massive wave in front of me.

I thrashed beneath the chilling depths, not knowing which way was up. When I finally surfaced, I rubbed my eyes and craned my neck. The Canthi towered above me in icy rage. Even though it was far above, I felt the warm mist from its powerful nostrils on top of those three strange horns.

Nittles was right. How was I supposed to defeat it? It could wrap around my entire village! If Mother were here, she'd know what to do. She always had a plan.

Something stirred inside me, and I recognized the feeling. When I looked in my soul, the second candle, the one that remained motionless for so long finally burst to life. I remembered fighting Vision Master and I realized the problem. I had to be actively fighting for the candle to ignite.

Time slowed as a rift opened in the air. The Canthi ground to a halt, and even the waves grew motionless. An emerald crab the size of a horse emerged from the portal. Its ten legs clacked across the water as if walking on stone. Studying me with its six eyes, it raised its pincers made of ice and clamped down on both of my arms. I screamed as ice coursed through my veins and burned my insides.

When I blinked, the crab was gone along with the rift. Rotating my arms, I found no wounds. As I treaded water, my hands glowed softly, turning a portion of the water around me the same emerald green as the crab. I claimed it. Without understanding, I knew I had claimed all the water within arm's reach, about a barrel's worth. I'd broken its will. I was its master, its god!

The Canthi snapped its head toward me, and its black eyes widened. Another puff of misty air shot from its horns. I raised my hand as it struck, and a lance of green water shot upwards. The surge bounced off its scaly hide, but the force was enough to knock it off course.

I willed the water around me, and it pulled me away. I shot another lance of water, but it was like throwing pebbles at a bull. I could only control a single wave and not with near enough force to kill it.

Roaring in outrage, it barreled towards me again. As fast as I was with the green water, the creature was faster. It would be on me in seconds. I sang the song quickly. "Next is the serpent that swimmeth below. The depths are its friend but also its foe." How can the water be its foe? It ruled the sea. It lived it. It breathed it. It—That was it!

Nittles swooped low. "What did you shoot at it? Can you do it again?"

"You came!"

"For what good it will do."

I pulled the dagger from my belt and rubbed it against my arm. Once I'd disappeared, I yelled, "Fly high and keep it still."

He furrowed his brow then shot upwards. I had to make this count. I summoned as much of the green water as I could and took a deep breath.

"Here goes nothing."

The sprackin flew in its face, buzzing in front of its eyes like a relentless wasp. The creature snapped at him, but he dodged and kept flying in front of its eyes.

I raised my hand and shot four lances of water at its face. One entered its open maw while the other three arced over its head and into the nostrils. The Canthi stopped mid-strike and shook its head. Clenching my fist, I held the water in place and cut off its airway. It lived in the sea, but it didn't have gills. It needed air, and I refused to let him have it.

The creature jerked and writhed, creating massive swells around it, but I held the water in place. The depths were its friend, but right now, it was becoming its foe. A wave pummeled me deep beneath the surface, but I couldn't control the water to bring me up. I dropped my concealment and poured all my focus into choking the Canthi.

Nittles dove in and stretched out his tail. Like before, I grabbed it and we took off. I gasped as my head reached the surface, and I risked a glance back.

The Canthi struck the water again and again, but its movements were sluggish. My grip on the water was slipping. Every second was exponentially more difficult. Just a little longer.

My hands slipped, and I struck the water hard, losing my concentration. The serpent coughed out the water and dove at me in pure rage. For once, I wished I couldn't see, but below the surface, the sea was clear, giving me the perfect view of a gaping mouth.

I would have screamed had I not been holding my breath. Holding my breath. Something else occurred to me, but I pushed it aside. I claimed the water around me and shot to the side.

The massive chomp shook me to my core, but it missed. I shot upwards and waited for it to emerge. Soon, its head peaked above the waves, and it let out a loud hiss.

The Canthi was large and could probably hold its breath longer than I could hold the water. But if I timed it right, things may be different. I swam, dodged, and struck with lances of water until I finally heard what I was waiting for.

A deep burble sounded as mist shot out of its horns. When the last bit of air left its lungs, I struck, shooting water as deep as I could.

It thrashed more violently than ever, desperate for air. The waves pummeled again and again, but I held on. I was so cold. Was I underwater? Everything was dark. Just hold on!

I gasped as my head reached the surface once more. The Canthi's eyes rolled back and it collapsed, creating a tidal wave. Nittles stretched his tail, and grabbed again, propelling the water forwards. Just a little more. Just…a…little…

The wave struck me from behind, and the cliff face raced toward me. There was pain and blackness. Something soft nudged my head, but I couldn't open my eyes. I had to hold the water in place. I had to—

A melodious voice rang out. "The Trial of Water hath ended."

CHAPTER 14

"The general is more vulnerable than his captives,
for the general believes himself safe."
—The Book of Clergy

There was no wind, no misty chilling air. Lily pads floated across the pond, disturbed only by the small waterfall at the other end. The peaceful scene was broken by Nittles laughing. It wasn't the normal condescending chuckles but the sincere mirth from the belly that would make others join in. "You killed the Canthi!"

My own laugh was cut short by my splitting headache. Daggers to the skull would not have produced more pain. I rubbed my temples and groaned. "Yes, we did it," I whispered.

After eating a lifespur, my mood improved. Nittles and I exchanged details of the event with him saying what it was like to fly right in the creature's face and me explaining my abilities to control water.

"Fascinating," Nittles said. "So, a giant lycinthrapod injected you with its venom and gave you a portion of its own ability. And you suffocated the Canthi with it. You aren't as dull as I thought."

From most people, the statement would be an insult, but from Nittles, it was the most glowing compliment I'd received. I gathered up the few supplies I'd brought and headed for home, a wide grin plastered across my face.

I glanced in my mind to see the candles. The single silver candle was half spent from the fight. The thick emerald candle in the center of the candelabra stood tall, probably awaiting the fight with the beast after the trials. One green candle remained on the left of the candelabra with three on the right. Two trials down and four to go. With how agonizing the first two had been, I shuddered to think what the others would entail. But for Minessa, I would do it.

"You!" A short woman with salt-and-pepper hair stood in the street and pointed a finger at me. "You did this!" She kicked a pile of black leaves. "All of this is your fault!"

My head throbbed, whether from my fight with the Canthi or the stress, I didn't know.

Tember was the woman's name. She was the wife of one of the men who died. I remembered her weeping near the pyre. For me, the funeral happened weeks ago, but for the rest of Ashwood, it was only yesterday.

An older woman, probably her mother, grabbed her shoulders. "Calm yourself."

"No!" Tember shook off the woman's weak grip. "She's a witch. We all know it."

I'm not a witch. I wanted to say the words out loud, but it wouldn't help. "I'm…sorry for your loss."

"You're sorry?" Her face wrinkled in disgust, her eyes still red and puffy from weeping. "I want Porthan back! But he's not coming back. He'll never come back, and it's all your fault."

"No, it's not."

"What's going on?" The head blacksmith stepped out, hammer in hand.

Tember faced the man and continued waving her finger at me. "This witch killed my husband!"

Mothers and children came out of their cottages and crowded around me. A stalky man strode towards me. "What say you? Are you a witch like your mother? Did she teach you her dark arts?"

The children raised their fists and chanted, "Witch! Witch!"

I dug in my pocket, but there were no glaidens. They had been washed away in the sea. If there was water nearby, I could claim it, but the only sea was the sea of jeering people gathering around.

"The ground opened up," a boy no older than twelve said. "It swallowed my brother whole. We didn't even have a body to burn."

I felt as though a snake had coiled around my chest and was squeezing the life from me. With each shout, my chest tightened.

"The monsters went away when Thrella died!"

"I saw dark clouds over her cottage."

"Did you see how she stabbed her sister's body?"

Tember spat in my face. "I think you sacrificed your sister in some twisted ritual. You should have died, not her!"

I couldn't hold back any longer. They hated me. They always hated me. I reared back and slapped the woman across the face. I didn't think. I just reacted and instantly regretted it.

The first blow came from the stalky man who pummeled my stomach. Tember backhanded my face, and the rest were a blur. So many faces, so much yelling. The numbness returned, covering me like a thick shell. I wasn't angry or fearful anymore; I just felt complete apathy. This was it. I survived the first two trials only to die by an angry mob. It's what I deserve, after all.

A flash of hot, white light blinded me. It was brighter than the sun, yet it didn't hurt. The numbness blanketing me dissipated like mist on a hot day. For just a moment, I felt something, but it wasn't anger. It was like a kiss from Mother, a hug from Father. The light. It was forgiveness. It was acceptance of who I was in all of my ugliness. It was joy!

The light faded as soon as it appeared, but my eyes never left the glowing runes on the cleric's staff. Old Shoff hobbled towards me, and the crowd gave him a wide berth.

Despite the intoxicating feelings radiating from the staff, the old man glared and stamped it down. "Ashwood is my home. I will not see it overrun by a mindless mob!" My ears rang from the abrupt silence that followed, making the cleric's voice all the more clear. "This is a time of mourning, for remembering the dead. We've all lost someone in the past few days, Sashel included."

Tember shook her head, tears filling her eyes. "We all know Sashel's responsible. She needs to pay."

Cleric Shoff placed a hand on her shoulder and gave an understanding nod. "When we fall, we never reach for the strongest branch, only the closest. Right now, you're reaching for Sashel. Justice is farther away, but vengeance is always near, always within reach." He turned to the crowd. "I urge you all to reach farther. It is painful and difficult, but one day, you may be the one pleading for mercy."

"So, we should turn a blind eye?" she asked.

"Justice is not blind. Her eyes are wide open, seeing every side, every detail. Justice seeks truth; vengeance seeks only blood."

The blacksmith raised his hammer. "But she's still a witch!"

"Then bring your evidence to Judge Fensin." Shoff raised an eyebrow. "You do have evidence, don't you?"

One by one, the crowd dispersed, most muttering to one another. Last was Tember who gave a slight bow to the cleric before leaving, never giving me the slightest glance.

Shoff looked down at me. "I would offer to help you up, but I'm afraid I'd just fall over. My legs aren't what they used to be."

I winced as I climbed to my feet. "They all hate me."

He gave me the same look he gave Tember. Part of me was convinced he cared about me, but I knew that couldn't be true. Ever since Mother died, nobody cared. But then why did he save me? Perhaps he wanted to appear wise and caring. But he could have done so and still condemned me.

"Sashel?" He tapped me with the staff. "Your mind is drifting again."

I shook myself. "I—what was that light that came from your staff?"

"Ah, yes. It's called Suthian's Gaze. It shows a glimpse of how he sees us."

"That can't be right. It felt like…"

He smiled. "Like acceptance? Understanding? A deep love that goes beyond the nurture of a mother?"

"I suppose."

"You don't believe he sees you that way, do you?"

I rubbed the tender bruising beneath my eye. "How could a god see me that way? He knows—I mean—how could anyone see me like that?"

"That's the difference between love and affection. When a woman is young and beautiful, her husband has affection for her. But when she grows old and feeble, only love stays strong."

"So, love is blind?"

"No. What is with you people and thinking everything is blind? Love sees more. It sees deeper and farther than the surface. Suthian sees past our mistakes and finds the precious gem beneath."

I gestured at my wounds. "I don't exactly feel loved right now."

Shoff shook his head. "The villagers are convinced you're a witch with no evidence. You, on the other hand, saw Suthian's light. You felt his love, yet you're equally convinced he doesn't love you. We're all as stubborn as a mule and twice as loud."

I bent down and placed the dagger back in my pocket. "I should be going."

The old cleric pursed his lips and sighed. He clearly wanted to keep talking, but he relented. "You should go to Healer Fendin. You took quite a beating."

I dusted off my sleeves and sniffed. "I'll be fine. Thank you for helping."

Halfway to my house, Nittles joined me and whispered. "Once we're out of sight, I'll make you another lifespur. You should be able to eat at least one more today without becoming ill."

"Where were you?" My words were more shout than whisper.

"I was beside you the whole time."

"Then why didn't you do something?"

Nittles glanced back at where I'd been beaten. "Trust me. I wish I could have."

"Now you sound like Suthian."

He wrinkled his brow. "If you're trying to insult me, comparing me to a god isn't the best strategy."

My blood boiled as I walked. "I've asked the cleric many times why the gods allow suffering. Every time he says, 'Suthian is always beside you. He cares when you suffer.' Then why does he keep letting me suffer?"

He leaped in front of me and locked eyes with me. "I will not speak for the gods, but I will speak for myself. Firstly, I lack the strength to stop an entire village. Before I melded with you, it would be a simple feat, but now I doubt I could stop even half the crowd before being overtaken. Secondly, even if I had the power, should I have wiped them all out?"

I gritted my teeth. "No, just…"

"Just the men? I'm sure the children won't mind losing their father."

"I didn't mean that."

"Then pray tell. What did you mean? Should I have killed the grieving widow as well? Very noble indeed."

"Stop!"

He stepped closer. "You think it's so simple. The gods should have waved their hands and stopped the angry mob from hurting you."

"Exactly!"

"So, the gods should control people like puppets on strings? If a man controlled you in such a way, chaining you against your will, you would call it slavery. Should the gods be slave masters?"

I didn't answer. I saw the trap in his words and knew anything I said would be turned on me.

He took another step. "So, if the gods stopped the mob against their will, the gods are monsters. And if they don't stop the mob, the same is true."

"They should have done something!"

"And what of Cleric Shoff? Maybe the gods helped you by sending him."

"And why didn't *you* help?" I asked. "You could have done something."

The sprackin sighed. "I couldn't do anything without revealing what I am. I waited. As painful as it was, I waited to see if the village would merely beat you. Lifespur can heal a simple beating. However, if the beatings continued, I would have intervened."

My muscles relaxed at his admission. "You would?"

"Yes. And there is one other reason I didn't stop them." He stared at something behind me and said, "He was watching."

I turned. "Who?"

"The zealot. The one you call Neerion."

Sure enough, the short, olive-skinned cleric stared at me from atop a hill. He was too far to make out any detail, too far to hear anything, but his gleaming staff stood tall in his hand.

"How long has he been there?" I asked.

"Since before the mob approached. I would bet my tail he sent her your way."

Realization struck. "He was baiting me! Neerion used Tember to see if I was a witch. He wanted me to use magic to prove he was right."

"Precisely. He is a wily one, and we must not underestimate him."

CHAPTER 15

"Do I recant my words? No. I denounce the clergy but not my faith in Suthian. My only crime is finding a magic slightly different. For that, I am sentenced to death."
—Words of Heretics

I opened my eyes and reached for some frenlock vines, but there was only a wooden stand. Something was wrong. It was too quiet. Where was the howling wind from the sea and the smell of salt and fish?

Everything slowly came back to me. After two weeks of making that infernal ballista, I passed the trial, and I was back in my room. A sack of glaidens and lifespur lay on the stand and my knife was hidden under my pillow. After yesterday's scuffle with the villagers, I was more cautious.

I peeked out of my room and sighed in relief as Father had already left for work. He had no doubt heard about me stabbing Minessa's body at the funeral. What would he think of me? Hopefully, I would finish the trials and bring Minessa back before I had to explain anything.

"Sleep well?"

I jumped back at the voice and raised my dagger. Nittles stretched like a cat near the stove. "My, you're lively today."

I sheathed the blade and placed it on the table. "What do you expect? I fought a sea monster then an angry mob beat me half to death."

"Oh, come now. Lifespur healed you soon after. You're good as new."

I opened the cabinets, finding them bare. There were two jars of jam in the back, but upon closer inspection, I realized they were made from lifespur and glaidens. I forgot about them. I wouldn't be putting them on bread anytime soon, not that we had bread.

"Looks like we're having potatoes for breakfast."

"Delightful," Nittles said dryly.

"You can eat sand if you don't like them."

He barked a laugh. "Using my words against me? Ha! It's been a while since someone was able to do that."

After we ate, I placed a water pitcher on the table and touched the surface. A green glow emanated from inside as I claimed it. The emerald water rose from the pitcher and formed a perfect sphere.

"Incredible," Nittles said. "Claiming is a rare skill, and on one of the basic elements is all the more impressive."

I ordered the water to form a ring around the pitcher, and it obeyed. I gritted my teeth as holding the water in place grew more difficult by the second. I forced it into a square shape then a triangle. How detailed could I make it? With deep concentration, I willed the water into the shape of Nittles with wings outstretched.

He perked up and spoke to the sprackin-shaped water. "My, what a dashing fellow! Finally, someone I can converse with who isn't a barbarian. You have no idea how dull it's been with only Sashel around."

I glowered at him. "You're not funny."

"Don't tell him that. Give him a chance. He hasn't even spoken yet. He'll grow on you."

My concentration slipped, and the water fell to the ground. Nittles looked at the puddle and then at me with an accusing stare.

I chuckled. "Sorry, I killed your friend."

He shrugged. "It's quite alright. I do it all the time." He opened his mouth to say more, but his ear twitched. "What is that scratching?"

Sure enough, there was a faint scratching coming from the front door. Was it another trial? Was it the Kral? An angry villager? It was sad how many possibilities there were. I drew my dagger and crept toward the door. Yanking it open, I raised my blade to see a young boy with charcoal in his hand. "DEATH TO THE WITCH" had been written all over, including on the old sign I'd hung to hide the last message. Profanities and vulgar symbols had also been drawn.

Bode, a short, stubby boy a year younger than I, dropped the charcoal and eyed my knife warily. "I don't want any trouble." He gave a weak chuckle. "Only joking. Didn't mean nothing by it."

My blood ran cold. "Were you the one who's been writing these messages on our door?"

Bode rubbed the back of his neck and stepped back. "I—I was only joking."

"The messages made my father angry," I said through gritted teeth. "Angry enough to beat my little sister."

His eyes widened and he shook his head. "I didn't mean nothing by it. I swear I didn't. I was told to, you see?"

"You were told to? You could have said 'no.' You *should* have said 'no!'"

As I stepped towards him, dark rifts splintered through the air like spiderwebs. I took another step, and the rifts widened, but I didn't care. This boy had caused my home so much heartache.

A slimy gray tentacle burst through the rift and constricted around his neck. Bode gasped and pulled against it, but his hands slipped off like grabbing butter. He gave me a look of desperation and said, "Please, please, I'm sorry. Make it stop!"

He thought I was doing this. I stabbed the tentacle, but its grip only tightened, cutting off the boy's airway. Pulling the dagger free, I switched my grip and used it to saw the tentacle off. Weeks of making a ballista made the work much easier. When it was completely severed, the slick tentacle dropped to the ground and Bode wheezed and coughed. Wasting no time, I poured heartfire into the rift and sealed it shut.

"What have you done?" Neerion asked. The cleric stepped out from behind a shed and stamped his staff down. "You summoned the beast to kill him, didn't you? The rotten fruit shall fall!"

Other villagers stopped in the street and stared. Like yesterday, Neerion had staged this to prove I was a witch.

"I didn't summon the creature."

The cleric turned to the boy who was still clutching his throat. "Speak. What did you see?"

The boy looked from me to Neerion and spoke in a raspy voice. "I saw nothing. Honest, I didn't."

Neerion knelt beside him. "You need not fear the witch. The clergy is stronger."

"She…attacked me. She attacked me! She muttered some incantation and summoned the beast."

The crowd murmured around us, and Neerion drew closer. The eagle on his staff glowed as he said, "To remove all doubt, I can probe your mind. If you have nothing to hide, all will be well."

I shoved his staff back. "Get away from me!"

"Afraid of the clergy's power?" he asked. "I thought as much."

A few in the crowd chanted, "Witch! Witch!"

I pointed at Bode. "The creature attacked him, and I cut the tentacle off. That's all that happened."

"And the rifts just happened to open right as you grew angry?" Neerion asked.

I paused. That's exactly what happened. Were the rifts responding to my thoughts? Did part of me want the creature to attack?

He nodded. "And how did the rift close? Only a witch can do such a thing."

"Witch! Witch!" the crowd chanted.

Silver light flashed, and the goddess's voice rang out. "The Trial of Sand hath begun."

A gust of wind stirred around me, blowing dust and debris until I couldn't see Neerion just a few paces away. When the dust cleared, the village was gone, and a massive desert surrounded me. The hot air dried my mouth, and the bright sun beat down on me.

In front of me stood a strange sand dune shaped like an hourglass the size of a mountain. It was several miles wide at the base and tapered upward to a fine point before widening at the top. Logic said the top half, a mirror image of the bottom, should fall since the middle was so thin, yet it stood firm as a mountain. A sandy pathway spiraled around the hourglass leading to the top.

The goal seemed simple enough: climb to the top. Still, I needed all the help I could get. Focusing on the link to Nittles, I sent heartfire through and pulled. The air shimmered in front of me as the sprackin came through.

"Is it sad that accompanying you on your third trial comes as a relief?" Nittles looked around and sniffed. "I'm not surprised it's a desert. Maybe we—" Upon seeing the hourglass, he froze with a look of absolute horror. "Send me back! Send me back now!"

"What's wrong?"

"Get me out of here!"

As much as I wanted him with me, I tried sending him back. I poured fire through our connection and pushed, but nothing happened. "I can't."

"What do you mean you can't?"

"I mean I can't. It's like pushing a rope. I can pull you closer just fine, but when I try to push you away, the line goes slack. I'm sorry, but I can't send you back."

He rustled his wings in irritation. "You don't understand. It's the Great Hourglass!"

"I figured. You mentioned it before."

"But it's a fable. It's nuanced with symbolism. I didn't think we'd have to climb the actual Hourglass!"

"And what of it? The Canthi was a myth, yet we fought it. We can do this as well."

He crawled up my dress like a squirrel and met my gaze. "Maybe this will show you the gravity of the situation. Many refer to this place as the Banished Realm or the Land of Damnation. The most depraved souls are said to wander this place with no hope of escape. Are you getting the picture now?"

My heart sped up. "But we're not banished here. This is a trial. Surely if we reach the top we could—"

"The mirages. You don't know about the mirages."

I looked at the mountainous hourglass. "Mirages? As in a trick of the eye? I thought they form by heat and sunlight or something."

"Not these. They manifest as different creatures, and if they touch you, you'll be forced to relive a memory."

"That's not too bad." I tried to stay optimistic, but my heart sank by the second.

He hopped off my shoulder and shook his head. "They are the worst memories we have. The moment the memory begins, sand grows around you, starting at your feet. If the sand reaches your head before you escape the memory, you'll be trapped. You'll be cursed to relive your most painful memories for eternity."

Nittles' desperation to escape finally made sense. It was the place of the damned, and Nittles and I had to suffer its torments.

"Tell me everything you know about the Hourglass," I said.

Nittles looked at the mountainous structure and pointed his tail to the bottom half which was mostly tear-shaped. "The Great Hourglass is divided into six sections, three on the top half and three on the bottom. The first three sections represent shame, fear, and guilt. If we make it past those, we should have a respite in the center." He pointed higher up. "The second half is different. The last three sections represent time, and the sequence is future, present, and past."

As I squinted through the sand blowing in my face, more details emerged. Each section had different colored sand like layers in rock. Red sand rested at the bottom, then orange, yellow, green, blue, and violet at the top, creating a dark rainbow throughout the Hourglass. Each section would represent the six stages Nittles described. At the base of the structure, a wide pathway made of red sand spiraled up the first section.

I grabbed a glaiden from my dress pocket. "Should we run?"

"No. The base is at least a few miles in diameter, and we'll be walking in a spiral pattern around it. So, unless you plan on sprinting several miles uphill through the sand, I suggest we walk. Besides, if we go too fast, we're more likely to be touched by a mirage, and that's the last thing we want."

"And you said we can rest halfway."

"Correct. And I know I've already told you, but it bears repeating. If you're pulled into a memory and don't escape in time, you'll be trapped forever, and I don't think the trial will end. This realm is merciless."

I knelt beside him. "Again, I'm sorry I pulled you into this. I had no idea—"

"Enough. Let us begin" His eyes never left the pathway as if it took all his will not to run away.

We both stepped onto the red sand, and the sun turned crimson.

CHAPTER 16

"The Hourglass was beautiful once, recalling cherished memories for all who traverse it. So much beauty before the Corrupt One came."
—The Book of Origins

"Walk slower," Nittles warned. "Mirages may appear at any moment from any angle."

I complied, looking around as I did. "Should I eat a glaiden then?"

"You can, but we have a full day's walk ahead of us. A few minutes of speed isn't going to do much good."

"What happens when we reach the top?"

His eyes darted around for any attacks. "If it is like other trials I've read about, there'll be an effigy of Kareli, usually a gold or silver statue. Once one of us touches it, we will both be sent back. We are not the first to travel in pairs during a trial."

I stopped. "Wait, what if you flew to the top?"

"That's...actually not a bad idea. I have the feeling this realm has something to hinder me from using such a cheat, but I'll take any chance of getting out." He flapped his wings, but nothing happened. "Send me some heartfire."

When I looked in my mind's eye, there was only a deep red chamber with no candles. For the first time in over a month, my soul was completely empty. "There's nothing."

"What do you mean?"

"I mean I have no candles in my soul. No heartfire, no emerald candles, nothing!"

He continued walking. "It's what I feared. Once we stepped on the Hourglass, we entered into a different magic. This realm nullifies much of the goddess's power. We'll still be taken back if one of us reaches the top, but it looks like we're on our own."

"If her power doesn't work here, then why did she send us here?"

"I don't know."

I looked around again but there was no sign of any mirages. "But why do you need heartfire to fly? Birds fly and they don't use magic."

"Birds are small, and they have hollow bones. I depend on heartfire. If I was at the top, I could glide down but I can't soar without fire. I'm too heavy."

I pulled out the glaidens. "Well, if the magic doesn't work here, then how come these still—" The fruit turned to ash in my hand and blew away along with any chance at making it out.

We trudged through the deep sand for only a few minutes before we saw our first mirage. A scorpion the size of a melon scuttled towards me. It was transparent and emanated a soft red glow. I jumped back, and its stinger sunk in the sand.

"Don't let it touch you!" Nittles cried.

"I wasn't planning on it."

The scorpion struck twice more before fading to red dust. We both let out a breath and continued, walking even slower than before.

"What's the difference between shame and guilt?" I asked. "I sort of use them interchangeably."

The sprackin looked around before speaking. "I'm not surprised. The difference is nuanced but important. Shame is how you believe others perceive you even if there is little to no basis. Guilt is grounded in mistakes we've made that we can't move past. For instance, if you've ever said something foolish, a very strong possibility for you, then you feel shame. You believe others think less of you, and you try to avoid seeing them for a while."

"That sounds uncomfortable but not deadly."

"If it can distract you long enough, it is worse than deadly."

"It still won't distract me," I said. "I don't care what other people think of me."

He gave a hollow laugh. "Then you are the first."

Before I could respond, a statue caught my eye. Sadly, it wasn't the statue of Kareli since it was neither made of precious metals nor at the top of the Hourglass. We crept towards it, careful lest it be a mirage, but it was far from that. The statue was opaque and dark red like the sand, depicting a massive man with a grizzly beard. His poleaxe hung limply in his hands, and his face wrinkled into the unmistakable expression—shame.

"What is this?" I asked.

Nittles sniffed it with his long snout. "It is not a statue. He is an unfortunate soul destined to live in shame for all eternity." He peered closer and gasped. "Tharinon the Vengeful! The crest on his ring is undeniable."

"Who was he?"

"A menace to Tal Miral. He was assassinated over five years ago. Who knew shame would be his downfall? Still, good riddance!"

"How do you know he was assassinated? Maybe he climbed the staircase and ended up here?"

Maybe it was the dim red light from the sun or the sand in the air, but I could swear I saw the corners of his mouth twitch as if suppressing a smile as he said, "I'm quite sure he was assassinated."

I gingerly touched the statue, or rather the entombed man. The texture felt rough like sand but solid as armor. Nittles was right. Once the sand grew around someone, there was no escaping.

"Sashel, look out!"

I spun, but the transparent scorpion pierced my calf. Instead of pain, a warm feeling ran up my leg, and when it reached my head, a memory struck me like a hammer.

* * *

I squirmed in my seat as Papa spoke to the mayor of Ashwood. Mama said this was a special dinner, and since I was only six, I needed to be quiet and let the big people talk. We finished eating a while ago, but Papa and the mayor still talked and laughed around the table. It was so boring.

Mama told me not to stare at the mayor's nose which looked as if someone pressed it in like it was made of clay. Whenever Mama looked away, I sneaked a glance at the man's squished nose. How could he even breathe through it?

The mayor's wife placed a hand on her large womb and turned to Mama. "I'm in my seventh month. And what of you, Thrella? Any chance of another child?"

Mama looked down. "I don't think so."

"Come now," the woman glanced at Papa. "Poor Tamble must feel outnumbered being the only man in the house. You must have a son next."

The mayor chuckled. "It isn't like she has a choice. Only Suthian decides if their next one is a boy."

"Nonsense," his wife said. "If you put ginger and lime in your tea every morning, and eat an onion before bed, the child will be a boy."

I wanted to ask about this, but one glare from Mama silenced me.

"Plain superstition," the mayor said.

"It is not. My sister, who has had six children, mind you, swears by it."

"The only thing an onion does at night is give you—" The mayor's wife shot him a glare, and he cut off his statement. "Well—uh—what of little Sashel here? Such a charming girl."

Papa smiled and patted my head. "Yes, she is."

"She's well-behaved." The mayor peered closer at me. "And so...focused."

Papa smiled. "She gets it from her mother. Her eyes are wide, drinking up everything she sees. She's curious too. She's quick as a whip and twice as loud."

The mayor laughed. "Well then, let's satiate her curiosity." He knelt beside me. "What questions do you have for me? I'm sure there's a dozen buzzing around in your little head."

I looked at Mama who glowered at me, warning me not to ask about his squished nose. She scolded me for asking too many questions, but this was my one chance to ask them.

I looked back at Mama and then at the mayor. His nose wasn't the only thing I wondered about. There was another question begging to be asked.

Placing my hand on his big belly, I asked, "Will your baby be a boy too?"

Mama groaned and buried her face in her hands. What did I say wrong? All I knew was Papa was laughing, and Mama was furious.

* * *

Nittles scurried up my dress and batted my face with his wings. "Sashel, snap out of it!"

Crimson sand covered my feet and ankles. A crackling sounded as the sand crept farther up, hardening like stone. I felt disgusted with myself. I felt so foolish, and that same memory plagued me countless times since it happened. I was an idiot, and I always would be. The feeling of shame was much stronger than I expected, and I couldn't shake it!

The sand covered my calves as the emotions swirled within me. How could anyone take me seriously? I always acted before I thought. I was a fool, and I always would be.

"Sashel!"

I shook myself and focused on the sand stretching up my calf. The shameful feeling wouldn't go away. I could tell myself I was a child and unaware, but that didn't take away the feeling. The sand grew further, and I couldn't feel my legs. Would this one simple memory doom me forever? With a grunt, I pulled free and broke its grip. After brushing off the sand, I couldn't help hiding my face in shame.

Nittles gave a high-pitched laugh. "The baby! Will it be a boy too? You should have asked about the mayor's nose. I would love to have seen that!" When his laughing finally stopped, he looked at me and then burst into another fit of laughter.

"You saw that?"

"We're melded," he said. "Vivid memories like that can pass through our link."

I rubbed my eyes, more to keep hiding my face than anything else. "That…doesn't help my mood."

"It helped *my* mood significantly."

"I was six!"

"I know. You were innocent and quite oblivious."

I quickened my pace through the sand. "It's not funny. I need to know how to break free of the memory next time before the sand covers me completely."

His smile fell. "I know. The memory was amusing, but you're right. Being trapped forever in painful memories is nothing to make light of."

"So, how do I fight it?"

He nodded as if chewing on the question. "It's a state of mind. You must first understand it's not wrong to care about how other people perceive you. If no one cared what others thought, we would all be quite rude, and that makes for a fragile society."

"That makes sense, but it doesn't take away the feelings of disgust I have. That small memory nearly consumed me, and I'm still struggling to shake off the feeling."

Nittles turned around, but there was no mirage. "The key is understanding that people don't think about us as often as we think they do. Case in point, your memory amused me. I laughed at it, but I didn't think less of you. The point is people may laugh for a moment, but they move on, and so should we."

"Moving on is easier said than done."

"Agreed, but shame keeps us humble. It reminds us not to take ourselves too seriously. We are attracted to people who know how to laugh at themselves."

I continued walking. All of what he said sounded good, but I didn't feel like it was practical. I wanted something I could do rather than some philosophy.

Nittles must have seen my frustration because he said, "If shame attacks you, admit what you did and learn from it. Tell yourself, 'I made a mistake, but it doesn't define me. It is not who I am. I am greater than my failures.'"

For the next three hours, we walked. The translucent scorpions attacked, sometimes in groups of three or four, but we avoided most of them. Nittles was quick and avoided their strikes, but without glaidens to help me, I was struck three more times. Each time an embarrassing memory penetrated my mind, the sand grew over me.

Apparently, the sand wouldn't grow until after the memory finished. The crimson sand fed on the emotions that flooded my mind in reaction to the memory. The quicker I shook off the feelings, the sooner I could break free. Each time I chanted what Nittles said. These are mistakes, but they're not who I am. It is embarrassing but no worse than what everyone else experiences. This is not who I am. By the last attack, I even chuckled at the memory and shook off the sand before it reached my ankles.

"Great work!" Nittles said. "You're learning how to deal with shame."

A scorpion burst from beneath him and grazed the sprackin's back before he could move. His memory shot into my head through our connection, but it was brief, only a second or two. Other sprackins sat near him, and Nittles blew, just blew in the air, and his friends all laughed. Then the memory ended, and he shook off the sand from his feet.

"What was that?" I asked.

He cleared his throat. "It was nothing."

"Come now. You've seen four of my memories, and all I get is a peek?"

"Yes."

I turned the memory over in my mind, but I couldn't see anything embarrassing about it. Could it be a cultural thing? Maybe to sprackins what he did was vulgar.

Nittles halted. "The next stage is just ahead of us. Be on your guard."

As we stepped into the orange sand, the sun changed to match its color. We looked around, even more cautious than before. Dread filled me as I remembered what the second stage of the trial was. Shame was difficult enough to fight, but fear was something else entirely.

CHAPTER 17

"The Hourglass was the first to fall, yet it was the greatest of all."
—The Book of Origins

A bright orange hawk swooped down and struck me in the face. As before, the mirage didn't so much as scratch me, but I was instantly overwhelmed by a vivid memory. It was the same memory that haunted me every night.

* * *

Minessa sat under the plum tree. Her skin turned pale white, and her left arm elongated into a sharp stinger. Her teeth were black and her eyes yellow. She looked at me with fear in her eyes.

After the Kral stabbed her, my sister reverted to normal with a gaping wound in her chest. Tears ran down her cheeks as she clutched her wound, then her body went limp.

* * *

Dark orange sand covered my feet. What if I couldn't save her? What if my mistakes doomed her to an early death? Nittles said something, but I barely noticed. I shouldn't have made all that fruit, and now my sister was dead. The trials were too much!

Another hawk swooped low. I tried to dodge, but my feet were locked in place. The transparent bird bit into my arm, and the memory surfaced.

* * *

Father stammered through the doorway and struggled to latch the door shut. He kicked the door which shook the cottage and spat out a string of profanities.

Minessa and I sat huddled in my room. A small dresser stood in front of my door, but I doubted it would keep Father out. His drinking was getting worse. How long would this go on? There was a crash in the kitchen, and I didn't have to look to know what it was. Father had thrown Mother's portrait again and probably broke the frame.

I squeezed Minessa and prayed to Suthian that it would all be over soon. "Bad things come to an end," I chanted. "Bad things come to an end."

* * *

I stared down as the sand coiled around my calves and up to my knees. What if I became like him? When Mother died, Father became a monster. What if Minessa's death affected me the same way?

"Sashel, be strong!" Nittles cried. "Nothing is inevitable!"

I shook my head as the dark orange sand grew up my thighs. I can't do this! I can't do this! What was I thinking? I never should have tried.

"You think you will fail," Nittles crawled up my shoulder and looked deep into my eyes. "You think all is hopeless. You're wrong."

I winced as the sand reached my waist. "I can't do this, Nittles. I'm not strong enough."

"You defeated the Canthi!"

My heart sped up and I struggled to breathe. "I can't do this!"

"You mustn't lose hope. There's always hope!"

Hope. The word was a curse to me. Hope always failed me. It gave me false promises and then relished in my disappointment.

I shook my head as my eyes watered. "I—can't—hope."

Nittles growled and sunk his sharp tail into my arm. "Then get angry!"

Angry. I could be angry. It's mostly all I feel these days. I looked at the sand growing up to my neck. *It was trying to imprison me. It was attacking me. No one attacks me. Not my father, not the Kral, and definitely not this infernal sand!*

I screamed in rage and the hardened sand cracked. I pushed harder. I was sick of not having a choice. I had been a coward for too long, but no further. I pushed with everything I had, and the sand covering my chest shattered. Bending down, I wailed against the hardened sand covering my legs, then I rotated my hips and yanked them free. The orange sand returned to normal, but I kept up my barrage of strikes. I hated it!

"Sashel, we must move."

Another hawk dove at me, but I rolled to the side. After it missed, the creature faded to dust. I let out a calming breath and continued walking. Once my anger faded, I realized how exhausted I was.

Hour after hour, we evaded the mirages, but our movements grew sluggish. Nittles was hit once but shrugged off the effects in moments.

"How do you defeat them so quickly?" I asked.

He panted as he walked beside me. "It's what I tried to tell you earlier. I cling to hope."

"Hope? Hope in what?"

"In many things. Truth for one."

"What if the truth is that there is no hope?"

"Nonsense. It's improbable that all of our worst fears come true. I reflect on all the difficult times I've experienced and realize I somehow made it through, and I will again."

"What if your life is nothing but failure?" I asked.

"Even the most successful people fail most of the time. They eventually succeed because they fail. They succeed because they have failed and then they rise again."

"And what if that doesn't work?"

He looked at me. "When all else fails, I trust Kareli."

I raised my hands and gestured around us. "Kareli brought us here."

"Everything she does is to teach us how to live better lives. Those who struggle the most will have mercy on others. Our trials make us stronger… if you let them."

We passed dozens of statues, or rather people encapsulated in the hardened sand. There were warriors, queens, beggars, fishermen, and many others, all wearing the same look of terror on their faces.

After passing an old man who appeared to be a cobbler, Nittles said, "Anger can block out fear for a time, but it's not sustainable. You must learn to hope."

"I may not need to." I pointed ahead where the sand turned yellow. "What's the third stage again?"

He swallowed. "Guilt."

"This should be the smallest section, right."

He nodded. "Yes. The closer we are to the center of the Hourglass, the smaller the sections are."

I noticed we were spiraling a bit faster around the structure, and I was delighted this stage would be quick. "You said we can rest at the halfway point?"

"Yes, but be cautious. The middle may be fast, but the mirages are faster still."

The sun turned a metallic gold as we entered the third stage. More statues appeared of people overcome by guilt; their faces scrunched in regret.

In less than a minute, the first mirage appeared. Nittles said they would be quick, so I'd thought of several animals they might be: a leopard, an eagle, maybe a snake? I was wrong. The mirage was a sprackin.

The golden creature shot towards me. I ducked, but the sprackin was too quick. Its wing connected with my arm, and the memory began. It was a simple one, barely a second. The memory was of the staircase. I had just taken my first step when the voice spoke. Kareli promised I would recover all that was lost, and I stepped off.

I should have gone further. I was such a coward. I doomed Minessa because I was afraid of disappointment. Gritting my teeth, I resisted. *No. I will do better. I will bring her back.* The golden sand shattered as I pulled my feet free. More sprackins charged.

No matter which way I moved, the sprackins were on me. *I shouldn't have made the fruit near the plum tree. I should have stopped before she died. I never should have let her go outside. What was I thinking? We were about to leave. We were so close.*

As the sand reached my knees, another sprackin connected. It wasn't just Minessa. Other villagers died because of me. I brought the Rending upon all of Ashwood because of my stupidity!

Nittles darted left to right from the barrage of attacks. "Sashel, you must forgive yourself. We all make mistakes."

"We all make mistakes. We all make mistakes." I said the words, but my heart wouldn't swallow them. I had to forgive myself. How was I supposed to do that? I hated myself. I—

A memory struck me, not from the mirages but what Nittles said about forgiveness. When the villagers were beating me, Cleric Shoff stopped them with the light from his staff, the Light of Suthian. In that moment, I felt loved, accepted...and forgiven.

The sand stopped at my chest, and my muscles eased. Most of my mistakes were out of ignorance not choice. I didn't know what would happen if I didn't climb further up the staircase. I didn't know Minessa would die. I regretted my decisions, but I didn't intentionally hurt people. And even when I intentionally did wrong, that wasn't who I am today. If an omniscient god can forgive me then I could forgive myself.

The hardened sand shattered, and I ran, Nittles right behind me. Each revolution around the Hourglass grew shorter as we spiraled upward. Just ahead was a flat surface of white sand surrounding the second half of the structure. There it was. Safety!

"I see it!" I yelled. "It's just ahead."

I turned to Nittles just as a mirage struck his side. His eyes widened as his memory flooded both of our minds.

* * *

Nittles soared through the emerald sky and laughed. "I'm gaining on you!"

Salar blazed her heartfire and sped up. His daughter was growing faster by the day which delighted Nittles to no end. Salar performed a complex maneuver meant to shake off her pursuers, but Nittles had taught her those moves and anticipated them.

Nittles blazed his own fire and poured his density into the front half of his body while simultaneously controlling the wind current around him for added propulsion. He then focused on the wind current around his daughter, and in mid-flap, he altered it ever so slightly. Salar jerked to the left, and Nittles grabbed her in a hug. "Got you!"

They reached the mansion constructed to resemble an Icklewood tree which sprackins were known for living in, and two of his sons leaped on his back and wrestled him to the ground. Nittles could have fought them off, but the sooner they thought they won, the sooner it would be over.

They all flew over the fountain, and onto the balcony branching off from the main building. Falonia sat cleaning their youngest son. His wife wouldn't stop licking until every blemish was gone from Cobin's white fur.

"Did you win?" Falonia asked.

Salar slumped. "No."

Nittles chuckled. "But she nearly did. Our little girl will be a master in no time!"

His wife gave an approving nod and then let out a quick whistle, signaling the children to leave while the parents talked. Salar and the two older sons flew up to the third floor, leaving little Cobin to scurry up the ladder and join them. Falonia's smile faded as she watched him climb.

"I already know what you're going to say," Nittles said.

Falonia shook her head. "He's eight and still no heartfire. Children half his age already have theirs."

"Yes, but it's rare. Usually, they ignite around six, not four."

"But he's eight."

He sighed. "There's still time."

His wife straightened. "There's a master in transference coming soon. I want to take Cobin to him. There's a process where some of my fire can be sent to him."

Nittles scowled. "You mean melding."

"It's…similar, but he'll be able to fly."

"Melding is an anathema. It's abominable!"

"It's not like he'd be melded to a human. It would be to me. I could give him as much fire as he needs."

"I'll not have my son bound to anyone, not even you. And who is this master of transference? Is he a human?" When Falonia didn't answer, he huffed. "No human will tamper with my son's heartfire."

"But Cobin just wants to fly."

Golden light flashed across the room. Nittles turned to see the center orb on the pedestal glowing. "It's the king."

Falonia stomped her foot. "We're not finished."

He readied himself then looked back. "We'll talk later."

Nittles blazed his heartfire and shot towards the palace. Within a few minutes, he flew through the far left window of the royal court opened specifically for him. Lighting on the velvet pillow beside the throne, he bowed.

"Rise," the king said. "No time for formalities."

King Banathin, one of the few humans Nittles respected, seemed bothered. His short, gray beard hadn't been oiled or combed, and he wore a simple tunic instead of his fine silk. The only sign he was even a king was his crown garnished with rubies.

"What is it?" Nittles asked.

Banathin fiddled with his golden rings, a gift from a former associate of theirs, which made small ripples in the air. "Naisis broke through the East Flank."

"Impossible." The word came out despite himself. Nittles knew the king wouldn't joke about such things, but the West Flank? It was unthinkable.

"Believe it," the king said wearily. "It's quite possible."

"But how?"

He spun the rings faster around his fingers. "He woke the Balorinth. Nothing can stand in his way."

Nittles' stomach dropped at his words. "Your messengers must be mistaken. If this is true then the waters themselves will rise against us!"

Banathin stood and waved for the guards to leave. "Nittles, do you know the saying 'Desperate times, desperate measures'?"

Nittles eyed the guards leaving. "Yes."

The king paced across the crimson rug. "Naisis found a knife, and we need a sword."

"Some swords can wound the wielder more than the foe."

"Desperate times," he countered. "There is but one being who is a match for the Balorinth."

"And that is Kareli," Nittles said.

"True…but she does not always respond. We need something reliable, something practical."

He pulled a chord beside the throne, and the floor in the middle of the courtroom opened. A platform beneath raised up with a clinking sound. A dungeon lay beneath the court, and the king would raise special captives from below for sport to entertain the nobles. This time, there was no prisoner. A large metal cage covered the platform and inside was an ordinary fox.

Although Nittles didn't feel like he was in any danger, the feeling in the pit of his stomach didn't go away. "I don't follow, your majesty. What is this about?"

Banathin opened a locked box and plucked a single fruit with tongs. Black mucus dripped like syrup from the dark fruit. It called to Nittles as it did to everyone.

"Drethals!"

"Only one." The king dropped the fruit into the cage.

"No!" Nittles cried.

Too late, the fox snatched it out of the air, and the change began. Its furry tail morphed into a long sinuous stinger that moved like a whip. Its red fur fell from its body, leaving only pale skin behind. A wail came from the fox's throat as it grew to five times its size and black fangs grew from its mouth. The creature let out a roar and pounded at the bars, the cage held firm.

"What are you doing?" Nittles asked.

The king took a calming step back from the cage. "Sprawn beasts can make for a powerful army."

"You can't tame them. They're rotten. They will turn on you the moment they're released."

Banathin looked out the window. "There are...rituals that can fix this."

"Rituals? You mean..."

"The Corrupt One."

Nittles' wings twitched. "Surely you're not—"

"Desperate times!"

The king brought out a small cage containing a young fox no more than a few weeks old. Nittles' stomach churned even more as he realized it was probably the other fox's offspring. The Corrupt One always required the sacrifice of their own children.

"Your majesty, I beg of you, don't do this."

The king drew a dagger and in a single motion slid the blade through the cage and slit its throat. Ancient runes on the cage's floor glowed a sickening yellow, as did an obsidian ring on the king's finger. The creature on the platform fell silent as his eyes glowed the same dim yellow.

"Rise," the king said.

The pale beast stood up.

"Lift your tail."

It raised its stinger to the top of the cage.

The king raised a shaky hand to his mouth before saying, "Kill."

The beast plunged its stinger into its own back. Black smoke billowed from its wound as all its venom poured out. It writhed and gnashed at the bars, but eventually, it lay still.

"I can't trust Kareli to win us this war." Banathin pointed to the cage of the dead beast. "But this is consistent. It is trustworthy. You follow the instructions and receive the desired result."

Nittles' throat was dry as he said, "And the result is always death."

"Only death to our enemies. With an army like this, we spare our soldiers' lives. You cannot deny this plan has merit. It is certain to succeed."

"All rituals to the Corrupt One are all successful at first, but they leave you with an insatiable hunger. It is a fire which cannot be quenched. I implore you, not as your advisor but as your friend. Consider other options."

"And if I refuse?"

Nittles bowed. "Then I must relinquish my position."

He lowered his head and fiddled with his rings. "I was afraid of this, but I know you too well. However, we still need heartfire to make the drethals."

Nittles bristled at this. "Sprackins will never agree to make them."

"They will think they are making mandrils. None will suspect we let them rot into drethals. It's unthinkable to them."

He was right. Gods curse him, but he was right. "I can't let you do this!"

"Then we force you to eat a drethal as well. You will be a powerful ally in one way or another. Don't force me to do this. Work with me. Sprackins were used as chattel once, and they can be again. I wish it didn't have to be this way, but desperate times."

"The ritual to control me requires a sacrifice of my own kin. You need all the heartfire you can spare. You can't afford to kill a single sprackin."

Banathin's face contorted into true remorse. "But one of your children has no heartfire."

Nittles' blood froze in his veins. Cobin. Little Cobin would be the sacrifice.

The king waved his hand, and his golden rings removed the illusion. Surrounding the sprackin were eight men and women robed in black and yellow. All were masters in different magics, and all swore fealty to the king. They were the Grand Maestros.

Nittles spread his wings and shot up. Two of the maestros stilled the wind, and he fell. His wings would be useless, but his heartfire blazed within him. Time slowed, and Nittles altered his direction solely with the fire in his soul. He tripled his density and magnified his speed, aiming for the two maestros blocking the wind. Before they could raise a finger, both were crushed like old parchment.

The other six launched attacks, some with black fire, others with water or lightning. None hit their target. Nittles altered the direction of each attack so that they struck their fellow maestros. One fell to ash from the black fire, but the others shielded themselves. While they did, Nittles launched himself out of the palace.

He soared through the city at a breakneck speed until landing in his mansion. "Falonia, get the children and flee!"

His family rushed to obey, little Cobin riding on his mother's back.

"Nittles, what's happening?" Falonia asked.

"Go now!"

Just as they left, the five remaining maestros arrived. One rode a lion made of water while another flew on pure willpower. The earth shook, and the ground beneath him opened up.

Nittles spread his wings and caught himself just before the ground slammed shut like a mouth chomping its prey. That was too close. A whirlwind grew around him, and lightning crackled from above. A clever trap.

He reached out with his senses and felt the movement beyond the whirlwind. Maldak, the maestro of air, held out his runic staff to control the wind. Nittles couldn't manipulate his staff since it was joined to the welder, but he could control things around the maestro.

Nittles held his focus while dodging lightning strikes from above. It wasn't easy. More than once, his focus slipped, but finally he found what he was looking for. A leaf, a single leaf drifted near the maestro on the other side of the angry wind. None of the other maestros paid the leaf any mind. Why would they?

Nittles poured his density into the leaf and then manipulated the wind around it. The maestros sensed this, but it was too late. The mighty sprackin brought the leaf down like a heavy axe, lopping off Maldak's hand holding the staff. The whirlwind dissipated as the maestro's staff toppled to the ground.

A woman raised a sword crackling with yellow lightning. "Give up."

Nittles gave a sharp-toothed smile. "Yes, you should."

The woman prepared her lightning, but Nittles was far ahead of her. He couldn't affect their density at this range as they were too large, but he could create a false aura around them. In essence, he could trick the lightning into thinking two of the maestros were massive trees. When the woman released her lightning, the maestros on either side of her fell to the ground in a smoking pile of flesh.

"I could have sworn there were eight of you just a moment ago," Nittles said.

Another maestro launched a wave of water, encompassing the sprackin. He swam to the side, but the maestro held him firm. The woman raised her sword to strike the ball of water with her lightning.

Not good! Nittles blazed his fire as hot as he could and launched himself out. The jolt took his breath away and cracked a few bones, but he was free. A concussive boom sounded as the lightning struck the water.

Nittles collided with a tree and fell. The maestros warily approached him, apparently still deciding their next course of action. He was growing sick of these humans. He served a human king for decades, and for what? They saw sprackins as little more than livestock only good for harvesting their heartfire.

The woman's sword shook in her hand. "Give up!"

Nittles didn't know if he could take on the remaining three. He still had heartfire, but at this rate, he may lose. Better to defeat their spirit instead.

Nittles raised his head and smiled as though this were all a game. "I'm beginning to think you mean for me to give up instead of you." He blazed his fire as time slowed around him. He had a fraction of a second, not enough time to take out all three. But if he took out just one more like it was child's play, the others may retreat.

In a blink, he stood on the woman's shoulder, his spiked tail impaling her neck. "Give up? Sprackins never give up."

She collapsed, and the last two maestros turned and fled. Nittles watched them go, then turned to catch up with his family when he felt a peculiar sensation. His heartfire was being pulled towards the South. A human had climbed the Great Staircase. Since it came from that direction, the human was from another world.

Only a fraction of his heartfire would be taken, just enough to ignite the person's heartfire. Nittles' soul would be restored within the hour, but he hesitated. Reason told him to just let the fire go. No man should oppose the Staircase, but Nittles was no man. He was a sprackin, and he would not let a lowly human take even a fraction of his fire. They had taken too much from him, but no more.

The Staircase pulled, and Nittles pulled back. Pain coursed through his body, but he stood his ground. Part of him screamed to let it go, but he refused. It was his fire. His! A stream of silver fire seeped from his soul, but he grabbed it with his will. He knew he was being stubborn, but he didn't care. He was a master of Agrariance, master of two noble gems, and counselor of kings. He—

A translucent chord wrapped around his soul, and his heartfire poured out like a river. No! This can't be! He pulled against the chord, but this time a new entity, the climber of the stairs, pulled back. With that one pull, an emerald portal opened, and Nittles was ripped from his world. As he crashed into a pile of crimson leaves, he looked back as the portal winked shut. Tal Miral, the palace, his family, everything he knew was gone.

CHAPTER 18

"He sought them out, first the Hourglass,
then the Maze of Tirran. Only the Staircase remains
uncorrupted, but for how long?"
—The Book of Origins

I rolled over and opened my heavy eyes. Swallowing proved difficult as my throat was dry as the white sand around me. My tongue felt dry and my lips chapped. Even if the mirages didn't overwhelm me, I would die of thirst if we didn't make it out soon.

Nittles lay an arm's length from me, and the events of last night sluggishly returned to me. The sand had grown up to his waist before he broke free. After diving into the white sand, he didn't speak. He knew I saw the memory and didn't need to explain. After only a minute, he drifted off to sleep, and I followed.

I sat up and took a deep breath, resulting in a fit of coughs. My eyes were dry and the inside of my nose was sore and crusty. "I hate this place."

"You do?" Nittles stood and stretched his wings. "I say, this place is beginning to…grow on me." Despite the pun, he remained solemn as he stared at the desert below.

"Nittles, I—"

"Don't apologize."

"Why not?"

"Because it was my fault. I should have let the fire go. My hubris got the better of me."

"I still took you from your family."

He dropped his head. "They will be safe until I return."

I had many questions about his memory, but one stood above the rest. "Is melding to a human—I mean—is it actually—"

"Is it an abomination?" His silver eyes turned to meet mine. "I used to believe it."

"And what about now?"

He smiled, not a cunning smile or a derisive one, but a true, heartfelt smile. "We should be going. We can't last long without water."

I felt both delighted and disappointed by his reaction. He was right that we needed to move, but I had to ask one more question. "How come I've never seen you fight like the way you did in the memory?"

"I haven't had much chance. I couldn't slay the Canthi with ten times my heartfire."

I wasn't letting it go that easy. "You could have torn Vision Master to pieces."

"Caster is quite formidable. He acquired special abilities from climbing the stairs."

"Still, you've never come close to fighting like you did before we melded."

The barb on his tail twitched in irritation. "You seem fixed on this point. Very well. I used a skill called 'blazing.' It's a way of burning heartfire hotter and brighter. It amplifies my abilities, but

I can't do it now that we're melded. Even if you transfer all your heartfire to me, I can't blaze anymore."

"Oh." I knew Nittles was separated from his world, but after seeing his memory and hearing about his abilities, I was only now realizing how much I had taken from him. I had reduced him to a fraction of what he once was. And his family, his wife, little Cobin! Would they be safe? What was this about Naisis and the Balorinth? Had I put his whole nation in jeopardy?

"And your mind has drifted again," Nittles said.

I rubbed my eyes. "Sorry."

He sniffed. "The next three stages of the Hourglass represent the future, present, and past. All will target our mistakes and deepest pain. Let us begin." He stepped onto the dark green sand, and the sun glowed emerald. "Beware of the future. It will only show what might be, not what will be. Mirages of the future are different from the others and can be difficult to shake off."

Scores of emerald statues emerged, all entombed in the hardened sand. Instead of having one expression like before, they each wore different emotions: curiosity, wonder, fear, and confusion. "Anything to distract," Nittles had said.

Ahead, one of the statues moved. No, it wasn't a statue like the others; it was a mirage, a human mirage. The young woman knelt in the sand and wept, an eerie green glow emanating from her transparent form.

"Keep your distance," Nittles said.

"But we have to pass her. There's no way around her."

We crept close, ready for an attack, but the woman remained on her hands and knees and wept. Despite the heat, my blood chilled at her words. "They're dead. They're all dead."

As I passed her, my attention drifted to her feet. The tendons in the back of her ankles had been sliced clean through, rendering her crippled.

"They're all dead," she wailed.

Nittles nudged me and whispered, "Keep moving."

The mirage looked up, and her hair brushed away from her face. It was me. Staring back at me was a mirror image of my face. She cocked her head in confusion, then her eyes fell on the sprackin at my feet.

"Nittles, you're alive!" She reached out to embrace him, but he jumped back. The mirage turned back to me. "Sashel, I was wrong. Mother—" The mirage flickered and then faded away.

"No!" I yelled. "Bring her back!"

"We need to keep moving," he insisted.

"What was she going to say?"

"Sashel, move."

"She mentioned my mother. She said I was wrong. What did she mean?"

Nittles said something, but all my focus was on what I just saw. It was a mirage about the future. My future self was trying to tell me something. Nittles grew louder, and I tried to ignore his yelling. Her ankles were cut. She was crippled. She said that everyone died!

The sprackin nipped at my hand, and I grunted. "Stop that!" I bent down to swat at him when I realized what was happening. Green sand covered me up to my chest.

"Let it go, Sashel. The mirage was only one possibility."

"But my mother! I—"

"You can think about it later. Now is not the time!"

I winced as every part of me wanted to keep thinking about the mirage, but I shook myself from it, and the sand slid off.

A green glowing sprackin stood before us. It was Nittles, or rather a version of him. He wore a glimmering crown and jewels ornamented his wings and tail. The mirage scowled at the real Nittles. "Pathetic," it said. "You will never attain true power again with leeches attached to your soul." Its eyes darted towards me at the word "leeches." Turning back to Nittles, it said, "You are an anathema to your kind. Kill the girl or kill yourself."

"No," Nittles said as green sand crept up his legs.

The mirage strode closer. "You could become me. You could be powerful, more so than the king."

Nittles clenched his teeth. "Power is a means, not an end. It is a tool to be used, nothing more."

"Spare me your righteous reasoning. We both know those beliefs hang by a thin thread. Cut it. Free yourself from the anchors holding you down."

Nittles wriggled in the sand hardening around him. "Without anchors, we will shipwreck. Our beliefs do not hold us back; they keep us afloat."

The mirage stood nose to nose with his real counterpart. "But we are sprackins. We do not float. We fly!"

"Away with you!" Nittles wrenched himself free, and the mirage vanished.

The only sound he made as we continued was his heavy breathing, but I didn't know if it was from fatigue or if he was wrestling with his thoughts.

Before I could say anything, another mirage appeared. It was me as an old woman. She leaned on a staff covered in green runes, and a shimmering tattoo of a serpent coiled around her forearm. The woman raised a bottle to her lips and downed half its contents.

Nittles nudged my leg. "Sashel, keep moving."

My eyes never left the old woman as I asked, "What do you know of my mother? What was the other mirage going to say?"

Her eyes drifted up to meet mine. "It doesn't matter. The war. All the worlds I've traveled. None of it matters."

"My mother," I repeated. "What about my mother?"

She drank again. "The Hourglass would stop me the moment I tried to help. It's merciful, you see? It doesn't allow for hope."

The mirage winked out, but the sand grew as despair blanketed my thoughts. *She's right. Hope only prolongs suffering. It is bait on a hook filled with false promises. When we sold the fruit, I began to hope again, and Minessa died because of it.*

"Sashel!"

I shook myself as the sand grew again. I tried to be angry, but the numbness returned, feeding on my despair. I knew I should fight, but what was the point?

"What you saw was only what might be, not what will happen," he said. "My future self only reflected my base desires, the worst parts of me, but that is not all of who I am. I choose to be more, and so should you!"

I am more. What did that mean to me? I am more than my despair. I am more than my failures. When I fall, I will rise again. Something burned deep inside me. It felt like anger, but there was something different about it. The feeling was pure, untouched by bitterness or wrath. It gazed at the sand growing up my shoulders and said, "No!"

I recognized the feeling. I felt its spark when I considered entering the Scarlet Forest so many weeks ago. The forest warned me to stay away, and the feeling said the same word, "No." As the sand spread up my neck, I knew what the feeling was, and I embraced it. It was defiance!

Once more, I burst from the sand, but this time with a strength I could never have mustered before. Another mirage appeared, but I walked straight through it. I didn't care what fears the future held. *When I fall, I will rise again.*

The fifth stage arrived as we stepped on the deep blue sand, and the sun changed to match. There was only silence save for the wind. Strangest of all were the statues, or rather, the lack of statues. Only azure sand lay before us as we trudged onwards.

"I don't like this," I said.

Nittles looked around. "There are no memories here. The present is where we make memories."

"So, we're safe?"

"In a way."

As we turned on the spiral pathway, a faint chuckling sounded. I turned to Nittles, but he looked equally confused. A sapphire monkey as tall as my waist sat before us with a manic smile. It let out an eerie laugh but didn't move. It simply watched us, its crazed smile never fading.

"Why is he laughing?" I asked.

"Since they can't attack us, the Hourglass is saving its power for a final assault. The mirages are aware of this and find it amusing."

Another monkey appeared, then another, and another. Soon, a row of transparent monkeys lined either side of the pathway, all grinning from ear to ear. Their laughs shook me to the bone, but we had no choice but to walk through them.

Mile after mile we walked, and I felt the mirages would pounce at any second, but they never did. Their laughs felt like they all shared a joke I wasn't part of, and their smiles seemed to say, "We have a surprise for you."

As we drew near the final stage, a strange humming sounded. It wasn't like the manic laughter I'd grown used to. This noise was more constant like a waterfall. The sapphire sand morphed into deep violet, and countless statues like a scattered army stood before us.

"Careful," Nittles said. "This is the past, and it'll attack us with everything it has. Remember what you've learned."

No sooner had we stepped into the purple sand when an ethereal wasp the size of my hand shot towards me. Maybe it was fatigue, but I reflexively swatted at it. Too late I realized my mistake as my hand passed through it, and the memory came.

* * *

I clutched the sack of coins and shifted from foot to foot. I hated waiting in lines, but the soothsayer would be worth it. Ten people stood between me and her tent, and most would use the full fifteen minutes allotted to them.

Porthan and Tember pushed the maroon flap back and stepped out. Tember placed a hand on her swollen womb and smiled.

"How was it?" a man in line asked.

Porthan grabbed his wife's shoulder and laughed. "It's a boy, and he will grow into a strong man!"

The crowd cheered, and the next man stepped inside. I wondered why Ashwood was avidly against witchcraft but not soothsaying. The clerics explained it once in the temple, but I still didn't see the difference. Enough of the village was against it; so, the woman's tent had to be pitched outside the gate. After several minutes, the man stepped out and scratched his head.

"Well?" an old woman asked.

The man looked back at the tent. "She said I shouldn't plant potatoes this year." He walked away, muttering a string of curses.

My heart sped up as the line shortened. The soothsayer was never wrong. But could she really see the future? Could she commune with spirits as the stories say? I squeezed the sack tighter and waited.

One by one, the people came and went. Not all were happy, but each seemed resigned to what they heard. Finally, it was my turn, and my stomach churned from the anticipation. This had to work.

Inside, animal fur of all kinds covered the walls and floor of the tent. The soothsayer, Tenari, knelt behind a short table with a bowl of burning incense on top. The woman had an olive complexion, but she didn't seem to be from Gran Mala. Strewn across her forehead were copper frontlets, jewelry I'd heard was common farther West.

Tenari gestured for me to sit across the table, purple silk draped loosely over her arms. The last thing I wanted to do was sit. This was my last chance, and I couldn't relax.

"Your spirit seems troubled, child." The woman's words were muffled by a deep blue veil covering her mouth, and a slight Derlic accent bled into her voice. "You are shaking like a cornered rabbit. You see? Would you like some tea?"

"No thank you." I bent my knees and sat stiffly.

She nodded as though expecting my response. "What can I do for you?"

I clutched the bag and swallowed. Time and time again I failed, but this would be different. The soothsayer never failed. She was never wrong, and I had the coin. But still, I hesitated. I wanted this so bad, I couldn't bear the rejection. I would have vomited, but my nerves wouldn't let me eat this morning.

My hands shook as I slid the sack across the table. "Twenty coppers. I was told that's the price for speaking with the dead."

She paused then brushed the corner of her veil in thought. "I do not take this request lightly. You see?"

"I don't ask it lightly."

Tenari nodded. "Have you ever been starving then only been given a small bit to eat?"

"I…think so."

"The crumbs do not—what is the word?"

"Um, fill? Satisfy?"

"Satisfy. The morsel only reminds you that you are hungry. It makes it worse. You see? Speaking to the dead is like this."

"I don't want to speak with her."

She raised her eyebrows along with her frontlets. "Oh?"

Taking a deep breath, I said, "I want you to bring her back. I want you to resurrect my mother."

The soothsayer sighed and gave me a look that said I was a foolish child. "It cannot be done."

I pulled another sack from my waist and slammed it on the table. "I can give you forty!"

"Most of the dead do not wish to come back. They move on to a better life."

"Not my mother. I need her, and she'll understand."

She stood. "Child, you do not know what you are asking."

I dug in my pockets and brought out another five coins. "Forty-five. Forty-five coppers for you to try."

"But—"

"My father's getting worse. My sister's barely one, and I don't know what I'm doing! Ashwood won't help me. Please!"

She eased back down and tapped the table. "I will contact her and see what she says. We will let her decide. You see?"

I relaxed at her words and nodded. The soothsayer opened a box and retrieved a black chord with five knots evenly spaced. After arranging the rope into a circle, she chanted in a guttural language. Her eyes glowed red as did the circle inside the rope.

It was working. I was going to speak with my mother. My eyes watered as I gazed into the circle. It had been over a year since I heard her voice. What do I say? I hadn't thought this far ahead. I guess I'll tell her about Father first, then Minessa. Surely she'll want to come back when she realizes how much we need her.

Raising her hands above the circle, the woman said, "Spirit from beyond, speak with us. Commune with your daughter and—" She clutched her head and screamed then fell to the floor. As the red glow faded from the circle, she climbed to her feet.

"What happened?" I asked.

Tenari pointed a shaky hand at the coins on the table. "Go. Take your coppers and go."

No. This couldn't be happening. I was so close. The knot in my stomach grew as I shook my head. "Try again. You must try again."

"No." She shouted something in her native tongue before saying, "There is darkness around her. I cannot bring her back."

"Please. I beg you!"

She shouted in her language, and her husband came from behind a tent flap. After a moment of whispering, the man turned to me and said, "You go now."

"Please!" I meant to grab her shoulder, but she moved, and I yanked her veil from her face.

The soothsayer stared at me in horror before her husband lifted me up and threw me out of their tent. He drew a curved dagger and pointed at my throat. "You no come back. You see?"

The tent flap shut, and the crowd yelled for me to move so the next person could enter. My feet moved without my knowledge, and I was halfway home before realizing I still held the woman's blue veil. Looking back towards the tent, I choked down a sob. The dwindling flame of hope flickered inside me, and I snuffed it out. I would never try again. Hope was for the fool.

* * *

I opened my dry eyes as violet sand encapsulated my legs. Why did I try? Why did I keep going? I would always be disappointed. The sand traveled up my waist, but I couldn't shake the feeling.

"Rise again!" Nittles yelled. "When you fall, rise again!"

The memory still clung to me. That was the day I gave up. I still did my best to raise Minessa, but deep down I stopped truly living. Now I was asked to rise again. Countless statues surrounded me, all people who had given up. I couldn't be like them. I had to rise again.

I broke from the sand, and we continued. The memories were too much. They piled on me, one after another. How much more could I take?

We ducked and dodged, but we had precious little energy to spare. Each mirage was quick, and it took longer to break through. Even Nittles struggled. Sand reached his waist and covered his wings more than once.

Neither of us spoke as it took far too much effort, and our memories weaved together so that we struggled to remember who we were at times. When we finished our last revolution around the spiraled pathway, we reached the top and found a golden statue of Kareli two hundred paces away. Between us and our way to freedom was a swarm of shimmering angry wasps.

At this point, I was too tired to be brave. I couldn't think about overcoming fear or shame or anything else. I just focused on the goddess's statue and thought of water. I needed to get to water. Nothing else mattered.

Nittles and I ran with everything we had. Memory after memory surfaced in our minds, but we pressed onward. One hundred paces. Fifty paces.

A wasp collided with my face, but instead of a memory emerging, there was only blackness. It was like a veil shielding me from the memory. It was the day Mother died, the day I couldn't remember.

A nearby wasp buzzed angrily and stung my arm. Like before, the mirage didn't hurt, but the same blackness washed over my mind. More wasps turned in my direction like sharks catching the scent of blood. They wanted the memory.

Five wasps, then ten, then twenty attacked me. Only memories from right before and right after the blackness emerged, but the wasps kept attacking, hungry for the one blocked memory. The black veil tore ever so slightly, and there was movement beyond. There was a flash of light and a loud noise, but I couldn't make out any details.

I crawled on my knees as my vision blurred. Just a little further. Nittles shook himself free from the violet sand and turned, seeing a hundred wasps swarming me.

"Get to the statue!" I yelled. "Only one of us has to touch it."

A look of panic crossed his face at the sight of every mirage focused on me. Then his will firmed, and he took off. His steps were clumsy, but he continued. Forty paces. Thirty. Twenty.

The veil opened further and wails came from my mother. What happened to her? There was shouting. My newborn sister crying. Blackness. So much blackness. The buzzing grew louder as the mirages attacked again and again.

"Got it!" Nittles yelled.

Light flashed across the sky, and the buzzing cut off. The goddess's voice was barely a whisper, but I heard it all the same. "The Trial of Sand hath ended."

Cool wind struck my face, and for a moment there was silence.

"Look at me!" Neerion yelled. I looked up as the cleric pressed his staff against my head and said, "I will pull the memories from you and see what secrets you hide."

Memories? Secrets? I couldn't think. Screams. Blackness. The wasps. Where was I?

The silver eagle on Neerion's staff glowed, and something inside me cracked. The memories from the trial had piled up and threatened to overwhelm my sanity. When the cleric used his staff, my memories found an escape. Like a ruptured dam, my memories burst free and poured into Neerion in waves.

He dropped his staff and convulsed, but the memories continued. The shame, the guilt, the fear, all of it washed over him. "Make it stop! Make it stop!" he yelled.

As he screamed, I looked around, my thoughts returning to me. Water. I needed water. Nittles and I staggered inside the cottage and reached for the pitcher, but it was empty. I had practiced controlling water with it, and it had spilled on the ground.

We ran outside and found a water trough a dozen paces away near a stable. Not giving Neerion or the confused villagers a second thought, we buried our faces deep inside and drank.

The water was rancid and muddy from half a dozen horses and mules that drank from it, but it was bliss. The parched tissues in my throat greedily absorbed the moisture, and the burning inside me faded. My stomach churned, but I held it in. I lay on the ground and shut my eyes. I had made it!

"What have you done to the cleric?" a man asked.

"Witchcraft!" another yelled.

"Death to the witch!"

The crowd huddled around me, but all I could do was stare up. I had nothing left, not even the willpower to claim the water and fight.

"Leave her alone!"

At first, I thought the words were from Cleric Shoff as he had stopped the crowd last time, but the voice was feminine.

Grinda, old, fair-skinned Grinda, pushed her way to the front and knelt beside me. Her gray hair was pulled up in a bun and she placed her hand covered in golden rings on my cheek. "You poor thing!"

"We should kill her while she's weak," a man said.

Grinda glared at him. "You'll do no such thing!"

"She brought these monsters to Ashwood."

"Right now, you're the monster! And if you kill her, you'll have to kill me." She elbowed her grandson, Shaidin, a burly young man at seventeen with sandy hair.

Without a word, he lifted me like a child and carried me to Grinda's cottage. The bed was softer than anything I had slept in, and a thick quilt covered me.

Grinda brushed a hand through my hair before rubbing her fingers together. "Is this sand? I swear it looks blue. What happened to you?"

I mumbled something, but not even I knew what I said. I was so tired.

My stomach rumbled, and the old woman pursed her lips. "When was the last time you ate?"

"I'm fine."

"Nonsense." She stood and rummaged through the cabinets. "I have bread straight from the bakery. Had I known I would have you as my guest, I would have more at the ready. You must let me know next time."

Why was she doing this? She must want something from me. All of Ashwood hated me. The fruit. Grinda had always been a faithful customer of mine. She would buy dried fruit and jam from me, especially jam. That must be it. If she treated me well, she would expect a discount from me later on. Part of me whispered that she was simply nice and cared about me, but I couldn't accept that. That was wishful thinking. All she cared about was her jam.

She turned with a plate of thick slices of bread. When I brought one to my mouth, there was a sweet smell. Only after I bit into it did I realize that each slice was slathered in dark jam.

"Blackberries?" I asked.

"Why, yes. Delicious, isn't it?"

"But…they're your favorite."

She cocked her head. "Of course they are, and you did a fine job making them. Now eat."

The voice inside me grew louder, yelling that Grinda loved me. No. There had to be another reason. I was a witch, and everyone hated me. But if she was only doing this to take advantage of me, then why would she give so much of her favorite jam? The answer was obvious, but I refused to believe it.

A single bite reminded me how hungry I was, and I all but inhaled two of the slices. I tossed one to Nittles who snatched it in the air.

Grinda cackled at the sprackin's performance and clapped. "How delightful! Can you train it to do other tricks?"

"He's too stubborn," I said through a mouthful of bread.

She laughed again and patted my arm. "You must come more often. Shaidin is a good lad, but I need more women in this place."

"Maybe," I said through a yawn.

Grinda grabbed the empty plate from my lap. "Rest now. I'll make sure those buzzards don't disturb you. Rest."

My eyes grew heavy as she left the room. There had to be a reason for her kindness. There had to be.

CHAPTER 19

"Armor protects the body, but what, pray tell,
can shield your spirit?"
—The Book of Clergy

Before I was even fully conscious, I sensed something was wrong. My eyes snapped open, and the air above me splintered into dozens of black cracks. Something roared on the other side of the rifts, a creature from the Sprawn Lands.

Pouring heartfire, I willed the rifts shut, but something pushed back. It felt like someone was opening a door, and I leaned on it with all my weight. The cracks widened as I struggled for a foothold. What had Nittles said about blazing his fire?

I focused on the silver candle in my soul and imagined it blazing hot, but nothing happened. When the rifts widened further, I abandoned the idea and diverted all my attention to closing them. I realized the rifts weren't exactly a door. I imagined them as such because they were similar, but they were still quite different.

Instead of simply pushing heartfire, I angled it, wriggling the silver fire like a whip. The fire followed my imagination and took whatever form I wished. When I found an opening, I shaped the fire into a crude sword. It looked impressive, but it couldn't be used in combat. The blade was ethereal, only good for closing rifts. Pressing with all my will, I heaved. The rifts shrank, and the creature had time for one last growl before the openings winked shut.

Nittles jerked awake. "What? What happened?"

I sank back into bed. "Just another day."

"I see. Well, we should eat."

"We just ate." I glanced at the light peeking through the window, but the sun was still out. In fact, everything seemed brighter than before.

"Do you feel hungry?"

I realized I was ravenous and thirsty, so thirsty. Why?

Nittles chuckled. "My best guess is we slept for nearly a day."

"What?" I stood and opened the shutters. Village folk bustled about, and children played in the street. It was the following morning.

Before long, Grinda arrived and prepared breakfast. I assured her she didn't have to, but she would have none of it. She made porridge, more sliced bread with jam, and milk, fresh milk. I couldn't remember the last time I drank it, but it was divine.

After eating, Grinda begged me to stay, but I insisted I had things to do. Once we were out of earshot, Nittles turned to me. "You seemed bothered by her niceties."

I hated how well the sprackin could read me. Every bite of food I took was a struggle. My body wanted more, but my mind wanted to spit it out. Accepting things from Grinda just felt wrong, somehow.

"We should go to the forest," I said.

"Clever misdirection. Very subtle indeed." His dry tone made it clear he wasn't ready to end the conversation.

I sighed. "Grinda is—I don't know. I just don't like her."

He swatted me with his tail. "The woman is an absolute gem. The problem is not with her but with you."

"No, it's not."

"She slept on a mat in the other room while you snored on her plush bed."

"I told you, I don't snore, and—wait. She did what?"

"Didn't you know?" he asked. "She has to be at least in her late sixties, and she let you have the bed."

The relentless voice continued to whisper that she cared, but I couldn't believe it. If I let Grinda come too close, she would only betray me. *She can't hurt me if she doesn't get close.*

As we left the town gate, Nittles gave me a pitying look. "You've been neglected for too long."

"What do you mean?"

"You've developed mental calluses. Soldiers develop them during wartime, but some fail to readjust afterward. The calluses remain, and the soldiers handle love like it's a poisonous adder. They're terrified of being vulnerable."

It irritated me how accurate he was. "What would you know? You've barely known me two months."

"I know you well enough to know you do in fact…snore." He cracked a smile and took off into the woods.

Despite myself, I laughed and ran after him. We made lifespur and glaidens then tested my dagger's capabilities. Although it had the ability to turn me invisible, the blade could only make one thing invisible at a time, and the wielder had to be holding the item. There was also a limit to the size of the item. A branch was easy enough, but an entire tree was out of the question.

Next, I practiced controlling water. If I held the water firm enough in my will, I could lift other objects with the water. Hour after hour I shot balls of water at a tree, and by the end of the day, it had fallen from my barrage of attacks.

My practice ended as Nittles spotted a dark rift near the stream. I poured most of my remaining heartfire into it, and eventually, the cracks sealed.

"There has to be a way to close all the rifts at once," I said.

"I told you, only through dark arts can it be done. Are you willing to kill an innocent child to appease the Corrupt One?"

"No." I remembered Nittles' memory of his king contemplating that very thing. "Desperate times," he had said just before trying to kill the sprackin. I wouldn't be like him. I wouldn't let desperate times pressure me into taking innocent lives.

Nittles gave an approving nod. "If you did, it would nullify Kareli's agreement, and you wouldn't get your sister back. All who serve the Corrupt One are cursed by the gods. If you die, you, yourself, could never be brought back. Completing the trials is the right way. Every rift should vanish if you succeed."

"What about blazing heartfire? You said you couldn't do it anymore, but can I?"

He hesitated. "You might. I think you have the mind and will for it, but it's a skill, an incredibly difficult skill, which takes years to learn and decades to master. I wouldn't try it for the time being."

"Why not?"

"Think of it this way. Do you know why younger snakes are more lethal than older ones?" When I shook my head, he said, "It is because the young ones don't know how to ration their venom. They inject everything at once. After years of practicing, you might be able to affect your heartfire, but you'd still be like a young serpent and burn all your fire in a second. You'd have nothing left, and in a fight, you're good as dead without fire."

CHAPTER 19

I had imagined blazing my fire like Nittles did and slaying the beast I was supposed to fight, but of course, it couldn't be that easy. I let the issue drop as we made our way back to Ashwood. The cold dreariness of my home permeated the air as we entered. Luckily, Father hadn't returned yet. Throwing off my sand-covered dress, I slipped into my old blue dress and cinched my waist with a crimson sash.

Nittles shook himself. "Why is it always so cold in here?"

"It's from all the joy surrounding the place," I said dryly. I grabbed a cleaver and chopped an apple into fine slices.

"That's a large knife for cutting fruit."

I shrugged. "It's what my mother used."

The rhythmic, cutting motion was soothing. It made my mind drift, and for once I let it. I defeated a sea monster. I'd been sliced and diced by a sadistic illusionist. I climbed an hourglass-shaped mountain made for condemned souls. And…I'd go through much more to get Minessa back.

The door swung open as my father walked in, but I kept slicing.

"I heard what you did to her body," he said.

I grabbed another apple and sliced. "Yes. You *heard* what happened because you weren't there."

Slice. Slice. Slice.

"Why did you stab her?"

"Why didn't you attend? You were the one that should have spoken for her, not me."

Glass clinked and I turned as father held a half bottle of mead.

"That's what you were doing instead of standing beside me. Drinking!"

I spat out the last word like a curse, for that's what it was.

Father put the bottle down, but his hands itched to grab it. "I couldn't go."

"You couldn't or you wouldn't?"

"I couldn't see her like that. I couldn't see her small body beside the others."

I sunk the knife into the cutting board. "You hated her. You called her a mutt!"

"I didn't mean it."

"Then what did you mean? Ever since mother died, all you've loved is your mead."

"Don't you think I want to stop?" He stared at the bottle. "But what else is there?"

"It doesn't help!"

"It stops the pain."

"But at what price? Minessa feared you, and I—I hate you!" I had never said the words to him aloud. I thought it would be freeing, but I felt horrible the moment I said it.

Father nodded. "That makes two of us."

I balled my fists as my face heated. "The mead makes you a monster."

"I have two monsters: grief and anger. When I drink, grief is locked up while anger is loose. What I wouldn't give to restrain both at once! Maybe that's what death is."

"Then get it over with!"

I covered my mouth, but it was too late. Like an arrow, there was no catching it once released.

Father took a deep breath and slowly let it out. "I keep forgetting you're still a child. I shouldn't expect you to understand."

"A child? You're the one that hasn't been weaned from the bottle. You're the child, not me."

His face hardened. "Which one of us stabbed her on the pyre? Which one of us is responsible for that creature killing her?"

My stomach dropped. He knew. Somehow, he knew.

He nodded. "You think you're the only one who knows about the staircase? Why do you think I told you not to enter the forest?"

"How do you know about it?"

"Your mother climbed the first step but couldn't go further. She became obsessed with it, always trying to climb higher but never able to."

This confirmed what I was shown in Neerion's memory, but I didn't know she hadn't made it past the first step. And I had no idea she was obsessed with it.

"I didn't know."

"Of course you didn't know," he said. "You travel the forest and think you know the world. You know nothing. And don't forget I've seen your little weasel fly…and talk."

I'd forgotten he'd spoken in front of Father when Minessa died. It had been ages for me, but for him, it had only been a few days. Weeks of building a ballista past in a blink for the rest of the village.

Nittles stood. "I'll leave you two alone."

Father stepped back at his words. He remembered him speaking but apparently wasn't used to it.

The sprackin stopped at the back door and looked at Father. "Tamble, was it? Hear me well. Not only is your daughter the only source of my former powers, but I count her as my friend. Harm her and I'll kill you."

Without another word, he left. For nearly a minute Father stared at the door before shaking himself. "I warned you not to enter the forest."

"And why should I have listened to you? You took every copper I had."

"I warned you!"

I stepped closer and looked up at him. "I did it for Minessa. I used the magic to earn enough silver and leave."

"And where has that gotten you? A new dress?"

"And what has drinking gotten you?"

"Minessa is dead because of you!"

"I can bring her back."

"You're dabbling in things you know nothing about."

"Anything is better than staying with you!"

Father turned and struck the door. An ear-splitting crack sounded as one of the panels broke in two. Pulling his hand back, blood dripped from his knuckles, but he didn't seem to notice. He grabbed his cloak and left, leaving the broken door wide open.

Rain pattered the ground, and the scent of a coming storm filled the air. Had I just driven out the only family I had left? I thought finally saying everything I felt would be freeing. But no. It was like shaking a beehive for a few drops of honey.

The temperature dropped as the rain picked up. When I tried to shut the door, it stopped a foot from the threshold, the broken panel wedging it open.

Grunting in frustration, I hit the panel, and pain exploded in my hand. I squeezed my hand tight and cradled it as blood trickled down my knuckles.

"I'm nothing like him," I whispered. "I'm nothing like him."

I wrapped my hand in a sash and lit the fireplace. There weren't many logs left, but they would last until the storm passed.

I stared at the fire, listening to the soothing crackle of burning wood. What was I becoming? Would I be just like my father if I'd gone through the same thing? But I had gone through the same. We both lost Mother. We both missed her. But was it the same?

The flames flickered faster, orange cinders dancing in the air. The fire dimmed to crimson then pooled across the floor. I covered my nose as a pungent odor burned my nostrils. It was the scent of blood, the scent of death.

A soft voice echoed in the cottage. "The Trial of Spirits hath begun."

CHAPTER 20

"The drink does not pacify sorrow. It feeds it. Though it be soothed in drunkenness, it returns with a vengeance."
—The Book of Clergy

A crimson hand burst from the blood and latched onto my ankle. It was warm and slick but held like a vice. No matter how I yanked and twisted my leg, there was no escaping its grip. The arm elongated into five joints that twisted at odd angles and then flung me across the kitchen.

My breath tore from my lungs as my stomach collided with the table. Scrambling to my feet, I wheezed in a shallow breath and raised a cleaver. But the arm was gone along with the fire, leaving the cottage cold and dim once more.

I frantically sucked in deeper breaths as I spun around with the blade held out. All was still, not even the rain breaking the silence. It was a deafening, smothering, suffocating silence until a grinding voice scraped at my ears.

"All is well. All is right."

Against the wall near my father's room sat an old woman rocking on the floor. Her weathered skin wrapped tightly around her bones, and thin white hair covered her face like a veil. Dark strings hung from her hands as she braided them and hummed a hollow lullaby.

Holding the knife in front of me, I recalled part of the song for the trial.

"The spirits within come out to play. Burn their name or drink them away."

"Who are you?" I asked.

The old woman continued braiding and rocking in the corner. "All is well. All is right. My sisters come to stay the night."

I searched for the strand connecting me to Nittles, but there was nothing. For the first time in weeks, our connection was simply gone.

I took a single step closer, never lowering the cleaver. "Whoever you are, you need to go."

"Go? You invited us."

As she lifted her head, her thin hair slid to either side, revealing gaping wounds covering her face. Her milky eyes stared at me as she broke into a smile, opening the wounds further.

"I'm making a necklace for you, like your mother's." She nodded as her smile widened, revealing broken yellow teeth. "I think you'll like it. Silver is difficult to weave, but it's so beautiful."

I bent low to examine her work. The dark strands were loosely braided in a long loop with either end running into her forearms. My stomach churned as realization struck. The woman wasn't weaving string or silver. They were her own veins pulled from her flesh and pulsing to the beat of her heart.

A scream leaped from my throat as I flung the front door wide to see…my home. I opened the door again and stepped directly into…my home. Standing in the doorway, I turned to either side, seeing a mirror image of the same dim cottage with the old woman in the corner.

A single flame flickered from a lantern on the small kitchen table, illuminating a young woman shuffling cards. Her ebony hair contrasted with her pale skin and when she laid down the cards, she revealed a low neckline covered in gold jewelry. She sipped from her wine glass and gestured at the seat across from her.

"I wish escape were that easy, dear one, but there's always a chance if you play the game."

With few options, I sat in the wobbly chair, cleaver still in hand. The woman deftly dealt my hand and then placed a single card on the table. The image was of my sister smiling and wearing the yellow hat I'd bought her.

Slipping my free hand in my pocket, I felt the real hat still inside. I looked around, but the old woman in the corner simply rocked back and forth muttering, "All is well. All is right."

The younger woman tapped the card with a fingernail that glittered gold. "You must lay one from your hand that can bring her back. She's such a darling, isn't she?"

I placed the knife in my lap and spread the nearly twenty cards in my hand. One had a picture of me giving a copper coin to the cripple while another showed a scholar holding a quill. A third showed me praying with Cleric Shoff in the temple, and a fourth was of me sitting, apparently doing nothing. Finally, I found a silver card with the staircase in the forest. I laid it on the table and looked up at the woman.

She nodded and spoke in a sultry voice. "Very good. The stairs have done much for you, and the goddess herself promises to return her."

She placed a second card of my father laughing and splashing me in the pond. "Lay another."

"Can I pass?"

She raised a thin eyebrow. "Have you accepted what he's become?"

"I've just given up on him."

Icy ropes coiled around my ankles, binding me to the chair. Dropping the cards, I pulled against the restraints, but my fingers went numb upon contact.

She tsked and raised her wine glass to someone behind me. "Saying that has grabbed the attention of my other sister. Be a good dear and don't upset her."

As I turned, a figure cloaked in shadow held a long strand of rope covered in frost. The figure bent down and sluggishly tied my calves as silent as darkness. I reached out to stop it, but my arm dropped. What was the point? My legs went numb, and I found I didn't care. Nothing mattered. Everything I did resulted in failure. I tried again, but the same sense of hopelessness overcame me at the thought of untying myself.

I recognized the spirit. It was the same feeling I had in my darkest moments. It would surround me like a thick blanket and block out all feelings, leaving me empty.

Staring at the cloaked figure, I said, "You're the numbness."

"Yes," it whispered. "But what is our name?"

Their name. The song said to burn their name or drink them away. What did that mean? I forced my eyes back on the table as the dealer laid a third card showing a pile of gold coins. I rubbed my hands for warmth and picked up my cards. Another card of the staircase appeared, and I laid it.

"Good." The woman stretched out the word the way a parent would congratulate a child. "The glaidens have already brought you wealth. Excellent choice, darling."

The shadowy figure tied my waist, and thoughts flooded my mind. What if the sprackin died? I would have no more glaidens. In that moment, I only thought of Nittles as a way of making money. I was a horrible person! And the more glaidens we made, the more rifts would open. I couldn't close them all. The harder I tried the worse everything became. Why should I even bother?

The fourth card was the portrait of my mother. I shook my head, trying to clear it and get out of my deep stupor. Could the staircase bring her back as well? My eyes fell on the card of the cleric in the temple. The day mother died, I asked the cleric if Suthian could bring her back. Shoff only shook his head and prattled on about how a few decades apart is nothing compared to eternity together in the afterlife. None of that helped me in the here and now.

I slammed the staircase down once more, anger boiling within me. A deep-throated growl rumbled from father's room, and the dealer shushed me.

"You mustn't wake her. My third sister is more agitated today." She looked down at the card and sighed. "Sadly, you don't believe the stairs will bring her back. It was a poor choice to lay. You should have gone with the cleric or maybe the scholar."

The cloaked figure bound my arms and shoulders to the chair, and I went numb from the neck down. The old woman walked over, carrying a bowl and spoon.

"You must be hungry, child. How about some hot soup for such a cold night?"

As she raised the spoon, shards of broken glass glittered in the lantern light. Blood dripped from her mouth as she said, "I've already tasted some, and it's delicious!"

Against my will, my mouth opened, and the spoon of glass drew closer. Anger boiled inside me as sensation returned to my hands. I hated being powerless. I hated these women. I hated my father. I hated everyone!

The icy ropes cracked then shattered. I tried to rise but stumbled as my legs were still numb. I crawled to the counter and reached for a pitcher. Sinking my hand deep inside, I claimed the water just as

I had in the last trial. The cool liquid glowed green and shot out, passing straight through the shadowy figure. I summoned the golden dagger, and it shot into my hand. Unsheathing the blade, I slashed through the air, and…nothing. All three entities stared at me, then drew closer.

"All is well. All is right."

I whipped the water towards the old woman, but it splattered harmlessly off her. The growl from the bedroom grew louder, shaking the entire cottage. I needed something else. The blade and water were doing nothing.

The third emerald candle in my soul stirred, and a bright rift appeared. I sensed only two things from the other world that could help, one would require an enormous amount of fire while the other had almost no cost, just the barest amount from the candle. This was the first time I could sense how much something would cost as well as sense other options. Maybe the other trials had no other choices. Maybe I was just getting better at sensing through rifts. I still had two trials after this one, and I couldn't afford to waste anything. After a slight tug, the smaller item flew towards me, and I caught it with a soft clink. A large bottle of ale rested in my hand.

What? No. There had to be a mistake. The three sisters halted and stared at the bottle.

The dealer moaned in ecstasy. "Spirits! Such sweet release."

"What do you mean?" I asked as the bottle shook in my hand.

"Why do you think they call them 'spirits?' The drink quiets us. It eases us into blissful slumber."

"Will you return if I drink?"

"Of course," she said. "But you'll pass the trial."

I ran the song through again. *"The spirits within come out to play. Burn their name or drink them away."*

"Drink. Drink," they chanted as they approached.

"The trial will end," the dealer said, taking another step. "You'll be one step closer to getting Minessa back."

I stared at the murky brown liquid. She was right. The song said as much, and my power only summoned things that would help me, but...I would become my father. I knew deep down if I drank, it wouldn't be the last time. My pain would go away, and I wouldn't be able to resist it the second time.

The spirits stepped closer, and I clutched the bottle. I could save my sister and take her away from my father. But if that happened, I'd become a monster as well. Others could drink occasionally, but I knew that wouldn't be my outcome. I would drink my sorrows away; then swear I'd never do it again, but I'd return to it. Minessa would go from the frying pan into the fire. There had to be something else. I pulled deep at the rift, searching.

A silver banner came into focus reading "Eyes of a Truth Seer." I could sense it would help, but it would cost three entire candles. I may not have enough to finish the trials if I summoned it. I looked down at the ale. Minessa needed me.

I raised the bottle and smashed it on the old woman's head. I pulled on the power, and my eyes burned. Light flooded the room, and I could see everything! The Eyes of a Truth Seer revealed all.

The old woman was even more gnarled than before. The dealer's face was painted white, but beneath, her skin was scarred and burned. The shadowy figure was now solid, wearing a gray cloak, and beneath her hood were empty eye sockets.

The old woman grabbed a fork and charged. I burned more of my fire, and her thoughts became visible. I could see her aiming for my left eye. She intended to take away my new sight. I ducked and then swiped with the broken bottle. The jagged glass raked across her face, but she felt nothing. Her thoughts were as clear as day. She was deluded, seeing and feeling only what she wanted.

What did the song mean by "Burn their name"? My eyes darted around the room until they landed on a single word emblazoned in crimson letters. There it was!

My father's door burst open, splintering the wood into hundreds of pieces. The scaly creature lowered its head to step through the doorway. Its blood red eyes locked on me as inky venom spewed from its mouth.

I raised my arms to shield myself, and my skin burned from the acidic spray. The creature barreled forward, and I spun to the side. One of its talons grazed my side, and pain erupted. Their name. I had to destroy their name! Only then did I realize where it was written. Of course. These spirits were as sadistic as they were mad. In large letters, across the face of my mother's portrait was the word "GRIEF." The song echoed within me. "Burn their name or drink them away."

Deep down, I never accepted her death. Maybe since I didn't see her die, part of me clung to hope. Why couldn't I remember? I prayed to Suthian for him to bring her back. I refused to believe my mother was gone just as I refused my sister's death.

As I grabbed the painting, the spirits froze. Beneath the word "GRIEF," I studied the portrait one last time. I took in her raven black hair, her silver medallion, her forest green dress, her favorite sash across her waist made of fox fur, and her eyes, her deep caring eyes. I grabbed the lantern from the table and tossed it in the fireplace. Flames erupted from the oil and lit the wood.

I lowered my head and kissed my mother's face as tears dripped onto the canvas. "I love you, Mother. I miss you so much, and I always will… but I have to let you go."

The instant I set down the portrait, flames rose and consumed it. I was reminded of my sister's funeral. This was why the village burned the bodies. It was why Cleric Shoff insisted that the loved ones be present. They needed to see for themselves. They needed the reality seared into them.

One by one, the spirits vanished until I was alone once more. As I expected, the goddess's voice rang out. "The Trial of Spirits hath ended."

Rain pelted the roof, and a chilling wind blew as the broken door creaked open. I stared at the fireplace as heavy boots stepped behind me.

"I'm sorry," I cried. "I had to. I'm so sorry."

Father didn't reply. He didn't reach in to try and save the painting. He only stared as the fire consumed it. His watery eyes reflected the orange firelight as a single tear ran down his cheek.

"She's gone," he whispered. "She's gone; isn't she?"

I nodded and wiped my nose on my sleeve.

Pulling out part of the frame that wasn't consumed, he stammered, "I never saw her body burn. I guess, part of me always thought she'd come back. This is why I would throw the painting down when I was drunk. Part of me knew I hadn't accepted she was gone."

He looked at me. "Do you remember when I had that thorn stuck in my hand?"

"Yes."

He rubbed his palm absentmindedly. "It was a deep one. I yanked it out, but it could never quite heal. A week later, I realized part of that bugger was still inside. I had to reopen the skin and dig it out before it could properly heal."

Placing the broken frame back in the fire, he said, "This is the thorn, and we need to heal."

I buried my face in his chest and sobbed.

"She's gone. Mother is gone. Minessa is gone, and I miss them so much."

"I know."

His massive arms pulled me close. He was hugging me. His clothes were soaked, he smelled of mud, and it was wonderful.

His hug tightened. "I miss them too."

He stood and walked towards the door. At first I thought he was leaving, but instead he merely retrieved something from the table. A half a bottle of mead. The dark liquor looked black in the fire light, and a hint of burnt apples wafted from it. His grip tightened as he looked at it longingly.

"I guess this belongs in the fire too."

As he poured, the flames grew. The burning stench filled the cottage, yet it was sweeter than lilies.

He shook his head. "I don't know if I can do this."

I placed the empty bottle on the hearth. "We'll do it together, one day at a time."

I told him everything that happened after I climbed the staircase, and he listened. In turn, he told me how mother found it years ago but could never make it past the first step. As the years passed, she grew distant and never let him know why.

We shared other memories of mother, fond memories. We laughed and cried as the fire burned. For once, it was warm in the cottage. We sat by the fire as the wind howled and raged as the storm inside me had finally, blissfully calmed.

CHAPTER 21

"Words of a lover may fade, but the words of a father are etched in stone."
—Words of Shoffilem

I woke to the scent of eggs and fried fish. Opening my bedroom door revealed father setting two plates on the table. He placed a third on the floor for Nittles who still slept by the hot stove.

"What's going on?"

Father looked up. "I made breakfast."

I sat at the table dumbfounded. I couldn't remember the last time he cooked anything. He sat across from me, his massive frame swallowing up the chair.

My eyes widened as I took a bite of the eggs that tasted of garlic and herbs. "These are good."

He nodded as he shoveled half his eggs in his mouth. "I used the spices you bought in Sennevar. They're, uh—they're good."

He looked from side to side, apparently thinking of something else to say. He reminded me of a nervous boy courting a lady for the first time, floundering for a better conversation.

His eyes brightened, and he pointed a thumb behind him. "I found a few jars of jam in the cabinet. We could have some with bread afterwards."

"I would like—" Realization struck. Those were from the glaidens and lifespur. "No!" Father flinched at my reaction, and I hurried to explain. "Those are made from special fruit. It—it has to do with the staircase."

"Oh." He furrowed his brow and continued eating.

As I bit into the fish, it became apparent he hadn't cooked much. The bottom side was charred black, and the middle was dry. But since father made it for me, it was delicious.

"What type of fish is this?" I asked.

"I'm not sure. It looked strange, but the two fishermen said it was some exotic delicacy from up North. Anyways, I need to leave soon."

I squinted at the orange sunlight peering through the broken door. "I thought you'd already be at work."

He nodded as he took another bite. "The masons won't have lime till later today, but I still need to prepare for the mortar. The duke's house is only half done. He wants an archway ten feet high with two columns on either side."

I smiled as he prattled on. He might be awkward at patching things up with me, but once he started talking about masonry, he was as eloquent as the rest.

He paused. "What are you smiling at?"

"You got up early to buy fish for us?"

He returned the smile and cautiously placed his hand on mine. "I did a lot of thinking last night. I haven't been a good father to you or…Minessa. I'm trying to do better."

He looked around the cottage. "I've neglected you as much as this old shack. It needs mending, and so do we. The money I spent on mead could have turned this place into a mansion."

"We can fix it up."

He looked down at his empty plate. "I...don't think that's possible."

"Why not?"

"I still have debts."

The fork of eggs froze near my mouth. "Debts? Even after..."

"Yes. Even after all the coppers I stole from you. And I'm gonna make that up to you as well."

"How much debt can you have? You couldn't have drunk that much mead."

He ran a hand through his frizzy gray hair while his other reflexively clenched as though holding a bottle. "I gamble when I drink at the tavern. I'm in debt with almost half of Ashwood. I may lose the cottage if I don't pay."

I dropped my fork. "The cottage?"

He had never mentioned this. No wonder he was so depressed. It wasn't just mother's death that bothered him but the accumulating debt he owed. Despite the poor shape of our home, it was still worth far more than the one I was saving up to buy in Sennevar.

He glanced at the empty space on the wall where the portrait used to hang. "After Thrella died, I just stopped caring. The deeper into debt I got, the more I was convinced I could win it all back next time."

"Father, I—I didn't know."

He shook himself. "Sorry. All that's for me to worry about, not you."

I continued eating, but I didn't enjoy it as much as before. Why was I now concerned about him? Wasn't I planning on leaving once I passed the trials?

After eating, he strapped his boots then paused. "You know that lockbox mother kept under the bed?" I nodded and he continued.

"I've never opened it, even after finding the key. I guess part of me always thought she'd come back. After work, I thought maybe we could open it together and go through it. Maybe share memories of her?"

Again, I was struck speechless. He never talked about her. Now he wanted to go through her lockbox.

He must have taken my hesitation for a "no," because he looked away and said, "It was a foolish idea."

"It's perfect!" I blurted out. "I'd love to."

"Good. We still have to talk about the staircase and all you've been through. But I can't afford to miss work. Take it easy today and rest."

An hour after he left, I finished dressing and braiding my hair. I folded Triska's robe and placed it in a sack. I'd forgotten about it and needed to return it to her. When I opened the door, the wooden sign which said, "Dried fruit for sale," clattered to the ground. I had forgotten Father broke the door panel last night.

I brushed my fingers over the smudged message in charcoal—"DEATH TO THE WITCH!" Beneath read a second message someone had recently written, one filled with profanity and vulgar words. Unlike before, I wasn't afraid of Father finding out. I didn't fear his anger if he saw the message. Rather, I didn't want him to be hurt by it.

Then an idea struck me. I ran to the water pitcher by my bed and reached inside. The water glowed emerald green as I claimed it then raised itself out and followed me to the door. Once I ensured no one outside was watching, I commanded the water to press against the door and scrub the message. The green water moved faster and faster till it sounded like a miniature waterfall. In seconds, every bit of charcoal had been wiped away, leaving the wood cleaner than I ever remembered seeing it. Holding the water with my will became harder by the minute, so I released my claim, and it splashed to the ground. Nittles walked over and gave me an approving nod.

The squeaky wheels of a cart rolled past our cottage followed by voices. "Horn fish! Get your horn fish!"

Nittles looked up. "Are those the two imbeciles from the fishery?"

Two men, one tall with a straw hat and one short, pushed their cart of fish. The shorter one, Grad I remembered, said, "I saw a school of eels this morning on the West Lake. We should try our luck there next time."

Bordig tipped up his straw hat and wipeD his brow. "Nah. Them be wimble eels. One bite of them's got enough poison to kill an elephant."

"What does that matter? We're not elephants."

He paused as if chewing the words. "Grad, sometimes you—"

His words cut off as he saw me and plastered on a smile. "Ho there! Would you be liking some horn fish? It's the freshest in all of Ashwood."

"Today's the last day to buy," Grad added. "Whatever we don't sell, we're taking to Sennevar. They're already salted and ready to go. You best buy some while they last."

"No thank you." Something occurred to me. These men were going to Sennevar where I sold the glaidens. "When will you be leaving?"

"Noon at the latest," Bordig said.

I looked at Nittles then back at him. "I sell fruit to the constable there. Could you deliver them for me?"

Grad shook his head. "Sorry, but we don't make deliveries."

"I'll give you ten percent. That would be at least three silver."

He shut his mouth and looked up at Bordig, who nodded. "We'll be at the village gate at noon. Bring what you can, and we'll deliver it. We'll be back with whatever you make in three days' time."

I went around picking as many fruits as I could find. Before long, I had a basket full of cherries, wild blackberries, and apricots. The kinds of fruits didn't matter since they would be transformed.

"Are you sure now is a good time to make glaidens?" Nittles asked. "Shouldn't you be preparing for your trials?"

"We can do both! I'll save a good amount for us. I want plenty with me at all times in case a trial comes, and while we make them, you can tell me all about Tal Miral. The more I know about your world, the more likely it is that I'll succeed."

He nodded. "And if the trials keep progressing, I'll be leaving soon. This may be the last batch we make."

I dropped a cherry in the basket and looked up. "What do you mean?"

"Well, three trials have already come and gone. It seems like only a few more days before you finish. After that, you'll be able to return me to my world."

"I see."

My mind was a jumble of emotions. The fact that I might see my sister soon was more than I could wish for. But I'd also grown fond of Nittles, and I didn't want to see him leave. Then there was the fruit. Nittles was my friend, but he was also the key to selling glaidens. My father had more debts than I thought, and he needed help. And I wouldn't have cared about that, but last night changed everything.

For the next hour, we transformed fruit while Nittles spoke. Since much of the song from the staircase was vague, he couldn't be certain of what to expect. The Canthi was considered a myth, but that didn't stop us from having to fight it; so, he proceeded to tell me all he could.

He spoke of bats the size a man, flesh-eating fish that swim in the earth, and birds made of pure water. My interest piqued when the sprackin told legends and folktales from his world. It wasn't the stories themselves but the energy and expression he used.

Nittles was secretive of what serving in the king's court entailed, but whatever he did, telling stories had to be part of it. Even with my problem of focusing, my mind seldom drifted as I hung onto every word he said.

By the time we stopped, Nittles' voice was weak, and my mind was heavy with information. Mentally, I felt like I had eaten a feast and couldn't take another bite. A mountain of glaidens stood on the kitchen table with a smaller pile of lifespur beside it. It seemed like my heartfire grew with each trial as we made twice as much as before with plenty of fire left.

I rubbed a glaiden between my fingers. "Nittles, if you return to Tal Miral and I choose to stay here, is there a way for me to make fruit without you?"

"Only sprackins can make them."

My heart sank. "I see."

He rustled his wings. "I thought you wanted to come with me. You said you wanted to take your sister away and see Tal Miral."

"I did, but…"

"You're thinking of staying with your father."

"I—I don't know. After last night, he seems different."

He straightened. "Well, either way, I'm returning to my realm. I have a life there. I'll help you make fruit until then, but I have no intention of staying here."

I placed the fruit back on the pile. "So, if we become un-melded, I won't be able to make more."

"Correct."

Life was simpler before the staircase. It would have been easy to leave him before, but now I didn't know if I could. But he hurt Minessa. He beat her and yelled at her. But that was drunken Father. Sober Father was kind, funny, and caring. Was I trying to excuse it all away? Nevertheless, I wanted to help him.

I picked up a healing fruit. "You know, it's too bad we can't—"

"We're not selling the lifespur," he said.

"Look, I know you said they're sacred, but they'd be so valuable, and we may not get another chance to make them."

"Dignity has no price."

"Says the one who's lived in a royal palace. It's easy to keep your dignity when you can make money with a flap of your wings. When you leave, whatever we make now is all my family will have for life."

He stepped in front of the lifespur and spread his wings protectively over them. "It's not my fault your father is a drunken fool. No one forced him to drink and gamble. His choice, his consequence."

"He deserves another chance."

"I will hear no more of this!"

It was quiet for a time until Nittles cocked his head. "Wait. You won't even have time to dry the fruit. How do you plan to sell them?"

I knew he was changing the topic, but I let him. Plus, I was excited to show him my idea. "Watch this."

I had tried it earlier on an apple; so, I knew it would work. I pressed my finger against a glaiden, but nothing happened.

"I must say, I'm impressed," Nittles said dryly.

I shot him a glare, then focused on the glaidens. Maybe I had to make contact with the inside. I sliced the skin with my thumbnail and touched the dark purple juice. Instantly, I felt a connection. The fruit glowed green as I claimed the water inside, pulling out every drop of moisture and leaving a perfectly dried fruit behind.

Nittles' eyes bulged. "Well, well! It is not beneath me to admit when I'm wrong. It was one thing to kill the Canthi with your ability, but you seem to find more and more uses from it. Can you do the same to living creatures?"

"That—that's disgusting!"

He shrugged. "So was suffocating the Canthi. It's always good to know your limits."

I reluctantly agreed. I continued drying fruit while Nittles caught a field mouse. I winced as the poor creature squirmed in his maw.

"You could have at least killed it first."

He shook his head but couldn't speak with his mouth full. I touched its gray fur, and like the fruit, I couldn't connect with the water. After making a small cut on its back, I touched its blood, but I still felt no connection.

Nittles spit out the mouse. "I didn't think it would work."

"Why not?"

"You don't use your heartfire to control it. You use a type of will power, don't you?"

"Yes. It's very exhausting."

"I see. Claiming is an art I've never mastered, but I know it's much harder if someone else has possession of it. You can claim the water in the sea because no one else claimed it. The mouse's blood is rightfully his; so, you can't claim it. Not even when it's dead will you be able to."

I had to take several breaks while drying the fruit, and by the time I finished, my eyes were heavy. Forcing them open, I wrote several lines on parchment.

Nittles peered close. "What does it say?"

I hesitated. As sophisticated as the sprackin was, I forgot he couldn't read my language. He'd told me we could speak because the gods united the tongues, whatever that meant. But apparently written languages were quite different.

"It's a list of how many glaidens were made and how much they're worth," I explained. "It also says the fishermen have taken them on my behalf. The constable will sign it and give it his seal. This way the fishermen won't be tempted to skim extra for themselves."

He gave an approving nod. "At first, you struck me as a simpleton the way you lose focus so easily. But now I see you're a sharp sword beneath a thick scabbard."

His words were touching, and I felt a pang of guilt as I wrote an additional paragraph. We made it to the town gate where the fishermen, true to their word, waited for us. Placing the sacks of glaidens in the cart, I explained where the constable's office was and what to tell him.

"You'll get ten percent of what we make." I glanced at Nittles and said, "And my weasel gets another horn fish."

Bordig barked a laugh. "I think that can be arranged. He can—"

Nittles pounced, ripping into a fish with gusto. When he was halfway through his meal, I bit my lip, resigned with what I had to do. While he was distracted, I slipped the sack of lifespur in the cart.

I remembered Father itching to drink when he spoke of his debts. If we lost our home, the stress would drive him straight back to the bottle. He was trying so hard to change, and I wanted my father back. He deserved a second chance. *Once Nittles leaves my world, I can't make any more fruit. I have to make these count.* I pulled out the note to the constable and read the last paragraph before giving it to Bordig.

"You will notice one sack of fruit is different than the others. These are called 'lifespur" and can heal recent injuries. Feel free to try one out for yourself, but I'm sure you'll agree they are worth double."

I felt bad, but I didn't share the sprackin's beliefs, and Father needed this. I was reminded of our conversation was had when I first met him. I said that some women choose to be harlots because they need the coin, and he responded by saying, "the most horrid things imaginable are done in the pursuit of gold." I shook my head. No. Lifespur was fruit, nothing more.

Once they left, I turned to the temple. My one remaining sack held Triska's robe she lent me. I nearly forgot about it as she lent it to me weeks ago. No, that wasn't right. For me it had been a while since the battle with the Canthi lasted weeks and the

Hourglass trial lasted almost two days, but for the rest of Ashwood it had been only a few days. I rang the small bell near the door and waited.

Nittles looked at the two wooden doors with engravings of the gods Robius and Suthian. "Open for the repentant. Locked for the stubborn."

"What?"

"The doors. That's what they say."

I looked at the runes beneath the pictures. "You can read them?"

He straightened. "Of course. It's Old Bremic. The royal court uses—"

The door opened to reveal Neerion's scowling face. "You are no longer welcome here."

I really didn't want to deal with him right now. "I'm here to return—"

"You misunderstand," he interrupted in his Gran Mallish accent. "I received approval from the Hierarchy only yesterday. You and your father are shunned from the temple."

Shunned? He can't do this.

"Shoff would never allow this!"

Neerion pointed his staff at me, the silver eagle on top only a hand's breadth from my face. "Cleric Shoffilem has no say in this matter. The Hierarchy has spoken. And if I hear so much as a whisper of witchcraft from you, I'll hang you myself. And there won't be an honorable burning for your body. You'll burn in private for no one to see like your mother."

My grip tightened around the sack. *He'll hear far more than a whisper of witchcraft. I should—*

Nittles nudged my leg, evidently seeing my rage. Through gritted teeth, I said, "I've come to return Triska's robe."

Neerion's scowl faded, and he turned. "Triska, come."

A clinking sound came from behind the door, her many hair clips and hoops rattling about.

"Thank you," she said softly.

She took the sack, looking down and hunching, clearly not wanting to be in the middle of this.

"Triska, is your grandfather here?" I asked.

Her eyes darted from me to Neerion, but before she could speak, Neerion said, "He is not your concern."

"I want to talk with him."

His long black braid whipping around as he faced me. "I warn you, Sashel. You are walking on thin ice, and you will fall. Now go."

I grabbed Triska's arm. "I want to speak with Shoff!"

Silver light flashed across the sky like lightning as the goddess's voice echoed. "The Trial of Secrets hath begun."

The wind howled, the sky turned gray, and snow fell in heaps. The temple vanished along with the rest of Ashwood, leaving a valley blanketed in snow surrounded by towering mountains. All was quiet, the type of quiet only heard in the midst of a heavy snowfall.

The silence was broken by soft clinking as Triska spoke. "Holy judgment! Where are we?"

CHAPTER 22

"When a man plays some mischievous shenanigan, we call it foolish. When a god does the same, we call it divine."
—The Book of Heretics

Triska was in the trial. How? Not even Nittles was with me.

"Where are we?" she asked again.

I shook my head. "I don't know."

Beneath the gray sky, sharp mountains surrounded us. Green and silver light shimmered high above like a meandering pathway. It reminded me of the auroras I'd seen in paintings from the far North. The path of light led directly towards the tallest mountain.

Pointing towards it, I said, "I think we're supposed to climb it."

"Are you mad?" The many hoops in her hair clinked as she shook her head. "We don't know what's up there. We don't even know where we are."

In my pocket, I squeezed Minessa's blood-stained hat. I didn't have time for this. I needed my sister back, and Triska would just be in the way. But there had to be a reason she was here. What if she was important for the trial?

"Do you have a better idea?" I asked.

She gazed at the lights leading towards the mountain. "No, but…" Her eyes furrowed as she looked down. "The snow!"

Did she really just notice the snow? It was halfway up my calf and still falling in heaps. Then I understood what she meant. The snow wasn't cold. I scooped a handful and peered close. It felt lukewarm like sand or earth. I pressed it together, and it became a ball of ice, yet it wasn't cold.

The lights above us flashed, and I looked at Triska. "We should get going."

"How did we get here? Did you do this?"

I didn't want to tell her, partly out of spite and partly because her grandfather was Cleric Shoff. She'd tell him the first chance she got.

"I didn't bring us here," I said. It wasn't exactly a lie. The goddess was ultimately responsible, and I didn't choose the trial. If I had, I would have brought Nittles instead of Triska.

The snow fuzzed for a second. Something inside urged me to use my new sight I'd received from my last trial. It would cost some of my heartfire, but I felt it was worth it. The silver candle in my soul shrunk ever so slightly as I opened my eyes, not my normal ones, but the eyes of a truth seer.

Dark faces emerged in the snow, faces of foul creatures hungry for flesh. Red eyes glowed beneath the surface, first one pair, then dozens, then thousands. Soon the entire valley shone crimson with bloodlust.

I screamed, and my normal vision returned. All was white beneath a gray sky.

Triska looked around. "What's wrong? What did you see?"

"We have to go. We have to go now!"

This time, she didn't argue, and we ran through the sea of snow.

Faster. We have to go faster! What did the song say about this trial?

"Secrets are heavy and shouldn't be borne.

Speak them aloud or flesh will be torn."

Speak them aloud? What secrets? I pulled a glaiden from the sack tied to my side and ate.

A cobra, pale white with bloodred eyes, burst from the snow. No, it didn't come from the snow; the snow became the cobra. Time slowed as the fruit took effect. Leaning to the side, I struck the back of its head, and it burst into thousands of snowflakes.

Three more emerged, their heads raised at eye level. Triska screamed as two of them lunged for her. I grabbed one by the tail and slammed it into the other, but the third bit deep in my forearm. The venom burned through my veins as the serpent chewed on my flesh. I wrenched it free and squeezed it until it burst into snow. Dozens of mounds rose around us coalescing into ten-foot long, ivory serpents.

"We have to tell them a secret!" I yelled.

Triska's mouth opened in a look of utter confusion.

"A secret," I repeated. "We have to tell them a secret."

My arm burned where the serpent bit as a tingly sensation formed around it. My stomach churned, but I didn't know if it was from the pain itself or a symptom of the venom.

"What do you mean?" she asked.

I groaned in irritation. It would take time to explain, but one of us had to say something. As the serpents snapped their heads back to strike, I yelled, "I'm a witch! I climbed a mystical staircase that gave me magic."

Mid-strike, the creatures burst asunder, covering us in snow. All was quiet once more save for our heaving breathing. We trudged through the deep snow for minutes before Triska spoke.

"You—You're a witch?"

I still hated the word, but I accepted it. Nittles said magic was only evil if you used it for evil. I clutched my arm which still burned. "Are you surprised?"

She looked down. "Sort of. I didn't believe the rumors of your mother."

"Really? What about the ones of her flying across the village and eating children? Surely those must be true."

I couldn't stop the cutting words from coming. I didn't know if it was from the bite marks or from the pent-up frustration. I was sick of the unfounded rumors! They believed everything they heard.

Triska's face firmed. "What's your problem?"

"What's *my* problem? You're the one who stopped talking to me after my mother died."

She trudged faster through the snow. "Not true. I spoke with you on Reverence Day."

"That was months later, and you didn't say much."

"I was eleven. I didn't know what to say to you. I felt like anything I said would only make it worse."

I shook my hand as some of my fingers grew numb from the serpent bite. "Well, anything is better than saying nothing. After she died, you avoided me like the plague. Losing Mother was bad enough, but losing my best friend made it so much worse."

She looked as though I stabbed her, and my heart sank. *Should I have said that? I probably should have phrased it differently, but at least I said something. Better to spit something out and fix it later than never say it at all.* That was what made us so different. Triska thought much and said little while I spoke first and thought later.

We walked away before Triska said, "I still have the drawing."

"Drawing?"

"The one of the shop."

The shop. I hadn't thought about it in years. Triska and I always dreamed of opening a shop together. We planned to sell dried fruit, jam, and even candy we had made from our own recipes. We used to talk for hours about what the shop would look like and how we would operate it.

"I still have the sign," I said. "The one that says, 'Dried fruit for sale.'"

Triska gave a weak smile. "I think it was the only thing we actually made for the shop. Everything else was just dreams."

A howl echoed nearby, but after a minute of silence, we continued. Pursing her lips, Triska asked, "What do you know about this staircase you climbed?" When I described it, her eyes widened. "It sounds like the same one from the Book of Clergy."

I stopped in my tracks. "The scriptures talk about the stairs?"

"Well, yes." She spoke faster, reverting to her usual nervous tone which was twice as fast as most people. "I'm not sure if they're the same ones, but several passages refer to them as the Forbidden Stairs or the Stairs of the Beyond. You've at least read the Meritori, haven't you?"

"Has anyone?"

"Absolutely. And there are many tomes in the temple archives that extrapolate on the topic."

"You read books that explain books?"

"It sounds odd saying it that way, but yes. The Meritori was written a millennia ago, and many passages use idioms that've been out of use for centuries."

The clerics had written about the stairs. Of course they had. The scriptures talked about everything. Did mother know this? Had she searched the tomes as well? I never paid the sermons much mind as Cleric Shoff spoke in a soft, pleasant tone that could lull me to sleep while Neerion spoke as though he hated everything and everyone. I winced as I caught my mind wondering yet again.

It was strange to see snow fall yet the air here was warmer than it was in Ashwood. As the throbbing in my arm grew worse, something finally occurred to me. I dug in my sack and ate a lifespur. The skin healed, but the pain still raged inside. Apparently, the fruit couldn't counteract the venom.

"Great judgement!" Triska covered her mouth. "The bite marks are gone! What did you just eat? Was that magic?"

"Yes."

"And it healed you?"

I tried to make a fist, but my fingers only bent halfway. "Kind of."

"You never explained about you being a witch, and where you climbed the stairs."

I considered holding the information in reserve in case more serpents appeared, but I figured they would just be details to the same secret and wouldn't count. Plus, I wanted to tell someone other than Father.

Talking to Triska reminded me how close we once were, and I wanted to tell someone close to my age. I had called Nittles my friend, and I realized I wanted another, someone I had more in common with. Maybe telling Triska would end the trial.

"She will betray you," part of me thought. *"Don't dare to hope for anything more. Hope is for the fool."*

I gave her a glaiden and explained what it did, telling her to only eat it in an emergency. As we walked, I told her about the stairs, the forest, and the song, emphasizing the part about this trial and how telling secrets would stop the creatures.

She grunted as she trudged through the ever-deepening snow. "And that's why the snakes vanished when you said you were a witch?"

I nodded. "We need to think of as many secrets as we can; so, if any more come, we'll be ready."

For the next hour, neither of us said much as we each made a mental list of secrets. The pathway of green and silver light in the sky shimmered as we moved ever closer to the highest peak. The only sounds were the crunching of snow and the clinking of Triska's hair loops.

"What constitutes a secret?" she asked.

I rubbed my eyes. They felt like needles were piercing them, and my entire right arm tingled. "What do you mean? Everyone knows what a secret is."

"It depends. Would a secret be anything you don't know that I do, or is it something I keep hidden that no one else knows?"

I considered. Most of the things I'd come up were small details like what color my kitchen table was and how many pots and pans we had. But what if she was right? What if they needed to be stronger? What if I had to see them as a secret?

I thought of one. It was deep and strong. No one would know it, not even father. I would try smaller secrets first, but I had the nagging suspicion that they wouldn't work.

The same howling echoed again, closer this time. Triska squeezed my hand for comfort, sending a searing pain up my injured arm. I screamed and tore my hand away.

She covered her mouth. "I'm so sorry! I forgot."

My headache pounded as I looked around, still not seeing anything but snow. My vision blurred, and I rubbed my eyes to clear it.

A lump of snow rose in front of us, much larger than before. A pale wolf stood eye to eye with me and let out a deep growled. My mind froze. What was I going to say? I had a secret, didn't I? But all I could think about were those teeth the size of my fingers and those crimson eyes.

A voice behind me blurted out, "I like to smell my feet!"

I turned and stared at Triska. Then the wolf stared as well, seemingly just as shocked as I was. She buried her face in her hands. "I like to smell my feet. I don't know why!"

The creature stood motionless, its red eyes flickering, then it took another step.

"That secret wasn't strong enough," I said.

"Then you say one."

I took a deep breath. "I…hate everyone."

The wolf stopped again.

"I hate my mother for dying. I'm still struggling to forgive my father. I hate the gods for abandoning me. I hate all of Ashwood for rejecting me. I hate everyone!"

Triska gave a single shake of her head. "I already knew that. I think half the town knows it."

"What?"

As the wolf advanced, Triska chewed her glaiden. "You're always angry."

I ate a fruit as well, stepping back from the creature. "I was angry because of how you all treated me."

The wolf stopped again.

"How did we treat you?" she asked.

"You wouldn't even make eye contact with me. You and everyone else treat me like a witch ready for the hanging, even before I climbed the stairs."

"You treat us like dross," she countered.

"I'm very kind, and you know it."

"Only to your customers. At first, I didn't speak to you because I didn't know what to say. But when I did reach out, you wanted nothing to do with me. I kept my distance because you're rude! You take everything I say as an insult. I gave up on being nice to you because you think everyone hates you, and they don't!"

"Yes, they do!"

"How do you know?"

The wolf's eyes flickered from white to red, but he didn't dissipate. It was like the magic itself was trying to decide if these were secrets or disagreements.

"They write messages on my front door and make warding gestures when I pass them."

"Only some of them," she said. "Two boys in particular wrote on your door, and my grandfather has scolded them for it. It doesn't mean the whole town hates you."

I kicked a mound of snow. "They tried to kill me twice in the last few days!"

"Neerion riled them, and you know it. They're grieving and scared, and Neerion took advantage of them."

"It doesn't matter. They still tried to kill me!"

Triska's timid demeanor vanished and she strode toward me. "And who stopped them? Who stopped the crowd from killing you?"

I paused. "Shoff."

"And the second time?"

"Grinda."

She threw her hands up. "So not everyone hates you."

"So two people in the whole village didn't try to kill me. What's your point?"

Triska glanced at the frozen wolf and then back at me. "What about before all this? Do you think everyone hated you before you climbed the stairs?"

I thought for a minute. "I see the way they look at me. I know what they're thinking. They see me like they saw my mother, like I'm an evil witch, putting curses on everyone."

"Maybe some people thought that, but many only see you as an angry person."

I wanted to shout at her, to tell her I wasn't angry. But that would only prove her point, and I just admitted I hated everyone. Before I could respond, the wolf pounced. With the glaiden in her system, Triska ducked and slammed her fist into its stomach. It landed and spun in the snow, not even phased by the blow. I drew the knife from my waist and rubbed the dark side of the hilt.

When I vanished, Triska gasped and looked around. "Sashel? Where are you?"

As the wolf lunged at her, I thrust the blade into its neck, and it shattered to snow. I reappeared, trying to conserve my heartfire, but the candle in my soul was shrinking.

Four more wolves took its place, all as tall and angry as the first. I didn't have time to disappear. I slashed one, then two. I missed the third as my stomach churned. Too many glaidens. Triska kicked one in the face, but it spun and raked its claws across her back, tearing cloth and flesh alike.

My head spun as the glaidens wore off. The glaidens, that was it!

I looked at the wolves and shouted, "I sold glaidens to Sennevar." They froze, and I continued. "I sold them because I knew they were enemies of Ashwood. I hid the silver near the staircase in the Scarlet Forest. I told myself I only did it because Sennevar was larger and wealthier, but deep-down part of me wanted them to conquer Ashwood...because I hated them."

The wolves were like ivory pillars, teeth bared in a silent roar. There was a gust of wind, and they blew away like sand in a storm.

Triska stared at me, mouth opened. The weight of the secret had lifted, but the weight of guilt had doubled.

CHAPTER 23

"Heavy gold lightens the heart, but heavy secrets burden the soul."
—Words of Shoffilem

"Sennevar?" Triska asked. "You sold the fruit to Sennevar!"

I looked down at the snow. "Yes."

"You wanted the entire village conquered?"

"No. I mean—I don't know."

Her hair clinked louder as she grew more irritated. "You meant it, or the wolves wouldn't have gone away."

"Fine. I meant it, but only partly."

"You did it because…you thought the villagers looked at you funny? Because you thought they hated you? Like I said, most of us kept our distance because of how you treated us. You'd glare daggers at us if we got too close. My grandfather has been nothing but kind to you."

"I'm banished from the temple."

"That's Neerion's doing, and you're just as angry as he is!"

She was right. I'd been so angry, and I assumed everyone hated me as much as I hated them. I thought of Grinda bringing me breakfast while I lay in her plush bed. My lip quivered and my chest heaved. She cared about me. I didn't want to admit it, but the woman loved me like a daughter. Tears flowed down my cheeks, and I couldn't stop it. "What have I done?"

My vision blurred, but I kept walking. Grinda loved me, and Healer Fendin did as well. There were children in the village I'd put in jeopardy, but I didn't care. I didn't think about anything but my petty feelings. My father wasn't the monster; I was.

Warm arms wrapped around me as I sobbed, and for once, I didn't push away. I needed a friend. I needed to trust. Once I regained composure, I realized Triska was still injured. Digging in my sack, I pulled out a lifespur. "Here. This will help your back."

After taking a bite, her wounds closed. She felt her back and moved around in bewilderment. "Unbelievable!"

I nodded and wiped my nose as we trudged through the snow. "It's called 'lifespur.' We can't take too many or we'll get sick."

Staring at my sack of healing fruit, she said, "When I searched for a blessing, there was none to be found. So, I feasted on curses where plenty abound."

"What?"

"It's a quote from the Book of Heretics. It means we can turn to dark things when we're desperate."

"Why would you read about heretics? Weren't they hung for witchcraft?"

"Some were, but it's more complicated than that. Grandfather says everyone has words of wisdom, even the heretics."

Was I a heretic? I was banished from the temple, and I'd already admitted to witchcraft.

"Part of me feels guilty for eating the lifespur." Her hair jingled as she scratched her head. "I was taught all magic that isn't from the clergy is wrong, but I was also taught that dark magic can't heal, only destroy. Now I see healing magic that isn't from a clerical staff. I don't know what to make of it."

I smirked. "Well, whatever it is, it can't be as bad as you smelling your own feet."

Her eyes widened and she chuckled nervously. "I was hoping you forgot about that."

I let out a snotty laugh. I laughed until my stomach hurt, and Triska joined me. It was probably the stress finally being released, but it felt great. I couldn't remember the last time I felt this way.

"Careful," the voice inside me whispered. *"She'll only disappoint you like everyone else. She can't hurt you if she can't reach you."*

Pain stabbed in my eyes. My head spun and I vomited.

"Sashel, what's wrong? Is this from the fruit?"

I wiped my mouth, only to realize my forearm was swollen and red.

"The vomiting might be from them, but I have bigger problems."

"The Healer can help. She's treated snake bites before."

"We need to climb to the top first."

Hour after hour, the pain grew worse, and my vision doubled.

"We're nearly there," she said.

I wheezed harder and harder, never able to get enough air in my lungs. My arm swelled to twice the size, and I leaned on Triska for every step. Even swallowing grew difficult, and my tongue felt thick in my mouth.

"I don't fink I'm gonna make it."

I tried to enunciate, but I couldn't control my mouth. Drool ran freely down my chin, which I stopped wiping a while ago.

A silver statue of the goddess glinted at the top of the peak. Of course, I saw two or three of them, but I assumed there was only one.

"We're gonna make it!" she shouted.

The snow around us shook as our legs sank deep into the snow.

"Sharks!" Triska yelled.

That didn't make sense. Surely, she meant something else. My eyelids were droopy and my vision blurred, but I made out the distinct image of a white dorsal fin charging towards us.

"I'm in love with Gashen!" she yelled.

I thought of the tall, lean young man from the cobbler's shop. He had the quickest wit and a silver tongue and gave a look that said he always cared about what others had to say.

"We all love Gathen," I mumbled. "That's not a thecret."

I couldn't think of a secret either. I was so tired. I stared at the snow as several fins circled us. Something about the snow tugged at my sluggish thoughts. Something about water. Snow was water, right?

Reaching out my hand, I touched the snow and claimed it. A barrel sized portion of the snow glowed green. I clenched my one good hand, and the snow condensed into a thick ball of ice. The first shark burst upwards, its open maw revealing countless chalk white teeth.

I slammed the ice against it, and the creature shattered. I aimed for its head, but I was lucky to hit its tail. A second charged, and I batted it away, missing twice before landing a hit. My will faded, and the ice turned to mush and plopped to the ground. I simply stared at the three fins making their way towards us. I couldn't even talk at this point. The venom was too much.

Triska bit her finger in fear, then said, "I'm sorry, Sashel, but… your mother was in love with Neerion. I overheard their conversations and saw them sneaking off to the temple alone. I'm sorry."

The sharks tore from the snow in fury, but like before when a powerful secret was revealed, they morphed into snowflakes and blew away.

I stared dumbly as Triska sprinted to the top of the peak and touched the statue. Silver light flashed across the sky and a voice sounded.

"The Trial of Secrets hath ended."

The snow spun faster and faster until all I could see was white. When I blinked, I was back at the temple grabbing Triska. My arm remained swollen, and my vision was still doubled, but one person remained clear in my vision—Neerion!

CHAPTER 24

"When we stare at our enemies, we are blind to our friends."
—Words of Fremma

Neerion glared at me from the entryway. "I said you are not welcome here!"

I crumpled to the stone floor. The pain was too much, and I gasped for every breath. Triska knelt at my side, but my eyes never left the cleric. He had slept with my mother, an action he, himself, spoke out against. He was a hypocrite! He was a slimy snake!

My vision blurred again, as Neerion bent low. "What's wrong with her? And what happened to your clothes?"

I tried to speak, but all that came out was slurring nonsense.

"She's been bitten," Triska said.

"Bitten?"

"She needs Healer Fendin."

Two Neerions stood side by side, taking in the situation. "Very well."

Without another word, he picked me up and darted for the Healer's House, still holding his staff in the crook of his arm. I wanted to protest, to wriggle out of his wormy hands, but all I could muster was a weak jerk of my legs.

I could do nothing but stare at his face. He didn't look angry as he ran, merely determined. He glanced down at me, and for a second there was a glimmer of concern. I still saw double, and my eyelids were heavy, so it must have been my eyes playing a trick.

"Lay her on the bed," Fendin said. "And tell me what happened."

"Cobra venom," Triska said.

"Cobra? Was she at a circus? There aren't any—"

"Trust me. It's a cobra bite."

I heaved for breath, but I felt like I was breathing through a thick rag. My arm burned and tingled from the bite, and my head spun.

"Do you have the snake with you?" the Healer asked. "I need its venom to mix with lintin root."

Triska locked eyes with me, and my heart sank. The snake! We couldn't go back. I shut my eyes and focused on my candelabra. Two emerald candlesticks remained, but they didn't burn. Apparently I could only use them while in a trial. I should have done something when I was back there. I could have summoned—

That was it. I couldn't summon a cure. I couldn't summon a blessing, but I could summon a curse. Unlike the bright green portals I could rarely open, the black portals were different. They begged to be open and required no heartfire, no candles whatsoever. My only struggle was closing them. If I could bring a blessing from the green ones, could I summon a curse through the dark ones?

I focused on the floor, but nothing happened. Fendin dug through cabinets and Triska sat beside my bed. No. It couldn't end like this. The one time I needed a dark rift to open, I couldn't do it.

Neerion rose from kneeling on the floor. Was he praying? I leaned closer, realizing how stiff my movements were. A white chord tied in three knots surrounded my bed. Could it be?

I focused outside the circle, and felt something, but I couldn't break through. Stiffly, I thrust myself off the bed, collapsing to the floor.

"Sashel!" Fendin yelled. "Get back in bed."

I tried to speak, but my mouth and throat felt numb. My right arm was swollen and numb as well; so I crawled with my left, pushing the white chord aside.

Neerion grabbed me. "Don't disturb the chord!"

As I tried to open a rift, it pulled at me, hungry for something. Heartfire. It wanted my heartfire. I transferred a small amount, and the rift opened. Thousands of creatures demanded to be freed, pounding at my mind like caged animals. I felt them all. They yearned for flesh, for blood, for souls. I pushed at them, but there were too many. I was holding back a dam about to burst. Picturing the snowy white serpent in my mind, I pulled.

"Great judgment!" Triska yelled.

A pale cobra slithered across the floor, heading for the healer.

Neerion released me and held out his staff which glowed silver. "Stop!"

The serpent froze in place as if it was carved from wood. The cleric calmly grabbed it, still holding out his staff, and handed it to the Healer. "Its mind is trapped. You can extract the venom."

She hesitantly took it, then after a moment, milked its fangs. Minutes passed in silence as Fendin added the venom to the ground up fissle root. She mixed it with several other herbs into a tea, then forced it down my numb throat. I coughed and gagged, but most of it made it down. After a few minutes my breathing eased, and I laid back in bed in sweet relief.

"Poor thing," Fendin said. "She probably saw the serpent and fell out of bed from fright."

"Yes." Neerion adjusted the chord around my bed. "That must be it."

Fendin opened her pantry. "No disrespect, but can you make yourself useful?"

The cleric sighed and waved his staff. Shriveled herbs of all kinds turned as fresh as the day they were picked.

"The herbs will wilt the moment I leave. You know this. They only stay fresh as long as I'm nearby."

She shrugged. "They'll last until I make another cup of tea."

"I still do not see how the serpent came here," he said. "Cobras are foreign to this region."

"No disrespect," Fendin said, "but aren't they from your country?"

"Gren Malla has been part of Melandria for over two decades."

"And the cobras?"

He shook his head. "I have never seen one of this color."

The Healer ground another shrine root with a mortar and pestle. "Lots of odd things come lately. Strange fish, blue vines growing in the cellar. Even the moon's got a green tint lately. This is the worst time for Naska to have a baby, but then again, there's never a perfect time."

Naska. She was a kind woman who bought several sacks of dried fruit from me. Like my mother, Naska developed cravings for fruit with her pregnancy. Fendin was right. This wasn't a good time to give birth.

Neerion looked up at this. "She is in labor?"

"Just got word before Sashel came in. Her water hasn't broken yet, but the first pains have started. Sometime tomorrow I'd guess the child will arrive. This is her first which usually takes the longest. Will you be here for the blessing? If so, I won't have you enter until she's ready."

I lay as motionless as possible, not wanting to draw any attention. It wasn't hard. My eyes were heavy both from the venom as well as climbing a mountain. I tried to listen to the rest of the conversation, but once my eyes shut, my grip on reality slipped, and all went black.

* * *

Silver light shined before me, but it didn't hurt as sunlight did. Rather, the goddess's face was soothing like the cool light of the moon.

Touching the silver candle in the center of the candelabra, she whispered, "Remember."

The candle sprung up and glowed silver like before. Two green candles burned at the far right of the candelabra. One for the trial and one to slay the beast.

"Can you refill my other candles?" I asked.

The goddess's face was too bright to make out, but I could sense she was amused by her posture. She placed a hand on my shoulder, and something tickled the back of my mind, something about her appearance.

"Remember," she said again, louder this time. Then she vanished.

I sat up in bed, the Healer's Hut now dark. Something nagged at me, but I couldn't place it. The town was quiet save for crickets and frogs. Fendin would be in the next room, sleeping just like the rest of the town.

I rubbed my eyes as my thoughts slowly returned. I passed the fourth trial without using an emerald candle. The goddess renewed my heartfire, and I had been cured of the cobra venom. What was I forgetting?

Father! He wanted to go through mother's lockbox with me. I felt a stab of guilt despite the fact it wasn't my fault. He would have waited up for me. Had no one told him about me? Fendin would have stayed with me. Triska may not have thought about it, and Neerion surely wouldn't have bothered.

CHAPTER 24

I wavered for a second when I stood, then everything became solid. Good. I grabbed my sack of fruit and dagger then crept out.

The village seemed eerie at night, like it was a different place. Everything had a slight green hue, and I couldn't shake the feeling something was watching me. It felt the same as when I summoned the serpent in the Healer's House.

The darkness circled me like a hungry wolf. Twisted creatures from the other world demanded to be set free. The cries were silent, yet they wriggled in my mind like flesh worms. I had to get away. I had to get into the light!

My steps quickened until I was in an all-out run. Cottages blurred past me, but the darkness was ever-present. It wanted out, and I was the only door. The tall plum tree from my backyard emerged. I was close.

My steps slowed as though a strong wind pushed me back, and all fell still. The chirping crickets stopped, the wind ceased, and even my footsteps were as silent as death. My ears rang from the sheer silence that pressed in on me like a crushing vice. I yelled, but the darkness swallowed it like a drop in the ocean.

The cottage door was only a few paces away, but it might as well have been a mile. Each step was slower than the last, and I feared if I leaped in the air, I would never land.

Then the darkness whispered, "Let us out."

Images emerged from the shadows: flesh-eating centipedes, grotesque amalgamations of humans and beasts alike, and something deeper that had no form. They struggled to break free from the cyclone of darkness around me.

I needed light! I needed to…cut the darkness. Unsheathing my dagger was an agonizing process as my actions were slowed like they were moving through syrup. Once it was free, I poured heartfire into the blade, and it shone with golden light. The darkness released me as though it had been stung, and my speed returned to normal. I slashed down and met resistance like cutting thick cloth. I poured more heartfire into it and heaved with all my weight.

A loud crack resounded, and the darkness melted away, leaving a dim but normal cottage before me. My shaky hands fumbled with the doorknob, but I finally opened it and shut the door behind me.

"I waited for you," a faint voice said. "I waited, but you didn't come."

My father sat hunched over the small kitchen table, a nearly empty bottle in hand.

No. He promised he wouldn't drink again, but then, he always promised. I didn't know why I thought this time would be different. I was a fool, still clinging to childish dreams. My father hadn't changed, and he never would. Nittles was right. I was a gullible simpleton.

Something crinkled in his hand. His left hand still held the bottle, but in his right was…parchment. It was a letter.

When I stepped closer, he held it up. "She was going to leave us."

His words struck my ears, but they didn't penetrate. I repeated them in my mind, trying to make sense of them. *She was going to leave us.*

"Who?" I asked numbly.

He slammed the letter on the table. "Your mother!"

He stood and kicked the lockbox, strewing stacks of letters across the floor. "Thrella was going to leave us for Neerion!"

"Neerion?"

The words slowly sank in, and I wish they hadn't. I didn't want to believe what Triska had said. I picked up one of the old parchments on the floor and read.

"My dearest Thrella,

I treasure the hours we talk, and I yearn for many more. Teaching you to read from ancient texts has been some of the best moments of my life, and your endless curiosity has made me see through new eyes. I was hesitant to let you read from Thresti te Morditatum, but I soon realized your hunger for knowledge is boundless as Robius Himself. Whether it is asking questions of my homeland or of the temple itself, your wonder of the world is intoxicating. My oath to the clergy binds me to my duties; however, I cannot ignore my desires any longer. You told me once you would leave your family if I asked, and I believe the time has come. I can have a bill of divorcement written for your husband within a week, so we can rightfully be together. Think long on this, but I know you will agree that we are destined.

Yours now and always,
Neerion

The paper fell from my limp hand. My mother had planned to leave us for Cleric Neerion.

INTERLUDE

Bordig set the sacks of fruit on the constable's table, wondering why there were five sacks instead of four. Had Sashel put another one in their fish cart before they left for Sennevar? No matter. The more fruit sold, the more silver he and Grad would receive.

"These be from Tenari in Lanvire," he said. "She told me you you'd buy them all."

Grad opened his mouth to speak, but Bordig elbowed him. Grad was a good lad, but he had the nasty habit of correcting him during sales. Bordig didn't know why Sashel insisted on going by an alias, but what did it matter? He'd call her Grinkle Finkle if that's what she preferred. Plus, a bit of caution was warranted when selling to Sennevar.

He dug in his vest pocket and handed the letter to the fair-skinned man. Come to think of it, the constable was more red than white with all those freckles. Even red-gilled snappers weren't as red as he was, which made Bordig not trust him. What was he hiding behind all those freckles?

The constable furrowed his brow as he finished the letter. Opening the sacks, he froze at the last one which held golden-brown fruit instead of the dried plums, at least they looked like plums. The man reread the letter before looking back in the sack. How complicated was it to buy fruit? He inspected the brown ones more carefully than jewelers examined their merchandise. This is why Bordig stuck to fishing, good old fishing.

A jolt of alarm ran through him as the constable drew a knife at his belt. His alarm turned to confusion as the burly man made a small cut on his own forearm. Was he insane? It's the freckles. They must be messing with his mind.

The constable took a small bite from the fruit and waited. Was he expecting Bordig to say something? What in the ten lakes could he be—

The wound on the man's arm vanished. Great judgment! It was just…gone like it had never been there. What devilry was this?

Beside him, Grad gasped. "What devilry is—"

Bordig elbowed him once more. No matter what they saw, Grad had to keep his mouth shut. They weren't in Ashwood anymore, and the lad didn't understand how life was outside the village.

A sinister grin grew on the constable's face. "I'll write up a receipt at once. She'll have three gold for the lot, but I need to speak with her as soon as possible."

Three gold? What was Sashel selling these men?

Once the two left the office, they only made it five steps into the street when Grad whispered, "What was that?"

Bordig removed his straw hat and wiped his sweat. "Don't quite know, but for judgment's sake, you can't be reactin' like that! Sennevar be far different than the Grand Realm."

"What do you mean?"

"I'll show you, but don't you be sayin' a word."

Bordig took him to the town square and his stomach dropped. He meant to show Grad an empty stage before explaining what would happen there, but the stage wasn't empty. A cleric robed in white stood shackled to the center post, his cheeks singed from where they burned off his beard. The two fishermen stayed in the back while a hundred people gathered to watch.

A thin man in a maroon tunic climbed on stage and cracked his whip. "Do you denounce the clergy?"

The cleric's voice was weak as though he had been screaming for hours, but he still managed to yell, "Never!"

"You clerics are all the same." The man lashed the whip across his back. "You call us evil, yet the clergy build their temples on a mountain of corpses!"

"The corpses of evil men," the cleric countered.

The torturer spat. "Men that *you* deem evil. What right do you have to impose your superstition on us?"

"The clergy gives everyone a choice."

The man cracked his whip just above the cleric's head. "A choice? Convert or die isn't much of a choice!"

"What you do to your children is abominable. Your sacrifices, your rituals. They're evil! They—" Another lash across his back cut off the cleric's words.

Bordig ground his teeth. He wanted to rip that infernal whip out of the coward's hand and strangle him with it. Bordig had seen far too much. Not everyone in Sennevar was this brutal. Many hated the beatings as much as he did. He preferred to stay in Ashwood, but when times were tough, they had to sell here or go hungry for the winter. Still, it wrangled him to see good men be beaten like this.

"Five!" a woman in the crowd yelled.

"Eight," another said.

"What are they doing?" Grad asked.

Bordig clenched his fist. He wanted to leave, but Grad had to see it. "They're betting how many lashes before the cleric recants."

After the twelfth lash, the cleric whimpered. "Please! I denounce the clergy! Please, stop."

Bordig groaned. *He shouldn't have done that.* The crowd cheered, and coins were exchanged.

The man on stage grinned. "I'm glad you see reason." He drew his sword and thrust it into the cleric's chest. Without another word, the man turned and strode off, leaving the blade behind. The cleric whimpered and slumped against the post he was chained to, blood pooling around his feet.

As the crowd dispersed, Grad stared at the body. "Why? Why did they do that?"

"It's the Sennavian Empire," Bordig whispered. "They see the clergy the way we see witches. Sashel was smart to say she be from Lanvire. They don't take too kindly to us."

"Sashel." Grad said. "Her fruit healed the constable's arm. Is she a witch?"

"Judge me if I know."

Grad's eyes never left the stage. "If they hate the clergy and the Grand Realm so much, why don't they attack Ashwood?"

"We be pretty evenly matched, and Sennevar don't want many losses without a big advantage, something to tip the scales." He sighed and turned to leave, but something caught his eye. Black, hairline fractures appeared in the air, splintering like cracks on a frozen pond.

"Demon!" A woman near the stage clutched her child and yelled. "Demon attack!"

As the people fled, a bell rang outside the town square. The fractures widened, and a gray creature broke free. It had the build of a bison with dark scales and a long tail that slithered like a serpent. It made a coughing sound before black fluid shot from its nostrils. The viscous liquid struck the wooden steps leading up to the stage near the screaming woman. The wood sizzled like cooked bacon before disintegrating from the noxious acid.

"Run!" Bordig yelled.

The two turned to flee but halted as a squad of soldiers poured in.

"Nobody move," the captain said.

The men raised their kite shields as the captain shoved something purple in his mouth and chewed. The creature tried to run, but the men flanked its right side. As the soldiers blocked an acid attack, the captain grabbed a spear and leaped to the left.

The monster charged, but the captain slashed its neck with ease. As blood gushed from its wound, it sprayed another stream of acid. The captain bent to the side, never slowing his pace. The beast lunged, and the man planted the back of his spear in the ground. There was a muffled grunt as the creature landed, a bloody spear impaling its stomach.

The captain brushed the dust from his sleeves and chuckled. "Child's play."

Once they were allowed to leave, Grad whispered, "I thought the attacks were only in Ashwood. And what the captain did wasn't human. I've never seen anyone move that fast!"

"The fruit," Bordig said. "It be the purple fruit he ate right before he attacked."

"We just sold it to them!"

"That we did."

"What does this mean?" Grad asked.

Bordig removed his hat. "It means the scales have just been tipped, and Sennevar has the advantage."

CHAPTER 25

"When tempted to run, we must walk.
When tempted to slumber, we must stand."
—The Book of Clergy

I sat in my bed and stared out the small window, hugging the dim lantern in my lap. I wanted to cry. I wanted to let it all out, but I felt…nothing. It was like the darkness that had surrounded me only a few hours ago, swallowing up all sensations.

Across the cottage, my father snored in his bed as his mead held him captive in a deep slumber. For once, I didn't blame him for drinking.

Nittles nudged the back door open and shook himself. "I expected you would be asleep after your trial today."

I continued staring at the silver moon, now tainted an emerald green. I should be concerned about that, but I found I didn't care.

The sprackin hopped on my bed. "I came to check on you in the Healing House after you were bitten. Are you recovering well?"

"Recovering?" I snorted. "No. I'm not recovering well."

He gave a concerned look and sat across from me. "I infer you don't speak of physical wounds."

"You inferred right!"

Father stirred then rolled over.

I bit my lip and spoke more softly. "My father was supposed to be the monster, not my…mother."

He cocked his head as I went on. "We found letters from Neerion. My mother planned to leave us for him. That whore!"

"That doesn't make sense."

"Why would it make sense? Why would any of this make sense?"

"You misunderstand. Why would your mother be in love with Neerion? Didn't you tell me she stole his staff?"

My hands loosened on the lantern as I thought. His staff. The memory Neerion shared with me was still clear as day.

"How do you know your mother loved him?" he asked.

"We have dozens of letters."

"Do you have any your mother wrote or only those from Neerion?"

"Well, only his, but it's clear they loved each other."

"Not necessarily. He could have been convinced she loved him, but it sounds like you don't have proof. This could be a case of unrequited love."

"The letters make it seem like she loved him back."

"He may be delusional," he said. "Obsessive types often grow angry when their love isn't reciprocated. Tell me. What exactly can his staff do? Why would your mother want it?"

I ran my fingers through my frizzy hair. "Well, it can keep plants fresh, but they wilt the moment it's out of reach."

"I doubt your mother was using it to have fresh daisies around the cottage."

"It…mainly affects the mind. It can share memories and stop—"

"Stop people entirely!" He flapped his wings. "What if she was afraid of him and took the staff to stop his advances?"

"That would do it." I placed the lantern on the table and paced in my white nightgown. "It would explain Neerion's anger toward us. But if she took the staff, why didn't Neerion just tell the authorities?"

He chuckled. "A man's pride is not to be underestimated. He would have to admit she took it from him, plus, they would ask why the two were alone to begin with."

I allowed myself a faint smile. I didn't know if our theory was true, but it fit, and I was determined to find answers.

* * *

A loud banging tore me from sleep. Sunlight poured through the windows and crevices of the cottage, yet I felt as though I had just fallen asleep.

Nittles, who was lying at the foot of my bed, yawned. "Doesn't this village ever rest?"

Cinching my gown tight, I headed for the door with the sprackin trailing behind. Before answering, I glanced at Father's empty bed. No matter how hungover he was, he always made it to work.

The door barely stayed on its hinges from Father hitting it a few nights ago, and I had to lift hard. When it finally opened, I was face to face with Cleric Shoff who stood just outside.

He bent low with his hand over his heart. "Sashel, I would ask if this is a good time, but I know it's not. I just heard about Neerion banishing your family from the temple. That ba—backbreaker!"

I rubbed my face. "Maybe later would be better."

Shoff held up a basket. "I brought apple pastries straight from the bakery."

Steam rose from the white cloth covering the pastries, filling the air with a rich aroma of glaze and cinnamon.

As we sat, I bit into the largest one, and for a second I forgot my worries as the flavors flooded my senses. The center which was filled with apples and spices burned my tongue, and I sucked in a breath to cool it.

The cleric leaned his battered staff against the table and raised a finger. "First, I need to say that I had no idea that Neerion had petitioned the Meritorium to banish you from the temple. I'll be working on getting it overruled."

"You don't have to do that."

"You don't realize what this means. It's not a law, but most businesses here won't let someone work for them if they've been banished."

"They won't let my father work? He's one of the best masons."

"I know, but many would rather kiss a porcupine than let him work. They'll see him as cursed when they realize he's not welcome in the temple."

I ground my teeth. Before, I wouldn't have cared what happened to my father. But recently, things had gotten…complicated. No matter how hard I tried, I couldn't see him as a monster. He was a broken man trying his best in a bad situation. It dawned on me that for the first time in over three years, I cared about my father.

"…to hear back from Talamin, but I'm sure I can convince them," Shoff stood and dusted the crumbs from his robe. "Well, I need to get back, but I wanted to put your mind at ease."

Something nagged at me, something about Neerion and my mother. I thought back to the letter he wrote her. Most of it was about his love for her, but he was hesitant to let her read something.

"What does 'Thirsty Mordium' mean?"

Shoff furrowed his brows. "It's…a tome in the temple library. It records a lot of pagan rituals to the Corrupt One."

"But what does it mean?"

He lifted his staff. "It's dark stuff. You shouldn't be asking about it."

I walked in front, blocking his way out. "Please, I need to know."

He sighed. "It's actually 'Thresti te Morditatum,' and it means 'Death to the Newborn.' I'll be speaking on your behalf to the clergy, so it's best if you don't ask about these things. It won't go well for you." With a slight bow, he left.

I stared out the doorway, twirling my copper bracelet in thought. "Death to the newborn. Why would my mother be interested in it?"

Nittles' head shot up. "Sashel, what if your mother didn't die in childbirth?"

"What do you mean?"

His silver eyes darted back and forth as he thought. "You told me monsters appeared around the village before she died, correct?"

"Right. Probably like what's happening now."

The sprackin's wings twitched as he spoke faster. "And when did the attacks stop?"

"The day she died." *What is he implying?*

"Remember how I said dark rituals can close the rifts?"

I nodded. "You said I should never do them."

"Correct, but what if Neerion did?"

"No. He's irritating, but he'd never go that far."

He flapped onto my bed and looked at me. "I think Neerion discovered your mother was responsible for the attacks and tried to sacrifice Minessa. Death to the newborn!"

"No."

He nodded and spoke more confidently. "It fits. Since your mother was responsible for the rifts, Neerion would sacrifice her child to make amends. His twisted morals would see it as justice. And when your mother tried to stop him, he killed her instead."

"No. It—it can't be."

I turned away, but Nittles flew in front of me and continued. “Minessa was missing two fingers on her left hand. How did that happen?”

“I don’t know.”

“How do you not remember such a tragedy?”

“It—it must have happened the day Mother died. It’s the only day I don’t remember.”

“Exactly! And who has the power to influence the mind?”

My eyes widened. “Neerion!” I threw off my nightgown and slipped on my gray robe.

“Sashel, wait.”

I strapped a small sack of fruit to my waist and shoved my dagger into my robe pocket.

“Sashel, you mustn’t confront him. He has the staff!”

I filled a waterskin and tied it to my other hip. “I killed the Canthi with water. I can do the same to him.”

“You don’t know what he can do, and my theory only answers some of the questions. It doesn’t explain how your sister survived. We need answers.”

“Then let’s go ask Neerion.” I ran to the temple, Nittles trailing behind. Neerion killed my mother. I was sure of it. I ran faster and faster, past the stone slab and up the stairs, then pounded on the door.

Triska opened it a crack. “Sashel?”

“I need to speak to Neerion.”

“He’s—he’s not here.”

“Then where is he?”

She opened the door wider. “He’s at the Healer’s House. Naska is in labor and Neerion wanted to perform a blessing for her.”

Realization struck. Once again, monsters were attacking the village, and there was only one sure way to stop them. Death to the newborn! Nittles and I locked eyes, and we bolted for the Healer's House, leaving a confused Triska behind.

My lungs burned, and my mouth was dry as dust, but I kept running. Neerion had killed my mother. I was sure of it. I wished to all the gods I could remember what happened. He burned her body in private, claiming that witches weren't worthy of a public burning. He was hiding the evidence. But why didn't he kill Minessa? Had the ritual failed somehow?

The Healing House grew larger as Naska's cries intensified. Neerion stood just outside waiting. He scowled at me, but I shoved past him and opened the door. Naska's face wrinkled in pain as she squeezed the healer's hand for comfort.

"Just a little longer," Fendin said.

Neerion grabbed my shoulder. "What are you doing here?" He spun me around. "Leave now or I'll do more than just banish your family."

"Does 'Thresti te Morditatum' mean anything to you?" I asked.

He froze. His eyes went from me to Naska. Then his face firmed and he raised his staff. I opened my pouch of glaidens, but the runes on his staff glowed silver, and my muscles stiffened.

"You!" He shook with rage. "You are just like your mother."

My jaw was stiff, but I managed to say, "Not exactly."

Glowing green water burst from my waterskin, striking his chest like an angry serpent and knocking him to the ground. He swung his staff, and a lance of pain shot up my leg. Naska screamed, whether from fright or childbirth, I couldn't tell.

"Get out!" Fendin yelled. "Get out, both of you!"

I focused on my water, but his staff hit me square in the face. My vision spun as he pummeled my stomach. I coughed as Neerion climbed to his feet.

"I knew you were a witch." He struck me again. "I always knew."

He swung again, but Nittles collided with his face. The cleric grabbed him by the neck and threw him, but the sprackin caught the air with his wings and looped around. His staff glowed, but Nittles seemed unaffected as he slashed his arm with his spiked tail.

I launched my water, but a flash of silver shone from his staff and my thoughts grew sluggish. Where was I? What was I doing here?

There was a loud crack as Nittles slammed against a wall then fell to the floor, dazed. He struggled weakly as the cleric picked him up and squeezed his throat. I looked down at my waist to see an open pouch of dried fruit. I felt like I should eat one, but I couldn't think.

The fire inside me burned, and a silver hue flooded my vision. The mental fog dissipated, and I could focus once more. I was seeing through the eyes of a truth seer. I extinguished the sight immediately as the special ability burned through heartfire at a prodigious rate.

Neerion pointed his staff at me, but I triggered my sight once more. His brow wrinkled, clearly not expecting me to shrug off his mental attack. I raised my hand and pinned him to the wall with my water, causing him to drop Nittles. My temples throbbed from holding him in place and keeping my special sight at the same time.

Naska clutched her stomach and grunted as her pain intensified.

"Please, go!" Fendin yelled. "We don't want any trouble."

I ignored her and stared at the cleric. "My mother. What happened to my mother?"

As his lips moved to speak, a message in silver lettering flashed above him saying, "SHE IS ALIVE."

I blinked, and my sight returned to normal. It couldn't be. She was dead. But my sight would only show the truth. It saw through deception. And…my mother was alive!

My will faded, and the water holding him in place splashed to the ground. Neerion gripped his staff in both hands. "The punishment for witchcraft is death."

"Where's my mother?"

He raised his staff high at the same time I drew my dagger. The runes on my blade glowed gold as Neerion's glowed silver, flooding the room in shimmering light. I brought my knife down but stopped as a familiar voice echoed in my mind.

"The Trial of Forests hath begun."

CHAPTER 26

"The flesh of family may satisfy,
but the blood of the newborn is bliss."
—Thresti te Morditatum

"No!"

I slammed the dagger down, but it sank into black wood. A gnarled tree stood before me, stretching higher than I could see with a trunk as wide as a house. Plants of every shape and size surrounded me, all glowing a faint azure hue. Strange noises echoed around me, and a crescent emerald moon hung in the black sky. I growled in frustration and yanked my knife free of the thick bark.

"Sashel, don't!" Nittles yelled.

Yellow bile spewed out from the opening in the tree, searing my hand and wrist. A scream tore from my throat as the noxious sap burned like molten metal. With my left hand, I dug in my pouch for a lifespur, but the pain made my muscles spasm, and the dried fruit fell to the ground.

The spracken drew near and sang. It was a soothing melody in a strong baritone voice. The sap slithered off like a retreating tide, and the burns on my skin faded.

"The song of Gralius will only work on lockin sap," Nittles said. "Sap from other plants aren't as easily cured."

I grabbed the dagger and scrambled to my feet. "Let's go!"

"Sashel, we need to proceed slowly through these woods. This is the Whisping Forest, and—"

"No! We have to go now!"

Neerion was about to kill Naska and her child. I was so close to stopping him! My eyes darted around until they landed on a silver pathway of shimmering light in the air, much like in the last trial. I dashed forwards, my feet crunching on dead leaves.

The spracken trailed behind. "Slow down!"

My mother was alive! Had Neerion captured her? Was she here in Tal Miral? What if the clergy had a dungeon specifically for witches? I gritted my teeth as I ran. The goddess was toying with me, sending me to this trial right before I could stop the mad cleric.

A thin branch stretched in front of me and collided with my neck. No sooner had I hit the ground when tendrils of branches coiled around my legs. I reached for my knife, but the branches yanked me forward, causing me to bounce like a stone skipping across a lake. My head knocked against stumps, bushes, and rocks faster than I could think.

"I need your heartfire," he yelled behind me.

I poured some of my fire into him, and he shot forward, slashing the branches with his spiked tail. I came to an abrupt halt in the damp leaves and stared up, too sore to move.

There was a light thump as Nittles alighted on my chest. "Fool! You can't run headlong into the Whisping Forest."

I shut my eyes, still dazed.

He sighed and spoke in a softer tone. "Back in the Healing House, you asked Neerion about your mother as your eyes flashed silver. What happened?"

I shut my eyes tighter as a tear trailed down my cheek. "My mother. She's alive."

There was a long pause before he said, "Nevertheless, we must be circumspect as we move. Travel slowly or walk alone. I am not chasing you again just because you wish to throw a tantrum."

I nodded. Slowly climbing to my feet, I rubbed my throat where the branch had struck. It was swollen and I found it difficult to swallow. I dug in my pouch only to find two glaidens and one lifespur. I looked around, but the forest all looked the same with a myriad of trees all glowing a dark blue.

"Can you make more lifespur?" I asked.

"What happened to the ones we just made?"

"I dropped them. I only have one left."

"What about the larger sack we made?"

I held out the three fruits. "This is all I have right now!"

"Then you best use it wisely. I cannot make any more."

"I have more heartfire."

"It matters not."

I rubbed my pounding head and moaned. "What do you mean?"

He let out a frustrated breath. "You recall how you couldn't claim the blood of the mouse yesterday?"

I remembered drying the fruit then trying my abilities on the small creature with no success. Had that only been yesterday?

When I nodded, he continued. "You couldn't claim the water in its blood because it was already claimed. Similarly, everything you see is claimed. The Whisping Forest has a life of its own. A consciousness."

I bit half the healing fruit and placed the other half in my pouch. My headache faded and the swelling on my throat eased, but I hadn't fully healed. It would have to do.

As we followed the glimmering light, Nittles asked, "Do you remember the portion of the song for this trial?"

It only took a moment for me to recite, "Travel the forest that sees you as prey. The scepter of runes will make them obey."

He gave me a patronizing look. "Well, summon the scepter."

I bit back a retort and closed my eyes. The candelabra appeared in my mind with the silver candle half burned in the center with three candlesticks branching off on either side with only two of the six still holding an emerald candle.

I focused on one of the green ones and imagined holding a scepter. Nothing happened. I imagined holding anything that could help—a sword, a spear, a shield. Still nothing. I thought about it. All the other times I hadn't sought a specific item. In desperation my mind just reached out.

I imagined being dragged through the forest mere moments ago. I thought of my injuries and my lack of healing fruit. Then I whispered, "I need help."

The green candle remained frustratingly still, not so much as a flicker from its flame. Something seemed off. It was as if the fire was saying that my statement wasn't quite right.

Opening my eyes, I kicked the leaves. Each trial was so different from the next. First, I fought an insane man. Next, I fought a sea monster, then horrifying spirits forced me to confront my innermost problems. And in the last one I had to tell secrets. Now I couldn't summon anything unless I asked a certain way?

Something crackled beneath my feat. Thick roots pinched my ankles and slowly pulled me into the earth. Faster than quicksand, I sank to my calves then it passed my knees. Nittles sprung into the air, but one of his wings grazed a patch of moss, and he stuck like a fly in a web.

At the base of the tree, a blue and yellow flower as large as a horse opened its petals wide to reveal a monstrous mouth. Its teeth were like dozens of beaks from hungry birds. The moss flowed downward, pulling the sprackin directly towards the open maw.

Something stirred inside me. I had said, "I need help," but that was wrong. The whole point of enduring these trials was so I could bring back my sister. I sold fruit to support her and build a better life for her. I fought Neerion to protect Naska and find out what happened to my mother. And then there was Nittles. No, I didn't need help. Nittles needed help. My sister needed help.

As the earth reached my chest, I yelled, "*They* need my help!"

The dim, green flame inside me burst to life. It glowed as bright as the sun and then consumed the fifth candle. Before me, a portal opened, and a silver staff shot into my hand. The runes glowed green as the entire staff vibrated like I was holding it under a waterfall.

Gripping it in both hands, I struck the roots pulling me downward, and the staff rang like a temple bell. The rage boiling inside me somehow poured into the roots. As the staff stopped shaking, I sensed the trees around me. They were angry, not at me, but at the roots beneath me, as if the plants shared my feelings. The staff had persuaded the trees that the roots were their enemies.

The mouth about to consume Nittles turned its head and lunged at the thick roots at my feet with a loud crunch. The mouth didn't harm me, but it attacked the roots with a visceral rage. The roots released me and poured all their effort into defending themselves, but the massive flower crushed them in mere seconds. Pulling myself out, I yanked Nittles free of the moss and ran. Once we reached the silver pathway, I ate a glaiden.

Nittles squinted at the staff. "It looks ancient. What does it do?"

"Um…it vibrates?"

He cocked an eyebrow. "I see."

I held it up and focused on the silver candle in my mind. Only one emerald candle remained nearby, but that would be for later. I poured a bit of my silver heartfire into the staff, and it vibrated once more.

"Brilliant!" he exclaimed. "When the trees attack, we can shake them to death."

I glared at him, then looked around. None of the trees moved, but I knew that wouldn't last long. A short sapling stood nearby with white bark and deep blue leaves. When I struck it, the staff once again rang like a bell.

The sapling looked the same, then something hissed behind me like an angry adder. With the glaiden pulsing through me, I rolled as a stream of flames shot towards the tree. Even from several paces away, the heat pressed against me, and I struggled to breathe. When it ceased, the sapling was nothing more than a smoking pile of ash.

The sprackin's eyes widened. "I retract my previous statement."

I stared at the staff. "It seems like it can command the trees to attack whatever I strike."

He nodded. "Try to use less heartfire next time."

I focused on a tenth of what I had just done. It was like holding a barrel of water and only pouring a few drops, but soon the staff shook but only slightly instead of the violent motion from earlier.

The branches and leaves rustled, but there was no wind. They stirred in motion with the staff. The tension built to a crescendo as the staff shook faster, the energy begging to be released. As I looked around for a target, a faint whistle sounded, followed by a sharp pain in my arm. An orange fruit covered in quills sank deep into my skin. Reflexively, I reached to pull it free.

"Stop!"

Before his warning could register, my fingers wrapped around the spiky fruit. As I yanked my hand back, chunks of skin tore free, leaving the fruit embedded in my arm. Blood pooled in my shredded flesh as whistling sounded in front of me.

I ducked as Nittles flew high, carefully avoiding the moss this time. Dozens of spiked fruits shot above me. Grabbing the shaking staff with my bloodied hand, I slammed it against the nearest tree. As it rang, another volley flew, and the staff fell still. I had a moment to sigh in relief before the pain in my arm redoubled.

"How do I get this thing out?"

Nittles landed and scrutinized my arm. "Thrinken fruit. I cannot help with this."

I clutched my torn hand. "Are you saying there's no cure?"

He looked down. "No. There's a cure. It's just..."

"It's just what?"

Grinding his teeth, he said, "You—you have to whistle to it."

"Whistle? Well, then do it."

"I can't."

"What do you mean, you can't?"

"I mean I can't whistle!"

"Oh." I wasn't expecting that. "Well, is there a tune I have to whistle?"

"No. You must find the right pitch. Whistle as high as you can then slowly lower it. The quills will release once you...pinpoint the right note." He winced at the unintentional pun.

I whistled as loud as I could then made my whistle fade to barely a whisper, but the orange quills remained embedded.

Nittles rolled his eyes. "I said high to low, not loud to quiet. Pitch, not volume!"

His words were harsh, but I couldn't tell if that was because of the circumstance, or if he was embarrassed that he couldn't whistle.

I took a deep breath and tried again, starting at the highest pitch I could then lowered it. The tension in my arm eased as I found the note. The quills released and the fruit dropped to the ground.

Tiny holes like needle pricks covered the area on my upper arm, but they were nothing compared to my torn hand. With a grimace, I ate the second half of the lifespur and hoped I wouldn't need more. As the tender flesh regrew, I retrieved my staff. It wasn't a scepter as the song said, but I guessed it was metaphorical.

Minutes went by in silence as we followed the silver light. Finally, I said, "So, sprackins can't whistle?"

He sniffed. "Many can, but not I. It's quite bothersome. I've mastered many skills, both mundane and divine, yet I can't perform such a simple feat."

I chuckled at the ridiculousness of it all. For just a moment, my worries eased, then I felt a bundle of soft fabric in my pocket. My grin faded as I pulled out a small, blood-stained hat. Minessa's screams echoed in my mind as the memory of her death washed over me.

Bringing the yellow hat to my lips, I held back a sob. "What if I can't do this?"

"What do you mean?" he asked. "You have the staff."

I shook my head and continued walking. "These trials are supposed to prepare me for some beast, some great creature to fight. What if I fail? What if I never see Minessa again?"

"Come now. You slew the Canthi."

"But I lost to Vision Master. He could have killed me, but instead, he toyed with me."

"You passed the Trial of Spirits."

I squeezed the cloth hat. "I don't feel like I passed. All I did was burn a painting. I thought my father had changed that night, but he didn't. He never changes. Nothing ever changes!"

"Sashel, control yourself. The trial is far from over."

"I'm tired, Nittles. I'm tired of trying. I feel like no matter what I do, nothing will change."

He looked around. "You see all these leaves?"

The leaves still on the trees glowed a vibrant blue while those on the ground were dull brown. I nodded to him. The numbness from Minessa's loss had returned, leeching away all care and hope.

"Can you count all of them?" he asked.

"Probably not."

"That doesn't surprise me."

When he saw his jab had no effect on me, he continued. "Hundreds of thousands, possibly millions litter the ground. Now, how many do you currently see falling?"

I sighed and looked around. "Three, I think."

"You only see a few falling. Then how can so many be on the ground?"

I shrugged, not wanting to humor him.

"One at a time," he said. "They don't panic. They don't get overwhelmed. They simply fall one at a time. The trees grow so slowly it's beyond our perception, yet they grow."

"I don't care about trees."

"Of course you don't. You're too preoccupied with the forest, you miss the trees. If you carry tomorrow's worries, you'll trip over today's."

"Shouldn't we be looking ahead?"

"Not when you're despondent. You'll be overwhelmed and expect the worst."

I squeezed the hat tighter. "I can't afford to trip. I can't lose her!"

"If you run from fear, you'll find it every time." He flapped his wings till he was eye to eye with me. "Your desperation to save your sister may very well be your downfall."

The numbness left me, and all my fear and anger burst from me as I yelled, "Then what should I do?"

"Accept the fact that you may lose. Only then can you make wise decisions."

"I can't do that!"

"You must."

I gripped the staff and breathed. I knew he was right. Father taught me desperate people are far more likely to be tricked. They see what they want to see, and nothing else.

As I brushed my thumb along the bloody handprint on the staff, something tugged at me. I ran the song from the staircase through my head again. It said, "The scepter of runes will make them obey."

The staff was called a scepter. It wouldn't just protect me from the trees; it ruled them. I was looking at this all wrong. With the staff, I was their queen, and they would obey my every command.

"That's it!"

Pouring heartfire into the staff, I sensed the predatory trees around me. When I found the one I wanted, I pulled the staff like a fishing line.

Branches shaped like giant hands grabbed us. I pointed my staff towards the shimmering pathway, and we lunged forward. A wide grin grew on my face as the trees blurred passed us. The same branches that dragged me through the forest earlier were now my way out.

Nittles wriggled in the branches' grip, but I held out a hand. "Trust me."

When they stretched as far as they could, they gently lowered us. A whistling came behind us, and I struck a log. The staff rang like a bell before several spiked fruits embedded themselves into the fallen tree.

Raising my staff, I commanded another tree to grab us, and we shot forward once more. A gnarled, black tree targeted us, but with the insight from the staff, I sensed its intention and poured more heartfire into the staff. A stream of flames shot above, scorching the branches carrying us.

"Perhaps we should slow our travel," Nittles said.

I sensed a tree which I instinctively knew would suffocate us with its thick, sappy bark. With a thought, the branches holding us grew around us like a shell made of twigs. I summoned the new tree, and large sheets of bark launched themselves at us.

The sprackin flinched, but the bark only struck the branches a few feet away, coating the shell of twigs until it was thick as armor. With a bit of concentration, a small slit opened for us to see through.

Nittles cackled. "We're traveling in a wooden eggshell across the Whisping Forest! Ha! This is a story I would tell in the royal court."

The cycle repeated. The branches carried our shell as far as they could reach, then I would summon another. Whatever I couldn't deflect with the staff, the shell took the impact. Spikes, flames, and acidic sap attacked, but none penetrated.

"How are you on heartfire?" he asked.

"About a third left."

"Good. At this rate, we should make it with plenty to spare. I can't believe it!"

I laughed in pure delight. "I can't believe it either! I thought we were done for when I lost the lifespur back there."

He didn't respond. Only a sliver of light came through the shell's opening, making it difficult to see his features.

"Nittles?"

After a minute longer, he said, "What happened to the lifespur?"

"I dropped them when the sap burned me. You were there."

"No. The larger sack of lifespur we made before your last trial. There were nearly fifty of them."

I swallowed. "They're back at the cottage."

"No." His tone slipped from curious to accusatory. "We made the glaidens and lifespur. Then you gave the glaidens to the fishermen to sell in Sennevar."

A silver statue glinted in front of us, maybe a hundred paces away. As I slowed, Nittles continued.

"After that we went straight to the temple. Once your trial ended, you were taken to the Healing House for your snake bite, and by then, the fruit was gone. You never went to the cottage."

The branches lowered our shell directly in front of the statue. If this was anything like the last trial, all I had to do was touch it.

"What happened to the lifespur?" he asked.

"I—I don't know."

"You lie!"

"I must have dropped them in the last trial."

"You don't remember dropping a large sack of healing fruit?"

"I was bitten. The venom messed with my head."

In the small wooden shell, Nittles' yells were deafening. "You sent the lifespur to be sold, didn't you?"

"I did not."

I opened the shell, and the branches released their grip on us.

"The fish," he said as he realized what happened.

"The what?"

"You told the fishermen to throw in a fish for me to seal the deal. That's when you placed the lifespur in their cart. You distracted me!"

I turned to see his reaction. His face went from angry to hurt. Through our connection, I sensed his feelings of betrayal and guilt. He helped make the fruit, and he felt equally responsible.

"I've called you a fool many times," he said. "But I was the fool for ever trusting you!"

I opened my mouth to speak, but he went on. "You never planned to take me back, did you? You didn't want to give me back my abilities. You used me for your own devices, and I let you!"

"I'm sorry."

As I reached for the statue, Nittles pounced on me with the force of a battering ram. I landed on my back, and my staff clattered to the side. When I reached for it, the sprackin bit deep into my shoulder. I swatted at him, but he spun and sliced my thigh with his sharp tail.

"Traitor!" He hopped off and panted. "I trusted you, and you betrayed me."

His words sparked a memory. Hadn't Neerion said something similar to my mother? I was pained by his words, but anger took its place. "I never bought into what you said. It's fruit. That's all it is!"

"Not to me! I didn't expect you to share my beliefs, only that you respect them. And yet, you used me! You made me commit sacrilege. I'm an anathema to my world now. Don't you understand? I'm ruined!"

My stomach churned as I realized how deeply I'd betrayed him. Then it occurred to me. Why did Neerion feel betrayed by my mother? What had happened? And there was something about him in the Healing House just before we fought.

A hiss sounded beside me, and my mind snapped back to the present. My cursed mind had betrayed me, and it was too late. I knew what the sound meant.

Orange light illuminated the sprackin's face. He saw the fire headed straight for me, and his will firmed. Like an arrow he shot forward, intercepting the jet of flames.

First, he wailed then screeched as the fire continued its relentless attack. The air filled with the stench of burning flesh and black smoke that stung my eyes. The flames cut off, and the forest returned to a calming blue.

"No!" I scooped up his limp body in my arms. "Nittles!"

He gave a weak groan but nothing more. A whistle sounded, and I ducked as spiked fruit shot towards me.

"Nittles! I'm so sorry!"

I grabbed my staff and placed it in the crook of my arm, not letting go of the sprackin. As more flames streamed towards me, I lurched to the side and touched the silver statue.

Time froze as the celestial voice spoke. "The Trial of Forests hath ended. Ready yourself for the battle to come."

I held Nittles softly against my chest as the flames, the statue, and the Whisping Forest itself faded away. Bright sunlight filled the Healer's House, and I let out a relieved breath. Wait, Healer Fendin! She could help Nittles.

As I turned, Neerion stood before me with a look of absolute malice. He raised his staff and swung. There was a flash of light, then pain, followed by blackness.

CHAPTER 27

"When we lie to others, we deceive ourselves most of all."
—The Book of Wisdom

"Remember," a feminine voice said.

I looked up as the goddess, Kareli, placed a hand on a short silver candle. The metallic flame brightened, and the candle grew to full-size once more. It still stood in the center of the candelabra with one remaining emerald candle at the far end.

Falling to my knees, I stared at her gleaming face that like before was too bright to make out details.

"Please help me," I whispered.

She cocked her head and pointed at the tall silver candle.

I nodded. "Yes, the heartfire will help, and I'm grateful, but…"

What could I say next? Your fire isn't good enough? I felt like those would be at the very least excuses and at the most insults, neither of which I wanted to say to a goddess.

Instead, I lowered my head and said, "I'm not ready for the fight."

Kareli's silver bracelets clinked as she pointed to the final emerald candle.

Without saying a word, she made a fair point. I could summon one more item. My eyes drifted to her bracelets, and something tugged at my mind, but I couldn't place it.

"How can I win?" I asked. "How can I defeat the beast?"

She grabbed my shoulders then pointed to my eyes. "Remember!"

* * *

My head pounded as I lifted my heavy eyelids. A single lantern shined through the bars of my cell, and when I sat up, my arms felt heavy from the thick chains around my wrists. Patting my pockets, I found they were empty. No dagger, no fruit, no staff, and…no Nittles.

As I reached out with my mind, I sensed invisible threads to the items I'd summoned. Most were lumped together about a half mile away, but when I pulled with my will, they remained still. They were probably locked up tight, maybe in the temple.

A single thread connected to something much closer, merely across the hall. The thread was faint and fragile like an old spider's web, and deep sorrow pulsed from it, sorrow and despair.

"Nittles?"

The hallway was silent, followed by a muffled whimper. Focusing on the thin strand, I pulled as softly as I could. Metal scraped against the cobblestone floor, but I continued, wincing at the noise.

Emerging from the darkness was a tall, metal birdcage. I continued pulling with my mind until the cage clinked against the bars of my cell, revealing a limp, wounded sprackin inside. Much of his fur was gone, replaced by dark red patches of burned flesh, and his wings contorted at awkward angles. No. One of them contorted; the other was missing. It had been ripped off, and jagged bones protruded from his back. The flames wouldn't have done that; Neerion must have after the trial.

"Nittles!" I tried to whisper, but it came out as a shriek.

He opened one eye, the other swollen and coated in blood. He just stared at me, not saying a word. I wanted to touch him, to hug him, but the slightest touch would aggravate his wounds.

"Why?" I asked. "Why did you save me?"

His bleary eye locked on me, and in a raspy voice he said, "Because…it was right."

"But you attacked me just before." I rubbed my shoulder. "You bit me."

He gave a light chuckle which turned into a cough. "That too was right."

Even in this horrible state, the sprackin never wavered. "Nittles, I don't have any fruit. Is there a way to heal you?"

"I will not make any more lifespur."

I shut my eyes and my heart ripped in half. "I'm so sorry I lied to you."

"The moment I leapt into the flames, I forgave you."

"But—"

"Stop. I will die soon; so, listen well."

His words carried the weight of finality, yet he was calm. He was at complete peace with death, something I couldn't comprehend. No. I wouldn't let him die! I focused on the green candle in my mind and thought of saving Nittles, but the flame remained placid. Only in a trial could I use it.

I went to my silver candle the goddess had renewed. Opening my eyes, I willed a portion of the silver fire into him. He rustled his wing, and his body spasmed in pain. For a minute, he could do nothing but grit his teeth before finally relaxing.

"The fire is useless without fruit," he said.

I patted my pockets again then searched the small cell. Nothing but dirt and chains with a straw mat at the other end.

"I considered the song," he said. "I think I know how to slay the beast."

I shook my head. "Tell me after we heal you."

There was no window in the cell, and no water I could claim. Neerion had seen my abilities and planned accordingly. But there had to be something!

"The head of an eagle will slay the beast," he recited. "I don't know what the beast will be, but the head of an eagle probably refers to the Emarli."

Would my own blood work? Maybe I could bleed myself then control the water in it. I might be able to...do what? I couldn't see any fruit nearby. Even if I had water, I wasn't strong enough with it to break chains.

Nittles coughed, then winced at the movement. "The Emarli are creatures of light. They're massive eagles with sapphire scales instead of feathers. They should be strong enough to slay any beast in the Sprawn Lands."

I knelt and grabbed the birdcage. "Listen. We're getting out of here, then we're gonna find a way to Tal Miral. I promise!"

The sprackin's mouth quirked into a shuddering smile, then his eye went distant.

I reached my hand through the bars and into his cage, caressing his face. "Nittles?"

Once more, his back arched in pain, then he relaxed. His chest fell but did not rise, and his small head went limp in my hand. No. I shook his head softly, then shook harder.

"Nittles?"

His body lay still. I swallowed but didn't pull away. My hand stayed outstretched though the bars, stroking his head until his body went cold.

CHAPTER 28

"We demand retribution until we ourselves stand in judgment, then we plead for mercy."
—Words of Fremma

A tap on the bars jolted me awake, and I reached for my knife. But of course, it wasn't there.

Cleric Shoff leaned his staff against the wall and sat. "Sorry to wake you."

The morning sun peeked through the window across the hall, illuminating my cell. My thin mattress lay at the other end, but I had slept by the bars, next to Nittles. Taking a deep breath, I turned to face the birdcage.

Strangely, his body didn't look…real anymore. His body was a mangled mess, but I didn't think of Nittles when I looked at him. Lifeless wasn't the right word. He didn't have the silence of a corpse, but rather the dull normalcy of an old rug. His body was just there with no semblance of the sprackin I knew. Nittles was gone.

Shoff placed a hand on the cage. "I see you cared for the poor thing. I'm sorry."

I nodded and rubbed my arms, warming them from the cool morning air.

"Ah, here." He pulled a blanket from his sack and pressed it through the bars. "I would have brought it last night, but Neerion makes a habit of not telling me these things. I knew nothing of your imprisonment until this morning."

After wrapping the blanket around myself, my shivers eased. "What hap—" I coughed and tried to swallow, but my throat was dry as sand.

Shoff passed a waterskin through the bars. "Neerion refused to let me give you this until he wrapped a three knotted chord around the entire prison. Great judgment, the man is a zealot. None but the clerics are even allowed to visit you."

I greedily grabbed the skin and drank. After downing half in one swig, I tried to claim the rest with my abilities, but just like in the Healing House when the chord was around my bed, my magic was blocked.

After drinking the rest, I asked, "What happens now?"

"Normally, there would be a trial for you attacking a cleric which would result in a few lashes if you were found guilty, but I'm afraid it's not that simple."

"I didn't attack him. I mean, we fought, but there was more to it than that."

"Fendin and Naska say you attacked him. That's two witnesses, three if you include her newborn son."

Her son? Neerion didn't sacrifice him. But why? Had I ruined his plan? I rubbed my face, feeling the deep marks where my skin pressed against the bars as I slept.

"Why is it more complicated now?" I asked.

"Because of Neerion. He's suspending the trial for a few days while he gathers as much evidence as he can."

"How much evidence does he need?"

"Not evidence of you attacking him. Evidence of witchcraft. He's offering ten silvers for anyone who can provide proof. He already has your blade and staff. Where did you even find those things?"

"I—I don't know."

"You're not helping yourself with answers like that. If I'm going to defend you in your trial, you need to be honest."

I stared at him, refusing to say more.

He sighed and rose to his feet. "The real reason I came was to test you."

"Test me?"

"Yes. One of the things my staff can do is reveal your ownership. Have you ever branded animals before."

When I shook my head, he shrugged and continued. "In any case, the gods do something similar with us, and my staff can show me. I'll probably see the mark of Suthian, but even if it's Robius's, it'll prove you haven't performed witchcraft. Otherwise, they'd remove their mark."

As he pressed the weathered staff to my head, the tip glowed a vivid blue. Unlike Neerion's staff which felt invasive and harsh, this one had a comforting warmth that touched the soul instead of the mind. His dark brown eyes flashed blue, and he backed up in shock.

"What? What did you see?"

He ran a hand through his thin white hair. "If it was Suthian, I'd see a broken whip, the sign of mercy. The mark of Robius is a gavel for judgment."

"So, which one was it?"

He licked his lips. "I saw silver eyes staring back at me."

* * *

Standing on the stone slab, I gazed at the crowd as the judgment began. Neerion had ensured a three-knotted chord surrounded me as well as binding my wrists and ankles with the same white rope. It had been two days since I traveled the Whisping Forest, two days since Nittles died.

Naska and Fendin told their account, relaying how I had burst through the door and fought with Neerion. I didn't blame them. It was exactly what happened, but they didn't know the reason behind it.

My father sat in front, his eyes locked on me. He came. Unlike at Minessa's funeral, Father came for me.

Lord Fensin sat beside his wife, Meleer in front of the temple. Their gold bands coiling around their arms and necks marked them as the lords of Ashwood and more importantly, the judges in my trial.

The judge brushed his clean-shaven chin. "I have only heard witnesses of her attacking a cleric. Why has the trial been postponed until now?"

"Because of *how* she attacked me." Neerion pointed his staff. "This woman has used witchcraft and deserves more than a simple beating. The sentence should be death by hanging."

My heart leapt in my throat despite Shoff preparing me for this. For the last two days we'd gone over everything he would say.

Judge Meleer raised an eyebrow. "And what proof have you?"

Neerion unsheathed the golden dagger and tapped the dark side of the hilt, turning invisible. I winced and turned to Shoff who stood beside me. I had hoped he wouldn't discover how to use the blade, but it was simple to understand and Neerion was relentless with his investigation.

The crowd gasped, and even the judges looked up at the display of power. Father wrung his hands when he saw him vanish, but the cleric wasn't done. Curiously, Neerion didn't reveal the staff. Did he want it for himself? Maybe it would make me seem more like a cleric than a witch if they knew I had a staff like them. If I could get him to reveal it, maybe—

Bile rose in my throat as he lifted the cage containing Nittles' decaying body. Wrenching the sprackin free, Neerion raised it high. "She has summoned a demon from the Banished Realm!"

The judge winced at the sight. "Many have seen her weasel. How is this proof?"

"And how many weasels have wings?" The cleric stretched out his one remaining wing and brought it closer. Fensin's eyes widened, and several in the crowd screamed as he threw the corpse before the judges.

I shook with rage as the body was callously displayed like a piece of meat in the butcher's shop. Even knowing the cleric was just baiting me, it took every bit of strength I had not to leap at him and claw his face.

Shoff stood and placed a comforting hand on my shoulder. "That's enough. She could have found the creature in the forest, and having the blade doesn't prove she's a witch. There are many items throughout the world that have strange abilities."

"She wished to sacrifice Naska's child!" Neerion shouted.

"Do you have proof of this?" the judges asked in unison.

"She said, 'Death to the newborn' in ancient Moralic just before she attacked," Neerion said.

"Did anyone else hear this?" Shoff asked.

Neerion held up his staff. "I can show the memory of it all."

"No." Lord Fensin raised his hand. "No artifact of the clergy shall be used to prove one's guilt. This has been a decree for some time. Furthermore, your disdain for her family has been apparent for years. I will not take any memory from your staff as evidence."

Neerion ground his teeth. "If we were back in Gran Mala, we would—"

"We are not in Gran Mala," Meleer said. "Now let Cleric Shoff say his peace, or I will deem the accused as innocent of all accounts including her fight with you."

Shoff nodded in thanks. "Sashel is a faithful worshipper of Suthian."

"She defiled her sister's body!" Neerion shouted.

"Only out of grief," he said quickly. "She had just lost her sister. Poor Sashel was like a mother to Minessa after their mother passed a few short years ago."

There was a shift in the crowd, his words making a clear impact. Father nodded as his face brightened. Neerion had made a mistake in mentioning my sister, and Shoff had capitalized on it. As my tension eased ever so slightly, I allowed myself a faint smile. There might just be a chance.

Shoff pointed his staff at the base of the stone slab where my father sat. "Tamble has fared little better at the loss of his wife." He cocked his head as though just remembering. "Neerion, wasn't it you that banished him from the temple?"

Neerion squeezed his staff but said nothing.

"Answer him," Judge Fensin said.

His eyes lowered as he said, "It is."

The crowd murmured, and hope rose within me. This was going better than I ever expected!

"Have you any further evidence?" Shoff asked. "Or do you wish to torture a grieving girl further?"

Neerion turned stone cold. After opening the box the dagger was held in, he pulled out a bag and slammed it on the table. There was a clink as the bag landed, and the judges squinted in puzzlement.

Opening the dirt-covered bag, Judge Meleer pulled out five silver coins bearing the emblem of a tree in the shape of a hand reaching up towards a crescent moon. Her eyes widened as the sack bore the same emblem, the emblem of Sennevar.

The judge scowled and looked up at Neerion. "Where did you find these?"

"A witness followed Sashel into the Scarlet Forest," the cleric said. "She was seen burying the sack shortly after returning from Sennevar." He proffered a crisp parchment to the judges. "This letter was found inside as well. You will see she didn't sell to a common merchant."

Fensin's grip tightened as his eyes darted across the words. "This is from the constable. It records how many troops will be aided and when to expect more."

The hope in Father's eyes faded, replaced by deep despair.

"Sennevar troops?" someone in the crowd asked.

I squinted. Something was off about all this. The sack looked like the one I buried, but there were several sacks, not just one. And each sack held ten coins, not five.

Shoff leaned in and whispered, "Sashel, is any of this true?"

Before I could answer, Judge Fensin looked up. "Who saw her bury this?"

"Since Sashel is being tried for witchcraft as well as treason, the witness has the right to remain anonymous."

Fensin pursed his lips. "I still need to question the witness in private."

Neerion grinned. "Of course."

"We are not at war with the Sennavian Empire," Shoff said. "And selling them fruit isn't illegal. Several folk travel there."

The judge set the paper down and tapped it, weighing what to say. For over a minute he and his wife whispered, and a knot formed in my stomach. The moment stretched out, and even Neerion looked taken aback. Finally, Fensin spoke.

"Skirmishes have been reported close to Ashwood. Tannekin was invaded yesterday."

My heart raced as the crowd murmured. What had I done? Had the soldiers used the glaidens to invade? They only last a few minutes, but soldiers would take any advantage they could.

I scanned the crowd. Who could have told them? Who knew about the silver coins? Who knew my…secret? My eyes fell on Triska, and we locked gazes. She shook her head and mouthed "no," but I knew. In that moment, I knew it was her. I told her exactly where I hid the coins. Of course she told. *I'm an idiot!* Once again, I let myself trust someone, and now I was reaping the consequences.

"How do you plead?" the lord asked.

Shoff straightened. "We will wait for you to question the witness before—"

"Guilty," I said.

I sold fruit to the enemy, and I was caught. I was so focused on supporting my sister, I didn't think about anything else. Why had I tried? Everything I touched turned to ash.

Shoff turned to me. "What are you doing?"

"I'm done."

"We can fight this."

"I'm done!"

His brow furrowed and a look of utter disappointment crossed his face. Nodding once, he turned to the judges. "She pleads guilty. But the witness should still be questioned."

"Agreed," Meleer said. "The trial is concluded."

"Sashel, no!" My father lunged toward me. It took seven men to hold him back as he thrashed and kicked. "You're the only one I have left. Please!"

As the temple bell rang, my fate was sealed, and I didn't care. Hope was for the fool, and I was the greatest fool of all.

CHAPTER 29

"Woe to them who worship the coin, for they shall be crushed by its weight."
—The Book of Clergy

"Why didn't you tell me?" Shoff asked. "I could have prepared a better defense if I'd known about Sennevar."

The old cleric sat hunching against his staff near my cell.

"Would you have helped if I'd told you?"

"Of course! It was foolish what you did, but you forget I wasn't raised as a cleric. I made more mistakes than I care to say." He ran a hand through his thinning hair on the sides of his head. "What else haven't you told me?"

I leaned my head against the bars. "It doesn't matter now."

"You've given up. Haven't you?"

"Nothing I do makes a difference."

"You don't know that."

My vision blurred as my eyes watered. "I try and try, but nothing happens."

Placing a feeble hand on my head, he said, "They say it's foolish to do the same thing repeatedly with no change."

"That's exactly what it's like."

He chuckled. "Then how do you chop down a tree?"

"What?"

"A tree." He swung his hands in as though using an axe. "You chop and chop and chop, seemingly with no results. Then, finally, the tree falls. You do the same thing over and over believing that something good will happen."

"And with my luck, the tree falls right on my head."

He poked my stomach with his staff. "Be sour if you wish, but don't ruin my analogies."

I barked out a laugh despite myself. It was an ugly laugh and my eyes burned as mucus ran freely down my face. Then my smile faded.

"Why are you here when my own father hasn't visited me?"

"Neerion's order still stands. Only clerics are allowed to come."

"But—"

The temple bell rang.

"Attack!" someone outside yelled. "We're under attack!"

Shoff stood. "Holy sh—sheep! What's going on?"

He shuffled across the floor as fast as his old legs would carry him. As he reached for the handle, the door burst open, knocking him to the ground. A soldier with a thick red beard stepped inside. He wore chainmail with a sigil around his arm displaying a tree shaped like a hand reaching up toward a crescent moon. A Sennevar soldier!

"Cleric!" The man spat the word like a curse as he eyed Shoff who struggled to rise. Without another word, the soldier drew his sword and thrust it deep into his chest.

"No!"

I grabbed the bars, but I could do nothing as Shoff bled out on the wooden floor, gasping and groaning. The soldier looked around, sparing me only a moment before dismissing me. As he turned to leave, he reached into a small sack on his side. My stomach dropped as he ate a slice of purple fruit before jogging out.

The glaidens! They were using them against Ashwood! Then I remembered. They asked where I was from, and I answered Lanvire. Foolish! They probably would have left the village alone had they known I lived here. I kicked the bars again and again. Once more, I tried summoning my items, but like before, the chord around the prison inhibited my abilities.

I turned as the door across the hall slammed shut. A thin, scraggly man stood with his back against the door, bracing it from any soldiers.

"Help me!" I yelled.

The man walked towards me, then stopped at Shoff's body. "Great judgement!"

"Help me! I need to—" I stopped as realization came. Jocksin! Crippled Jocksin walked toward me.

"Life used to be good, you know?" He shook a bony finger at me. "The folks here were good to me. Then you came!"

"I don't understand."

"The fruit! The cursed fruit healed me."

"But—"

"I didn't want change!" He paced around the room and wrung his hands. "Ashwood gave me a place to sleep, food to eat, and even a copper now and then. It was perfect."

"You can do more now. You can do whatever you want."

"What I want is my old life back. After the fruit healed me, I felt like a fraud. And it was only a matter of time before Fendin checked on me and discovered I'd healed. My perfect life was ruined because of you." He plucked a spear from a rack on the wall. "Day after day, I saw you come and go with that little weasel."

It finally dawned on me. "You followed me into the forest; didn't you? You were the one who told Neerion about the silver from Sennevar."

A banging came from the door across the hall, but Jocksin had locked it. He turned back to me as his spear shook with rage. "I was going to kill you then and there. That's when I saw what you hid. After I took it, I heard the reward Neerion offered for proof of your guilt. Ten silvers. I offered up five of the ones I'd found, knowing I'd receive double. Not only would I have enough silver to leave Ashwood, but you would suffer as well."

The pounding on the door grew louder, but my eyes never left the spear pointed at me. "I was only trying to help you."

He raised the spear to strike. "Well, you failed!"

The prison door burst open, and a massive form plowed into him. Jocksin scrambled for the spear, but the larger man grabbed it first. Jocksin tried yanking it away, but the burly man held it with a vice-like grip.

"Father," I said. "You came."

He nodded but kept his eyes fixed on Jocksin who quivered on the floor. "You dare harm my daughter!"

In that moment, my father wasn't a monster. He was what monsters feared. He was the embodiment of wrath. For the first time in what felt like ages, I felt protected, protected by my father.

"Tamble, please!" Jocksin held out a trembling hand. "I would never—"

"So, you wish to be a cripple again?" Father raised the spear and then turned to me. "Shield your eyes."

"What?"

"Do it."

No sooner had I covered my eyes than the sound of wood striking flesh began. There was a loud snap followed by an animalistic shriek.

When I opened my eyes, Jocksin lay on the floor wailing in agony. Father stood above him holding half a spear while the other half rolled next to the mangled legs of Jocksin the cripple.

Father grabbed a large, lumpy sack with one hand and grabbed my arm with the other. "Let's go!"

As he opened the door, my ears were struck by a cacophony of clanging swords, wailing mothers, and screaming children. Dozens of Sennevar soldiers ran from cottage to cottage stealing what they could, items and women alike. A boy, no older than seven, pulled against a soldier who wrestled with his mother. The man gave a single blow with the pommel of his sword, and the boy fell, never to rise again.

When the man turned back, silver light flashed, and his body froze. In a single motion, Neerion sliced the man's throat. Another soldier thrust his spear, but the cleric raised his staff, and the second man fell still. Blood sprayed across Neerion's white robe as the soldier's neck opened wide like the first.

The cleric continued his attacks as though dancing in the wind, freezing his opponents with his staff before swiping with his short sword. Flash. Slice. Flash. Slice.

My father yanked my arm to the right, and we sprinted for the Scarlet Forest. My heart leapt as the crimson trees grew large in my sight, but before we reached the edge, the earth shook.

The sky tore in half like a garment rent from seam to seam. Behind me, black mist billowed downward, covering the village below. The Scarlet Forest ahead of me blurred like a heat haze, and when it cleared, the leaves and bark were no longer red but a deep sapphire blue. Nittles was right. My world was rending as the Scarlet Forest was gone, and in its place stood the Whisping Forest of Tal Miral.

I spared it only a second of my attention as a giant, pale hand burst from the black rift above. Black talons protruded from each of its fingers, and a scorpion's tail lashed out from the rift a moment later. A thunderous boom shook the ground as the creature burst from the opening and landed at the village entrance. The Kral, the same cursed monster that killed my sister, had arrived.

The goddess's voice echoed from above, but I already knew what she would say.

"Slay the beast."

CHAPTER 30

"One shall stand. All others fall."
—Words from the Sprawn Lands

With one swipe of its stinger arm, the Kral obliterated the village gate. Even from the edge of the forest, its roar shook me to the bone.

Father grabbed my shoulder. "We need to leave."

"No. I have to fight it."

He gave me an incredulous look. "Absolutely not. I just got you back."

"If I defeat it, we might get Minessa back, maybe everyone."

"Minessa?" His face softened. "We can get her back?" I nodded, and his eyes went from me to the Kral in the distance. "I'm sorry. I can't risk it. You're all I have left."

"Not if I defeat the Kral."

His brow furrowed, clearly caught between a rock and a hard place. I placed a calming hand on his own. "You told me you were trying to fix your mistakes with me." I pointed to Ashwood. "Well, this is my mistake, and I need to fix it. Please, let me do this."

After a long moment, he lowered the sack from over his shoulder. "I'm not agreeing just yet, but...would these help?"

Only then did I notice my staff protruding an arm's length from it, emerald runes glowing softly. Ever since we ran, I hadn't so much as glanced at the oddly shaped sack. As I clutched it, the staff resonated with my heartfire, begging to be used. The dagger was next, glittering gold in the sunlight.

"How did you get these?" I asked.

"Once the trial ended, I sneaked into the back of the temple. I struggled to find them, but Triska came and showed me right where they were."

Triska. I was wrong about her. She hadn't told them about Sennevar despite the reward.

As I strapped the dagger to my side, Father raised two jars. "I found these in our kitchen yesterday. Will they help?"

My mouth dropped open as I stared. The jars were filled with jam made from glaidens and lifespur. Of course. I had made them weeks earlier before deciding to dry the rest.

The Kral roared again before impaling a mother carrying her child.

Father placed the jars down. "You said killing that thing will bring Minessa back?"

"I believe it will."

Silence stretched for a long moment before he nodded. "Alright, but you're not fighting alone. Now, how do we use these things?"

A dozen rifts opened around us, and my eyes watered from the acrid smoke. The same dark presence I had sensed before came raging back. Thousands of creatures pounded against the rifts, begging to be released. They wanted to run, to slice, to feed! I held them back with my will, but their minds pressed against me. Their doors were locked, and I was the only key.

"Sashel, what's wrong?" Father asked.

Tapping into my heartfire, I pushed against the darkness. Shrieks sounded beyond the rifts, and the pressure eased.

I let out a relieved breath. "If Nittles was right, we may not have to fight."

I took one last look at the monstrous creature wreaking havoc. Its left arm, like a scorpion's tail, stabbed at villagers and soldiers alike. Its right human-like hand lifted a wagon crushed a fleeing family.

Squeezing my father's hand, I shut my eyes and focused on the candelabra in my mind. The silver candle at the center burned bright, but all my attention was on the last emerald candle at the end. Every other branch of the stand was empty, but I hoped one candle was enough.

"They need help," I whispered.

The candle burst to life, and several possibilities became visible. I could summon a waterfall to push back the beast, but that wouldn't defeat it. A giant leopard made of pure wind could attack, but again, it wouldn't defeat it. Nittles had said with his dying breath that the Emarli was strong enough. They were mighty eagles made of light, and if anything could defeat the Kral, they could.

No sooner had I thought this when the Emarli appeared in my mind. As it raised its wings, its scales shone like shimmering sapphires in the brightest sunlight. Its beak glinted like a silver scythe ready for reaping, and its six legs bared talons that could rend a mountain in twain. The Emarli was the deliverer, the slayer of beasts. I knew. I knew as much as I knew my own name that this creature could kill the Kral.

"Sashel," Father said. "Sashel, who is that?"

As my eyes snapped open, a ghostly woman with long silver hair stood before us. She pointed at the Kral, but although her mouth moved, she was silent as stone.

"That's the goddess, Kareli," I said. "She's appeared to me before, but she's always silent."

"What is she saying?"

I tried reading her lips, but her form was misty and indistinct. She pointed at her bracelets then back through the dark portals.

Screams rang out from Ashwood as the Kral roared once more. I was out of time. I had to end this. I imagined the Emarli and reached for the emerald candle in my mind. But something tugged at me.

Why would Kareli appear to me? Why couldn't she speak? Nittles had said she never appeared to anyone in the real world, only in dreams. She just announced the final trial; so, why couldn't she speak now? I squinted at her once more. Her bracelets. They almost looked like… chains.

Vision Master had said he took prisoners. How had he worded it? "The last few I fought became my prisoners. Would you like that? I'll allow you to see your loved ones, but you'll be unable to interact with them. They will see you as a wraith, a haunting spirit. Truly wonderful. Wouldn't you say?"

Then it struck me. When I fought Neerion, the message over his head read, "She's alive."

She lifted her necklace, and I peered closer. A faint image of an eagle appeared on the front, and I recited the last lines of the song.

"After the trials, the beast will arise.

The head of an eagle will bring its demise."

I dismissed the image of the Emarli and focused on the woman standing before me. I focused…on my mother.

The emerald candle burned in my mind, and a shining portal appeared. As silver light struck the ghostly image, she turned solid. Her hair wasn't silver, but dull gray. Her skin darkened till it was the same as mine, and slight wrinkles appeared under her eyes.

Before I could speak, my father's voice quivered behind me. "Thrella? Is that you?" He stepped forward and reached out trembling hands. "It can't be."

Without a word, my mother leaped forward and threw her arms around the two of us. Father didn't just weep; he sobbed, and I joined him. My mother. She was alive! I squeezed her tight as my tears soaked her worn gray dress. My mother was alive!

Screams from the village tore my gaze away from her. I wanted nothing more than to talk with her, but the Kral came first. But we could do this together. Her necklace was somehow the key to—

Father grunted and clutched his stomach, and when he pulled his hand back, it came away dark red. Pat. Pat. Pat. Mother gave a wide grin as blood dripped from her thin sword.

He dropped to his knees and coughed. "Why?"

When mother spoke, my breath caught in my throat and every hair stood on end. It wasn't my mother's voice, but I recognized it. Oh, how I recognized it!

"Clickety clack,
The father lacks
A sword, a shield, or a knife.
The daughter has freed
The monster indeed,
The worst mistake of her life."

As she thrust the blade deep in his chest, her visage changed. Rags morphed into fine silk, and her hair shortened, becoming a metallic gold. I shook my head, begging it not to be true. My mother was gone, and in her place stood the regal form of Vision Master.

CHAPTER 31

"The greatest of lies we find on our own."
—Songs from the Staircase

I stood in stunned horror as my father collapsed to the cold earth. Vision Master looked around and cackled as he spun his sword. "Ah. What a ruse, what a ruse!"

Father tried to speak, but all that came out was a spatter of blood. Letting out a rattling breath, he lay motionless, his massive hand still resting on the gaping wound in his chest.

This didn't make sense. My eyes saw his body, but my mind refused to swallow. I summoned my mother, not Vision Master!

"You solved the riddle but missed the trap." He pressed the blade to my throat and tsked. "Part of me hoped you would see through the veneer, but alas, the cat always catches the mouse."

His words were like running water, a noise that couldn't translate. His blade pushed harder against my skin, and warm blood ran down my neck, not my blood, but my father's.

"You forgot the goddess's words," he said. "'The greatest of lies, you find on your own.' I had to convince you that I was your mother, but you would never believe such a lie all at once. No. You needed to eat it one morsel at a time. We're far more likely to believe it if we think we've discovered it ourselves, after all."

"How—How did you know what my mother looked like?" Part of me still didn't believe what I was seeing, but I had to know.

"I told you when we first met. I can see through the rifts, including the tiny ones in your miserable little cottage. What I neglected to tell you was I can cast illusions through the rifts as well. Granted, they're much weaker when I project them through the rifts which is why they were so faded. At first I made a vision of the goddess, planning to have her trick you, but once I saw your mother's portrait, I knew what I had to do. And it only took a small amount of tweaking to the image."

"No. I saw Kareli in my dreams. She refilled my heartfire. You couldn't have done that."

"Oh, that actually was her. I don't have the power to influence your dreams. But Kareli is limited in what she can say. I'm sure the sprackin told you the goddess hasn't appeared in the real world in ages, but once you saw the slightest possibility of getting your mother back, I knew you would abandon all logic."

But she had chains. No. That was just a vision. But the necklace! Again, merely an illusion. Too late I realized everything I'd pieced together was either a trick of the eye or words straight from Vision Master.

With his free hand, he lifted my staff and scrutinized it. Screams echoed from the village, and he turned. "I've only seen the Kral in the Sprawn Lands, never around crowds of people. I'm going to enjoy watching it rip their flesh. Such sweet agony. Remember, my pain eases when I see their pain. I need their pain."

He circled me slowly, never letting up on his sword to my neck. "I can't afford to kill you. I don't know if I'll be sent back if you die; however, I can't have you distracting me."

A swoosh sounded behind me, and pain erupted from the back of my ankles. I dropped to the ground and screamed, but he was already walking away, twirling my staff all the while.

I pressed my hands against the wounds, and the pain intensified. The tendons had been sliced clean through, rendering my feet useless. The lifespur! My eyes darted around, but there was no sign of the jars. Had Vision Master taken them? He wouldn't have left me alone had he known about it.

Crawling on my knees, I dug my fingers through the thick grass, frantically searching for any trace of the jam. As I drew near my father's body, a sweet sent reached me. It wasn't long before I realized my father had landed on them when he fell, crushing the jars completely.

With every bit of strength, I pushed, and his body rolled on his side, revealing shattered glass and smeared jam. A shudder ran through me as I scraped the golden-brown jam from my father's back.

Shutting my eyes, I held in a sob. If I started thinking of his death, I would never make it. Glancing at my ankles, I was reminded of what Jocksin had said. He wanted his old life back. He was terrified of change. Did *I* want change? Did I dare hope anymore? Every time I decided to keep fighting, things grew worse. My family was dead. The town was destroyed, and the Kral was loose. Vision Master was loose. And I…was a cripple.

Would I be like Jocksin? More importantly, did I want to be like him? I remembered asking Nittles why he saved me in the Whisping Forest. His response was simple. "Because it was right." Was it still right to fight even when the battle was futile? Nittles thought so. To fight was to hope, and hope was for the fool.

I stared at the smoke rising from Ashwood, and my will firmed. Better to die a hopeful fool than live as an empty king. I consumed the lifespur and stood. I gazed at the silver candle in my mind and breathed deeply. Live or die, I would do so with hope.

CHAPTER 32

"Wrath burns hot, but hope burns long."
—Words of Shoffilem

I looked for a waterskin, but there was none. The nearest stream was a half mile away, but I would have to travel through the Scarlet—no, the Whisping Forest to do so. Hearing the trees hiss and shooting barbs, I decided it wasn't worth it.

My nature told me to rush, to just fight and see what happened, but I couldn't do that. Fighting the Canthi had proven fruitless until I thought it through. A plan came to mind, more of an idea than a plan, but it would require luck, stupidity, and worst of all patience.

As Vision Master strolled toward the village, I raked a handful of purple jam from the grass. With two fingers, I scooped a small pile into my mouth, roughly the amount of one glaiden. Then I took another scoop, then another. My heart pounded like a hammer on an anvil, threatening to burst through my ribcage, but I could sense everything!

Part of me screamed, "What are you doing?" But it had to be done. The madman had toyed with me when we last fought, and

I needed the edge. And great judgement, did I have an edge! A mosquito flew past me as though swimming through honey, and I felt every beat of its wings.

Focusing on the thread binding me to the staff, I pulled with all my will. The staff was yanked from his hand, and Vision Master seemed to react at a snail's pace. As the staff clapped into my hand, I unsheathed my dagger and shot towards him.

When I had nearly closed the distance, the man vanished, but I continued running in the same direction. I slashed the air as I drew near, light rippling around the blade. The ground distorted where I would have stepped. He was trying to break my footing.

Before I could pivot, something moved towards my arm. Although I saw nothing, I trusted my heightened senses and I dodged. His rapier grazed my shoulder, but the cut was shallow.

A manic laugh rang out. "You forget, I too have climbed the stairs. Visions are not the only blessing I was given."

I thrust the dagger towards the voice, but it moved to the side seemingly of its own volition. *Patience!*

"Layers, layers," he chanted in a singsong tone. "You mustn't forget the layers."

Of course, he spoke of layering illusions. Last time, I failed to cut through them when he layered several on top of each other.

I poured heartfire into the blade and swung. This time, his sword appeared from nowhere, but his body remained invisible. Stepping back, I parried. *Patience!* The sword swung faster and faster, putting me on the defensive. How was he so fast? What other abilities had he gotten from the staircase? Then it occurred to me. I wasn't using all my abilities. With a thought, I opened my other set of eyes, the eyes of a truth seer.

Vision Master appeared but not the same one I expected. His beard was gray rather than gold, and the left side of his face was inflamed with a white and red rash. His chest burned a bright silver, and it took me a second to realize it was his heartfire. My special sight did far more than just pierce illusions. Most eerie of all were the long black worms slithering in and out of gaping holes throughout his body. I instinctively knew the creatures were symbolic rather than physical, so I paid them no mind.

His eyes widened as he realized I could see him. His face went from shocked, to ashamed, to pure malice. He knew I saw him down to his core, an exposure going far beyond mere nakedness. The ungarnished truth of what he was laid bare, and he hated me for it.

Up until now, he had been playful in his own twisted way, but no longer. He was as cold as winter stone, not a trace of a grin remaining. Raising his sword, he slashed with reckless abandonment. I parried, blocked, and dodged, but I kept having to back up until we had crossed the field. My back was up against the forest, and I dared not go further, but his blows were hard and merciless. My eyes grew heavy and my breathing ragged.

"How did it feel?" he asked. "How did it feel when you realized you'd been tricked a second time?"

I panted. "I'm used to being a fool."

My silver candle burned bright in my mind, but I held it back. I needed to save as much as I could. *Patience!*

"And what a fool you are!" Spittle flew from his mouth as he all but barked the words.

My stomach churned, and bile rose up my throat. Clenching my teeth, I held it in, tasting acid and blood.

He shook his head. "You don't look well. Too many glaidens, perhaps?"

My vision spun, and I keeled over, vomiting and heaving.

He pressed his rapier to my throat. "Perhaps if I removed your teeth, you wouldn't eat so much fruit."

He kicked my stomach, and I rolled farther back. I heaved again, and spots littered my vision. *Patience!*

Since I no longer had the balance to walk, I crawled away from him. For a minute, he allowed me, like a cat playing with its food. Eventually, he strolled up and kicked me hard in the side.

"Clickety clack. Clickety—"

I held up my hand; my fingers seemingly wrapped around nothing. He squinted, then his golden eyes widened as they finally pierced my illusion.

My staff shook like a bucking horse as I poured heartfire into it. The Whisping Forest roared with anger and pleasure in equal measure as every tree's attention was drawn to the staff. With my new sight, I saw his realization and horror. I had reached the forest inch by agonizing inch while keeping the staff invisible.

Vision Master spun around and leapt, but too late. I clipped his leg as I swung, and the staff rang like a bell. My ears erupted in pain from the concussive boom that followed.

He climbed to his feet and looked around. All fell silent, even the Kral in Ashwood. It was a powerful silence, like the moment before a judge declares, "Guilty." The verdict was reached, and the sentence was death.

The first barb pierced his arm followed by two more. He blocked a half dozen with his sword, but they kept coming faster and faster. Thick branches latched onto him like skeletal hands, but before he could cut himself free, a sharp hiss sounded from the forest.

I scrambled as far from him as I could, but I only made it a few paces before a gout of fire shot towards him. The smell of charred meat filled the air as he burned. The inferno roared like thunder, but the man's screams were louder still. As the flames devoured his skin and clothes, he dropped to the ground and flailed, discarding his sword.

Raising my staff, I gave a command, and the fire ceased. His skin sizzled and blistered, but he was alive. He lay on the ground staring up as his chest rose and fell.

I staggered to my feet and drew near, still using my special sight. "My mother. Where is my mother?"

His eyes drifted in my direction, but he said nothing.

"Is she alive?" I kicked his stomach. "Tell me!"

His mouth quirked into a smile, and he gave a shuddering laugh. His head turned to the Kral as he said, "She's alive…in a manner of speaking."

I looked to the Kral laying waste to the village, then back to him. "No."

His laugh turned to coughs. "Your mother is the very creature you must kill."

"You're lying!"

"Eyes of a truth seer." His mouth twisted in a rictus of pain.

Since the fire began, I had ceased my truth sight, but I opened it once more. The word "TRUTH" hovered above his head in white lettering. The word faded like mist as the life left his eyes. The black worms slithered out from him then faded as well, leaving Vision Master a lifeless husk.

The Kral roared in the distance. No. That couldn't be my mother. Vision Master told the truth, but he was a mad man. Maybe he only thought it to be true.

My thoughts drifted to that fateful day when my mother gave birth, but instead of a black veil shrouding the memory, the veil was transparent. My eyes of a truth seer had pierced the covering like it was a thin spider's web. I grabbed the ethereal fabric with my will and ripped it in half.

The goddess's voice echoed the word she spoke in my dreams, "Remember." Silver light flashed, and the memory of that day struck me like a wave.

* * *

"Sashel, open the window," Fendin said.

I raced to obey, opening the shutter in the Healing House.

"Another wet rag," she yelled.

My mother grunted and squeezed her hand. "It's time!"

"Great judgement! This one's coming much faster than Sashel did."

I dropped the rag and rushed to Mother. Sweat covered her face and bags hung beneath her eyes. She hadn't slept last night, but she thought the pains were false signals. It wasn't till after Father left for work that her water broke, and we made our way to the Healer's House.

Soon, the baby's head was visible, and my heart leapt. I hoped it was a boy, but a little sister would be fun too. Mother pushed again, and Fendin caught the baby with practiced ease.

"It's a girl!" she exclaimed.

I clapped in delight then looked at mother, but her face fell. She looked as though the baby had died. But the little girl seemed healthy to me.

Fendin cut the cord, sinched it, then wiped her clean.

"Merciful Judge!" she said, not noticing mother's disappointment. "Her eyes."

I stood on my tiptoes to see my sister's bright blue eyes staring back at me.

"They're beautiful," I said.

The healer peered closer. "Yes, but they're blue, bright blue."

"You told me their eyes can change when they get older."

"Not like this."

As I looked at her irises, I was reminded of the strange blue fruit mother loved to eat. Ever since she found out she was expecting, she'd been eating them religiously.

A knock came from the door, and Fendin looked up. "Probably the proud father."

"Give her to me," Mother said.

"Of course, let me just—"

"Now," she insisted.

Fendin's face wrinkled in confusion, but she handed the baby over.

The knocking grew louder.

"Keep your shirt on," the Healer hollered as she opened the door.

Neerion burst inside and strode to the bed where mother lay. "I will have my staff back now!"

"Get away from her!" Fendin yelled.

Mother reached under the bed, but the cleric slapped her hand away and lifted the staff.

Shaking the tip at her, he said, "I will be calling for a trial on you."

"For judgment's sake," Fendin said. "The woman just delivered a child."

He planted his staff. "It was the only time she would be vulnerable."

"Of course she's vulnerable! She just gave—" Her eyes widened.

Mother raised a knife, ready to plunge it into my little sister. "I'm sorry it has to be this way."

"Mother, no!" I yelled.

Neerion spun, and grabbed Minessa, but not before the blade sliced her hand. Two tiny fingers dropped to the ground as the baby wailed.

Mother violently shook her head. "No! No! No! She has to die!"

Neerion pressed the baby to his chest then with his staff pushed back the blanket on Mother's bed. Strange runes covered the sheets.

"I knew it!" the cleric exclaimed. "You are a witch, and you planned to sacrifice her. These runes are from the Corrupt One."

Mother looked down and gripped the sheets. "She has to die."

"Why?" Fendin asked.

She squeezed her eyes shut and rocked in her bed. "I can't close the rifts. There are too many."

Neerion narrowed his eyes. "What rifts?"

"I can't stop them. The creatures. The darkness. I can't!"

Blood from her knife dripped onto the sheets causing the runes around her to glow a sickening yellow. A voice rumbled through the room that shook me like thunder. "You have been claimed."

Neerion turned from her and handed the child to Fendin. "Find someone to nurse her. The witch will not come anywhere near the child. Thrella has been claimed by the Corrupt One!"

While the two talked, the bowl of bright blue fruit near the bed turned black. They called to me. The fruit needed to be eaten. My mouth watered as I stepped forward. They were mine. I had to—

My mother sank her hand into the bowl and devoured the rotten fruit. Black pulp dripped down her face, but she paid it no mind. Mouthful after mouthful went in with only a few chews before swallowing.

I reached out for one, but she batted my hand away. Pain snapped me out of my reverie as blood dripped from long claw marks down my arm.

As I cried, Neerion turned back. "What happened?"

My mother's nails grew and turned black while her skin was bleached of all color. Her black teeth sharpened to fine points, but she continued eating.

Neerion thrust out his staff, and the runes glowed silver, but my mother only growled. One of her arms lengthened, becoming a sharp stinger.

"Mother!" I shouted.

Her yellow eyes turned to me, and a spark of recognition crossed her face. She shut her eyes as if battling something in her mind. When they opened, only the beast remained.

She hissed. "One shall stand. All others fall."

A black rift opened in the air, and the wind stirred. It was as powerful as a tornado, but instead of blowing, it pulled, focusing all its might on my mother. She clawed at the walls and floor, but to no avail. The mighty gust swept her up, and the rift dissipated like vapor.

There was noise. It took me a moment to realize it was coming from me. I was screaming, and my sister echoed weakly. Neerion stood, and his face softened.

Pressing the child into my arms, he said, "No child should remember her mother like that." His staff brightened. "She was a good mother, and she died giving birth."

CHAPTER 33

"When we are young, our parents are like gods.
When we are old, we see them as devils.
Let us see them for what they are—human."
—The Book of Clergy

I gasped as my mind returned. It couldn't be. My mother had tried to sacrifice Minessa. But why? And the drethals. Where had she gotten them?

As slow as a gentle snowfall, everything fell into place. Mother climbed the staircase but couldn't make it past the first step. More and more dark rifts appeared, and she grew desperate to close them. She searched the temple library for answers, even seducing Neerion to gain access to forbidden tomes.

She learned a ritual that would close them all, but it required sacrificing her own child. The problem was it had to be a newborn, and Mother couldn't bring a child to term. Fendin couldn't figure out how she could suddenly have a child with no complications.

Nittles said that drethals were a corruption of a magical fruit that helped with strength and… fertility! Drethals were simply mandrils that had rotten. So, she summoned drethals then stole Neerion's staff to take away the rot, turning them back into pure magical fruit. That's why she stole it! She conceived and bore Minessa then arranged to sacrifice her, but she didn't expect Neerion to barge in.

When he retrieved his staff, the fruit rotted once more, leaving only the dark drethals behind. Mother was enticed by the fruit as I was, and when she ate, she became the Kral.

When I confronted Neerion a few days earlier, I thought he was going to sacrifice Naska's child. But what I actually asked him was, "Does 'Thresti te Morditatum' mean anything to you?" He had taken it to mean *I* was going to kill the child, and he fought to defend them. Neerion was in the right!

As dreadful as mother's plan was, it was clever and probably her only option. Even now, the twisted creatures beyond the slivers in the air demanded to be freed. They pushed at my mind like a river against a feeble dam. It was only a matter of time before it would burst, and mother felt the same. Better a single child die than the entire village.

Black smoke rose from Ashwood as the villagers screamed. The Kral was my mother, but if I didn't defeat her, none of this would end. Then I remembered what Nittles had said. If someone attempted a dark ritual like she had, there was no coming back. Even if I won the battle, she would not return.

With my stomach churning from the glaidens, I ran as fast as I dared toward the smoldering village. Several families past me to escape the beast, heading straight for the Whisping Forest.

"Stop!" I yelled. "Don't go in there!"

Two of the men looked back and glared at me, then continued running. Of course. I was a witch and a traitor to Ashwood. They wouldn't listen. Over a dozen people, men, women, and children, entered the woods. A moment later, their screams rang out, then all was silent.

I had to stop this! I had to kill the Kral. As I neared the gate, the heat from the fire struck me as though I'd opened a furnace. Smoke burned my eyes, and cinders meandered in the air. Although the creature was at the center of the village, its footsteps shook the earth around me.

The clanging of metal tore my gaze away, and I turned to my right. Dozens of enemy corpses littered the earth around Neerion as he continued fighting. Flash. Slice. Flash. Slice. His movements grew sluggish as sweat and blood poured from his face. His white robe was almost solid crimson from the blood with several gashes throughout. An enormous soldier ran behind the weary cleric and raised a massive war hammer.

Sinking my hands into a trough, I claimed the water inside. Emerald light emanated from the barrel-size ball of water as it rose high in the air. With a flick of my wrist, the water plowed into the soldier with a resounding crunch.

Neerion turned to see the fallen man, then he stared at me with an unreadable expression. "What are you still doing here?"

I pointed at the Kral over a mile away. "The creature! We have to kill it." Three more soldiers charged, but I brushed them aside with my water. "Hurry!"

He glared at me. "You are still a witch and tried for treason."

I pointed at the Kral. "Which one of us is the greater threat, me or that thing?"

The cleric looked at monster in the distance then back me. "Fine, but this does not pardon you." Without another word, he sprinted for the beast. With my nausea still present, I lagged at a light jog, but eventually, we made it. Clenching my fists, I commanded the water to charge, and a green lance shot towards the Kral. As it neared its mouth, the water turned inky black then dropped to the ground with a resounding splash.

The Kral turned to me and grinned, displaying rows of black, jagged teeth. That was it. My plan was to suffocate it like I had with the Canthi, but it somehow severed my connection.

Neerion raised his staff, and the eagle on top glowed silver. The Kral's eyes flashed silver, but with a mere shake of its head, its eyes returned to dark yellow as it faced us. With my own staff, I commanded the ivy covering the cottages around us to attack. But after coiling around its legs, they too turned black and fell lifeless to the ground.

"It is corrupt magic!" Neerion yelled.

As he gripped his staff in both hands, the silver eagle on top shook. Its beak lengthened and glowed until it resembled a scythe with an ethereal blade.

He grunted as though the action exhausted him. "This blade cannot cut human flesh, but it should work well on the beast."

Letting out a bestial growl, the cleric raised the scythe and charged. The Kral swiped its stinger, but Neerion leaped over it and sliced its leg. Instead of blood, black mist rose from the wound as the creature let out a howl of pain.

It reached for him with its long human arm, but Neerion sliced its hand, causing it to recoil and growl. Neerion let out a growl of his own as he reared his scythe back and buried it deep in its calf.

I looked around for something to use against it. I had to do something to help. I had to—

With the scythe still embedded in its leg, the Kral raised its stinger and pierced Neerion in the chest. Smoke rose from the wound as its fiery venom melted him from the inside out. As he fell to the ground and writhed, the Kral wasted no time in raising its elongated leg and crushing his body.

As I screamed, the beast turned to me with burning malice. Its eyes turned black, and my body stiffened. *I should obey the Kral. She is my master, the strongest of beasts. How dare I oppose her?* I took a step forward then another, and the Kral raised her stinger in glee. *The Kral is all-powerful. She is magnificent! She—*

I smelled smoke. Was something burning? I looked around to see several buildings engulfed in flames. What was I doing here?

The Kral snarled and again her yellow eyes turned black. The same entrancing feeling washed over me. *The Kral is glorious. She is everything. I should go to—*

My eyes wandered to the staff in my hands. *Why was it covered in green runes? What did they say? If I carved them into a normal staff, would it have magical properties as well?*

My mind refocused, and the Kral growled in frustration. It seemed to have the same hypnotic magic that the stairs had. I tapped the cross guard of my dagger, turned invisible, and ran for the forest.

The Kral lumbered after me, sniffing the air like a hound. Only when I neared the forest was I able to summon branches to whisk me away. There was a reason I had to lure Vision Master so close to the forest before I used the staff. The trees could only reach so far.

I was a mile ahead of the creature by the time I reached the staircase. The Scarlet Forest had radically transformed, but the stairs remained the same, and I prayed to all the gods that it would protect me like last time. I huddled beneath the winding steps as the thunderous footsteps approached.

"The Kral is not my mother," I said allowed. "My mother is dead, and this creature has taken her place." This gave me an idea, an awful idea.

The Kral came close, sniffing the air like a dog on a hunt. It swung its stinger arm towards me, but the invisible barrier around the stairs stopped it cold. It growled and raked its claws with its other hand, but whatever force protected me held firm.

A thin, black tree with streaked blue bark shot acid at the Kral, but the yellow bile splashed off its back like a stream against a boulder. With one swipe of its stinger, the beast snapped the tree like a dried twig.

I took a deep breath. *I can't believe I'm about to do this!* Reaching out with my mind, I sensed the dark portals all around me, begging to be opened. I searched inside me once more, but no green candles burned, and even the silver one in the center held only a flicker of light.

I searched the rifts until I found it. Using nearly all of my heartfire, I set it free. A bear-like creature made entirely of rock burst through the air. The Kral stood head and shoulders taller, but what the rock creature lacked in stature it made up for in strength and bulk. I couldn't control it as the beast was corrupted, but I remembered Nittles saying the Kral was territorial, and I hoped the two would fight.

The bear growled at the Kral, opened its mouth, and shot a blazing inferno towards it. The Kral held its arm out to block, but the bear capitalized on the distraction and pounced. The two swiped and grappled together, crushing dozens of trees as they fought.

Ignoring the pandemonium around me wasn't easy, but I managed. Summoning the creature was only the first part of the plan. The bear wouldn't defeat the Kral, but it would distract it and hopefully weaken it.

Now, I could only summon corrupt things from the Sprawn Lands, and like my mother, I had to make it work. But even summoning corrupt things used heartfire, and my candle was barely a flicker. Once more, I focused on the dark rifts and summoned what I feared most. The silver candle snuffed out, and in my hands lay a pile of black, wet drethals.

Instinctively, I shut my eyes, but I forced them open. The corrupt fruit called to me. I remembered how they lured my mother, how they enticed my sister, and now I was to be the next victim. As I stared, Triska's words echoed in my mind from the Book of Heretics. *"When I searched for a blessing, there was none to be found. So, I feasted on curses where plenty abound."* Pressing the fruit to my lips, I consumed.

It was bliss. My heart pulsed through my veins in pure ecstasy as I devoured more and more. I bit my lips and tongue with my jagged teeth, but I paid it no mind. The fruit was all that mattered. Flexing my arms, I felt raw, unadulterated power. My dark skin was leached of color, and my left arm elongated into a sharp stinger filled with potent venom.

Silver light flooded my vision, and my skin burned like fire. I thrashed and rolled away, and the burning cut off. When I reached out, my hand met resistance and with blinding sparks. Surrounding the steps was a flaming shield as solid as stone and hot as the sun.

Part of me worried, but I couldn't remember why. The stairs meant nothing to me. With each passing second, dark energy seeped into me, and I grew. Trees shot fire and acid at me, but they might as well have been attacking a mountain. I plucked the nearest one up as easily as a tulip and cast it aside. Then a savage roar bellowed from my throat as the intoxicating aroma of blood wafted towards me.

Another roar echoed my own, and I turned. The other Kral glared at me with venomous hatred as it towered over the motionless body of the rock creature. How dare this being stand before me! It was a wretched worm crawling beneath my skin.

"One shall stand," I growled.

"All others fall," my opponent responded.

She was older and larger than I, but I could taste her weakness. She was wounded from the fight, sagging forward and panting heavily. Swinging her stinger, she roared in defiance, but this was only to mask her injuries.

I sprang forward and lashed out with my stinger. She parried with her own, but it gave me the opening to rake my talons across her face, taking out an eye. I took a glancing blow from her stinger, but it didn't penetrate.

I rained blow after blow, always keeping her on the back foot. I smelled her blood, and I wanted it all. I would drink her dry. I would—

The nagging voice deep inside balked at this. *This was my mother!* As I shook my head to clear it, the Kral barreled into me. Trees flattened beneath us as we each struggled for leverage. A faint wheeze came from her throat, and she paused to catch her breath.

Before I could lunge, the ground crackled beneath me, and my left leg sank deep. Tendrils of black smoke traveled from my opponent to the ground at my feet, and my other leg sank. I could sense the magic she wielded and realized I could use it too, but I hadn't learned how yet.

The Kral strode towards me and let loose a barrage of strikes. Blow after blow shook me to my core, but with my held legs in place, I had no leverage for an attack. Clutching my throat, she squeezed, batting aside my futile swings. Spots littered my vision as I struggled.

With what little breath I could manage, I smelled a faint whiff of something that caught my attention. It smelled…clean, like the beginning of a rainstorm. The odor wreaked of purifying magic, and it came from the Kral's leg.

A scythe covered in silver runes protruded from her calf, dark smoke billowing from the wound. Since my legs were deep in the ground, I was just low enough to yank the scythe free. With a shriek of pain, the creature released my throat and clutched her wound. Gasping for air, I spun the scythe around and sunk it deep into her chest, letting out a spray of black, viscous liquid.

With the Kral writhing in agony, I ripped my legs free of the earth and pounced. Once more I pulled out the scythe and slammed on her chest with the blade. The pestering voice in my head screamed, but I brushed it aside. I would relish this moment. This foe had the audacity to challenge me!

She threw up a quivering hand, but I grabbed it easily and wrenched it, hearing the satisfying snap of bones. The Kral's cries were melodious to my ears, and I raised my stinger for the final blow. The voice in my head redoubled, screaming that this wasn't right. With a shake of my head, I pushed the nagging voice aside and plunged my stinger into the gaping wound of her chest.

Her back arched as my venom ran through her veins like searing oil. The Kral's yellow eyes widened as realization crossed her face. This was her end. A single tear ran down her cheek as she stared at me. For the final time, I brought the scythe down, impaling her through the heart. A moment later, her muscles went limp, and her head fell to the ground. I roared my triumph to the sky for all beasts to hear. "One shall stand. All others fall."

As if in response, a voice spoke from above me. Where my roar was deep and guttural, hers was soft as lilies, yet the strength behind it set mine to flight. Her words swallowed up all other sounds, conquering them like death itself.

"The beast has been slain. All that was lost, the new and the old, will be given in full when the story is told."

Silver fire ignited around me, growing higher and brighter by the second. The light was graceful, and the flames cool to the touch, yet it consumed me all the same. The fire spread out from me, like a ripple in a lake, engulfing everything it touched. But it didn't destroy; it restored. When the flames left me, I raised two normal arms which were cinnamon brown instead of the pale white from a moment earlier.

As the forest burned, it returned to its crimson color once again, leaving no trace of the Whisping Forest. Greatest of all, the dark, billowing rifts connecting my world to the Sprawn Lands faded away. The pressure on my mind I'd grown accustomed to fighting against vanished, and I gasped in relief. But the flames didn't stop. They spread farther and farther until all of Ashwood and beyond were illuminated in soothing, silver light.

CHAPTER 34

"Labor before rest. Cleansing before healing."
—The Book of Clergy

The Scarlet Forest was quiet, save for the chirping of birds. Not a glimpse of blue from the Whisping Forest remained, and not a single tree was broken, as if massive beasts hadn't just destroyed half the forest.

Patting my arms and legs, I sighed in relief as I discovered that all of me was human once more. Strangely, I wore the same blue dress I had when I first found the staircase. But it had been shredded several days earlier.

I sheathed my dagger and lifted my staff. Both were in perfect condition which comforted me. That comfort shattered me when I turned my head. The body of a woman lay motionless near the staircase, a gaping hole in her chest where the scythe had pierced her.

A lump caught in my throat as I whispered, "Mother?" She didn't move. I stroked her cheek as tears welled in my eyes. "Mother, we did it. The rifts are gone."

Silence.

I ran a thumb over her medallion. The engraving didn't show an eagle, but a wolf. "You would have loved Minessa. Had you known her, you never could have made the sacrifice."

Silence.

"You never loved Neerion; did you? You used him to take his staff. You only had eyes for Father."

A warm breeze struck my face and stirred the leaves. Still, she did not move. I squeezed her hand, only to realize it was cold and lifeless. "I'm sorry I couldn't save you."

Losing her now wasn't easy, but it was bearable because I had burned her portrait. On that stormy night after the Trial of Spirits, I learned to let her go. I would burn her body and give her the funeral she deserved. I needed sticks, kindling, and flint. Brushing a few strands of her hair, I kissed her forehead and headed for home.

While the forest was tranquil as a pond, my mind was a storm of emotions and memories. I killed my mother, but there was no other way. Was there?

A tingle ran down my arm causing me to suck in a sharp breath. It didn't hurt, but it felt like dozens of beetles crawling all over. For a second, I could have sworn my skin had paled and black talons grew from my fingers. But when I blinked, my arm was dark once more. Had I imagined it?

"Copper for the cripple?"

Jocksin sat, leaning against the gate post with an arm outstretched. One of his mangled legs stuck out from under the tattered blanket showing an injury that happened long ago. His smile was warm, and his eyes were soft. He didn't remember.

"S-sorry," I stammered. "Not today." Again, I looked at my arm, but it remained its normal dark brown.

Jocksin's eyes drifted from my dagger then landed on my staff covered in silver runes. "A cleric's staff. You planning to join the clergy?"

A laugh leapt from my throat. "Judgment, no!"

Past the gate, an older laugh echoed my own. "And why ever not?"

Cleric Shoff hobbled towards me, and I stared open mouthed at him. He had died because I sold the glaidens to Sennevar.

"Is something wrong?" he asked.

"I—I just haven't seen you in a while."

"You saw me not two hours ago in the shop. Where do you think I got the fruit from?" He held up a sack with a perplexed look on his face. When I didn't answer, he shook his head. "Well, when you get home, remind your father he has lantern duty on Reverence Day. It's coming up soon, and he always forgets to fill them with oil."

I paused. My father was alive too? And he hadn't performed temple service in years.

"But…Neerion banned us from the temple."

His face hardened. "When did this happen?"

Only then did I realize it probably hadn't happened. The goddess hadn't just resurrected the villagers. She'd apparently brought back much more—All that was lost.

"Neerion!" Shoff shouted. "Come here."

Dread filled me as the younger cleric approached.

"Yes?" Neerion asked.

"Did you banish Tamble's family without me knowing?"

He furrowed his brow. "Of course not."

"Never mind," I said. "It must have been a dream."

A smile stretched across Shoff's face. "I know the type. I dreamed my prize bull had died. Imagine how shocked I was when I saw him healthy as could be in the field the next day."

The silver eagle atop Neerion's staff glowed, and a flicker of recognition crossed his face. Silver light filled his eyes as he said, "Yes. Probably a dream."

I bowed to the clerics, but before I left, something Shoff had said struck me as odd. "What did you mean you bought my fruit from a shop?"

"I mean your shop… near the cobbler's." Shoff's face scrunched in concern. "Are you alright?"

I darted down the street; the road littered with velvety red leaves once more. My steps slowed as I reached a small shop that hadn't been there only yesterday. A small, wooden sign hung on the door which read, "Dried fruit for sale," and inside, a faint jingling sounded.

When I entered, Triska turned to me from behind the counter and spoke in her usual fast pace. "It's about time you're back. Grinda bought nearly half the dried fruit while you were out. Gods only know where she puts it all. You said you'd be back in a few minutes, but it's been almost an hour."

All around the room were shelves and shelves of jars. Different colored jams, dried fruit, and pickled vegetables surrounded me, and the sweet smell of drying fruit in the oven flooded my senses.

"Who—Who's shop is this?" I asked.

Triska placed a jar on the counter. "It's ours, which means you can't just leave for too long without telling me."

I swallowed hard and held in my tears. It was perfect! I had a hundred questions I wanted to ask about the shop, but it would have to wait.

"I need to go home."

"You just got back," she insisted.

"I'll make it up to you."

As I reached for the door to the cottage, I paused. Weeks ago, I'd been terrified to see my father; now, I feared I wouldn't see him. Would my father really be inside, or would he be dead like my mother? I knew that was unlikely, but I had hoped so many times and been disappointed.

I remembered the message written on the door— "DEATH TO THE WITCH." I remembered trying to scrub at the charcoal with no success. Then it occurred to me. The door was new. It was solid oak and stained red, matching the shutters around the cottage.

My heart leapt as a high pitch giggle came from inside. As I opened the door, Father tossed Minessa up in the air before flipping her upside down. Her laughter grew louder as Father tickled her feet until she gasped for air. Minessa was alive! And Father was not only alive but sober and… happy.

When I stepped inside, the cottage felt warm. A polished stove stood in the center of the cottage with freshly chopped wood stacked neatly beside it. Bright blue curtains covered the windows, and a thick wool rug covered the floorboards. My home was beautiful!

"Sash!" Father said. "How's my other favorite daughter?"

The dam holding back my emotions finally burst, and I fell to my knees and wept. I hugged them both and wouldn't let go. I lifted my sister and took in her bright blue eyes which matched her crocheted hat. I had no doubt it was supposed to be a blacksmith hat.

An hour passed as I told Father everything, showing him the dagger and staff. I finished with me coming back to gather supplies to burn mother's body. He nodded somberly and told me what happened from his perspective.

It seemed like most things happened the way I remembered. Neerion still claimed Mother died giving birth and that he burned her body before Father came home. However, instead of turning to the tavern for comfort, Father went to the temple. The pain hadn't vanished, but it was manageable. Cleric Shoff and others worked with him through his grief, and he moved on. He admitted he had turned to drinking for a few months, but he stopped when I burned the painting of mother.

What caught me completely off guard was when he said he had his eyes on a lady in the village and things were getting serious between them.

"But first," he said, "Let's speak of your mother. Is her body really in the forest?"

I nodded.

"It's not that I don't believe you. It's just—you told me quite a tale. It all lines up, but I still have trouble believing it."

A strong, regal voice spoke behind me, one I knew well. "I assure you she speaks the truth. Tal Miral is real, and I intend to return one day."

As I turned, two small silver eyes met my own. "Nittles!"

* * *

Father struck the flint, and the tinder ignited. The flames rose and consumed the body, illuminating the Scarlet Forest in bright yellow.

Turning to Nittles, I said, "Tell me again why the goddess couldn't bring her back."

He sighed. "Because she couldn't claim her. Much like how you can't claim water in someone else's blood, Kareli couldn't resurrect your mother. The dark ritual she performed exiled her. If she belonged to one of the other gods, it would be fine, but the Corrupt One is something else entirely."

"But the vision," I insisted. "When I first climbed the stairs, I saw a vision of my mother, father, and sister all together. The goddess promised to restore it all."

Nittles cocked his head. "Curious. Where were you in this vision?"

"I told you. I was on the staircase."

"No. I mean when your family was all together, including your mother. Were you in the vision as well?"

"I—no. I wasn't."

He nodded. "You still see yourself as a child. Don't you?"

"What do you mean?" Then it struck me. I didn't see my mother in the vision. I saw myself. The vision showed *me* hugging my father and sister, the same thing that happened when I entered the cottage only hours ago. The vision was misty, and I assumed it was showing my Mother.

"But why sacrifice Minessa?" I knew the answer, but I had to hear it from him.

"I told you. The sacrifice would close the rifts. You, yourself, considered it when you were overwhelmed."

"But why didn't she climb the stairs like I had? She obviously climbed the first step. Why not climb further?"

The sprackin looked puzzled. "I thought it was obvious. She simply couldn't go further."

"Why not?"

"All stories say the same. The steps pull the mind away like a minstrel charming a serpent. Few can see the stairs, and even fewer can resist the hypnotic pull. Surely you felt it."

I remembered. I was consumed with a desire to leave the stairs and never come back. I wanted to leap off like the steps were red hot. I rubbed Minessa's hair as she leaned against my chest. "But my mother was strong. If she couldn't resist, then how could I?"

He smirked. "Your weakness."

"What do you mean?"

"You can't focus on anything for long. Don't you see? Keeping your attention for only a few minutes is near impossible."

I nodded. "Like holding a squirming eel."

"We have no such creature in Tal Miral. Nevertheless, the stairs couldn't hold your attention any more than you could. Your lack of focus broke the enchantment, something even your mother failed to do."

That was exactly what happened. The stairs drew me away, then I was distracted by something, then I refocused on climbing. My weakness became my ally.

My father squeezed Minessa as he stared at the fire. That reminded me of the other question that had bothered me. "Nittles, why is everything different? The goddess didn't just bring back my family, she changed things, a lot of things."

He nodded. "Kareli promised to bring back all you had lost. When your father became a drunk, you lost the man he once was. When your mother died, you gave up on your dream of having your own shop. Kareli brought back everything you'd lost." He gazed at the pyre. "Almost everything."

My father stood and gave the parting words. He spoke of how wonderful my mother was. How she was sweet, caring, and in the end tried her best to do what was right. We made a prayer then continued watching the fire.

My eyes drifted to the staircase nearby. It spiraled upward as before, but the steps seemed solid instead of ever changing. The stairs reached as far as the trees around it, whispering to me, begging me to climb.

"Nittles," I whispered. "How exactly do I take you back to your world?"

He grinned. "You should know by now. Staircases always have a destination."

As if alive, the flames from the pyre stretched high in the dark sky, illuminating the stairs in crisp detail. At the top of the steps, so far up I could faintly see, stood a large wooden door.

ACKNOWLEDGMENTS

To my backers on Kickstarter who made significant contributions in making this book a reality:

1. Robert Bowen
2. Eric Marczak
3. Christ Killoy
4. Faith Reynolds
5. John Jensen
6. Pantheon Arts PDX
7. Chase McGlinchey

To my backers who made even larger donations on Kickstarter:

1. Jessica Brock
2. Will Wight
3. Paul Ray
4. Arthur Reich
5. Catherine Parker
6. Samantha Keil

To my friends and family who proofread my book and gave me priceless feedback early on:

1. Paul Ray
2. Krysten Ray
3. Faith Reynolds
4. Ely Reynolds

ABOUT THE AUTHOR

From a young age, Stephen Ray found refuge in storytelling and creativity. Diagnosed with Tourette syndrome at age ten, along with OCD and ADHD, he also faced the challenge of a severe stutter. Art became his safe space, a place free of judgment, that eventually ignited his passion for science fiction and fantasy.

Stephen met his wife while attending Bible college in the Chicagoland area, where he later taught classes for five years. It was during this season that he discovered his love for writing. Today, when he isn't working or enjoying time with his wife and their two daughters, Stephen devotes himself to crafting immersive fantasy stories.

Silver Steps is his debut novel, featuring a protagonist with ADHD, an experience Stephen deeply relates to. His goal as an author is to create stories that feel emotionally authentic while set in imaginative and fantastical worlds. He looks forward to expanding the universe of *Silver Steps* in future books, weaving in elements drawn from his own journey and challenges.

Readers can learn more about Stephen and his upcoming projects at **www.stingrayspublishing.com**. You can also find him on YouTube at **www.youtube.com/@RayofPower**, on Instagram at **www.instagram.com/stephen_ray_author**, and on TikTok at **www.tiktok.com/@ray_of_power**

Enjoyed the book? We'd love to hear your thoughts.
Reviews on **Amazon** and **Goodreads**
help connect this book with new readers.